Psalovw

16.00

Ann. E L.

CAWNPORE
AND
LUCKNOW

For my wife, Nancy

CAWNPORE AND LUCKNOW

A Tale of Two Sieges

D.S. Richards

Pen & Sword
MILITARY

First published in Great Britain in 2007 by
PEN & SWORD MILITARY
an imprint of
Pen & Sword Books Ltd
47 Church Street
Barnsley
South Yorkshire
S70 2AS

A CIP catalogue record for this book is
available from the British Library

Typeset in 11/13 Sabon by Concept, Huddersfield, West Yorkshire
Printed and bound in England by Biddles Ltd

Pen & Sword Books Ltd incorporates the Imprints of
Pen & Sword Aviation, Pen & Sword Maritime, Pen & Sword Military,
Wharncliffe Local History, Pen & Sword Select,
Pen & Sword Military Classics and Leo Cooper

For a complete list of Pen & Sword titles please contact
PEN & SWORD BOOKS LIMITED
47 Church Street, Barnsley, South Yorkshire, S70 2AS, England
E-mail: enquiries@pen-and-sword.co.uk
Website: www.pen-and-sword.co.uk

CONTENTS

DRAMATIS PERSONAE

Lieutenant Gordon Alexander	93rd of Foot
Captain R.F. Anderson	25th NI
Captain George Atkinson	6th NI
Mrs Katherine Mary Bartrum	
Major G.W.F. Bingham	64th of Foot
Ensign George Blake	84th of Foot
Mrs Corlina Maxwell Brydon	
Lady Charlotte Stuart Canning	
Mrs Adelaide Case	
Nanak Chand	Banker's Agent
Lieutenant Henry George Delafosse	53rd NI
Mrs Emma Sophia Ewart	
Colonel John Alexander Ewart	1st NI
Corporal William Forbes-Mitchell	93rd of Foot
Mrs Maria Vincent Germon	
Cornet Hugh Gough	3rd Light Cavalry
Lieutenant William Groom	Madras Fusiliers
Mrs Georgina Maria Harris	
Mrs Lydia Hillersdon	
Miss Amelia Horne	
Mrs G. Huxham	
Lady The Hon. Julia Inglis	
Mr John Lang	Barrister
Miss Alice Lindsay	
Miss Caroline Lindsay	
Miss Fanny Lindsay	
Mrs Kate Lindsay	
Lieutenant Vivian Dering Majendie	Royal Artillery
Captain John Francis Maude VC	Royal Artillery
Corporal Henry Metcalfe	32nd of Foot
Lieutenant Henry Martin Moorsom	Rifle Brigade
Surgeon William Munro	93rd of Foot
Major Charles North	60th Rifles
Subedar Sita Ram Pande	Bengal Army Pensioner
Ensign Hugh Pearson	84th of Foot
Mr L.E.R. Rees	Calcutta Merchant

Lieutenant Frederick Sleigh Roberts
  VC   Bengal Horse Artillery
Ensign J. Ruggles   41st NI
Mr William Howard Russell   *The Times* Correspondent
Mr William 'Jonah' Shepherd   Head Clerk, Commissariat
Mr John Sherer   Magistrate and Collector
Sergeant Ludlow Smith   48th NI
Mrs Elizabeth Sneyd
Mr William Oliver Swanston   Civilian Volunteer
Lieutenant Mowbray Thomson   53rd NI
Cadet Edward Spencer Watson   HMS *Shannon*

INTRODUCTION

On the last day of December 1600, Elizabeth I granted the 'Company and Merchants of London trading with east India' a charter enabling them to conduct business in gems, indigo, camphor and spices. Twelve years later, with the permission of the Moghul Emperor Jahangir, they were then able to set up a permanent trading post at Surat on the west coast. Thus Britain set foot in India as merchants and until the late eighteenth century the East India Company was content to prosper by 'sea and in quiet trade'. The French had also established a number of trading stations in India, notably at Pondicherry and at Chandernagor in Bengal, and until 1730 relations between the two rival companies were reasonably peaceful. Later, increasing tension between France and England in Europe persuaded the French East India Company to enlist native soldiers to protect their interests. 'John Company' was quick to respond by raising a similar army and when war came, Robert Clive gained an impressive victory at Plassey in June 1757 over the combined forces of the French and the Nawab of Bengal, Suraj-ud-daula, and established the East India Company as the principal trader on the subcontinent.

During the latter half of the century the East India Company, with the support of the British Government, extended its power and influence by assuming responsibility for the armies of the three presidencies of Bengal, Madras and Bombay. They were largely composed of native infantrymen or sepoys, and by cavalrymen known as *sowars*. Each regiment had its complement of native officers or jemadar, a rank equal to lieutenant, but all were subordinate to the most junior of British officers in the native regiments and were not even allowed to give orders to a British sergeant major. In addition to the Company's native regiments, there were also British Army regiments stationed in India, but by 1856 the ratio of British soldiers to Indian, was no better than one in six.

To the north-west of Bengal lay the Moghul kingdom of Oudh which had yet to feel the full impact of British rule, whilst further south, although the predominately Muslim faction had been brought under control, people nevertheless harboured a sullen resentment of the British. The many religions of India, together with the caste system, puzzled and appalled the average Englishman. The majority of Indians were Hindus and the caste system governed their entire social and emotional behaviour – unlike Islam whose followers embraced the Koran and looked upon Allah as being all powerful.

It is perhaps not easy 150 years on to appreciate that the political, social and economic welfare of some 250 million souls was supervised by a few hundred young English administrators supported by less than 13,000 British troops. The precariousness of such an administration was recognized at the time by a few discerning individuals such as Sir Charles Metcalfe who wrote: 'Our domination of India is by conquest; it is naturally disgusting to the inhabitants and can only be maintained by military force. It is our positive duty to render them justice, protect their rights, and to study their happiness.' It was a difficult balance to maintain in the face of widespread resentment, and John Sherer, a magistrate in Cawnpore, had no doubt as to the malign influence the Brahmins had on the Hindu soldiers. 'The Brahmins have always been the inimical force which is discontented with British supremacy,' he wrote. 'Not because it is British, but because it is Western ... because the political principles of the West are all opposed to any belief in caste – that is, caste as understood in India.'

The last half of the nineteenth century also saw an Evangelical Revival in England, and influential Christians like William Wilberforce believed that Indian society would benefit from a total conversion by way of a Christian education. Unfortunately, the subsequent proselytizing of European missionaries was to have a grievous effect on subsequent events and must surely bear some responsibility for the Sepoy uprising.

The Mutiny, when it occurred, developed into a savage cycle of senseless massacre and equally violent retribution, from which only the behaviour of the besieged women perhaps emerges with any credit. Their journals and letters reflect personal emotions and fears, but the courage shown is all the more remarkable in that the memsahibs had no part to play other than being supportive to their menfolk in the face of appalling violence, and to care and protect the children in the most horrific of circumstances. I have tried as far as possible to present the tale of the

2

two sieges through the comments and experiences of the men and women most intimately involved, in the hope that the atmosphere so created will help the reader to picture not only the full horror of their situation, but also the punishment meted out to the mutineers. Some observations will undoubtedly appear racist to the present generation, but it should be remembered that the average Briton of that period held firm patriotic views and was proud of the British Empire. It does not excuse, of course, the fact that many Britons of the period were also of the opinion that the British race was superior to that of most other peoples.

In acknowledging the assistance I have received in completing the narrative, I would particularly like to thank the staff of the India Office Library at Blackfriars and the National Army Museum at Chelsea, without whose excellent research facilities this book would not have been attempted.

No work of military history would be complete without some illustrations of the period, and those that appear in this book have been reproduced by 'Courtesy of the Council, National Army Museum'.

I would also like to thank Constable & Robinson Ltd for their permission to use extracts from the *Journal of the Siege of Lucknow* by Maria Germon, published by Constable in 1958, an excellent publication which graphically records the discomfort and dangers faced by the besieged, especially the women. My thanks to the Orion Publishing Group as well for granting me permission to reproduce extracts from the very interesting *Chronicles of Private Henry Metcalfe*, originally published in 1953 by Cassell & Company, a division of the Orion Publishing Group.

Finally, although every effort has been made to secure permission from persons holding copyright material, it is often difficult to locate such sources and the author apologizes in advance for any omission inadvertently made.

Chapter 1

'THE FAVOURITES OF HEAVEN'

For the many British families residing in Northern India whose duties bound them to the military cantonments of Oude, a province noted for its oppressive climate, there had been few outward signs in the months leading up to the fateful year of 1857 to suggest that they were poised on the brink of a catastrophe.

In October 1855, a new governor general had been appointed to succeed Lord Dalhousie in the task of governing the subcontinent, and it was Lord Charles John Canning's hope that following Dalhousie's controversial reforms, he would enjoy a period of peaceful calm. However, in a speech at a farewell dinner given for him by the Court of Directors before leaving for India, he admitted with commendable candour: 'I wish for a peaceful term of office, but must not forget that in the sky of India, serene as it is, a small cloud may arise, at first no bigger than a man's hand, but which growing larger and larger, may at last threaten to burst and overwhelm us with ruin.'

Although the era was long past when an enterprising individual could embark upon a career as a clerk with the East India Company and return with a considerable fortune, the officers and covenanted civil servants nevertheless pursued an existence as comfortable as the rigours of duty in a hostile environment would allow. Well paid by European standards and far from overworked, the Company's employees, both civil and military, were able to enjoy a lifestyle not dissimilar to that of an English country gentleman, at a fraction of the cost, with the added advantage of a host of servants to provide a degree of personal comfort unimaginable outside of India.

Henry Addison, on his first night ashore in the house of a friend, was scarcely awake before the mosquito net around his bed was parted and he became aware of a native busily lathering his face preparatory to shaving him. 'No wonder old Indians on their return to Europe fancy themselves sadly neglected by their

4

domestics,' commented an astonished Addison. 'I shall however shut my door tomorrow morning, and insist on dressing myself.' No doubt Henry Addison found the attentions of his friend's servants tiresome, but in this he was not alone. British India's First Lady, accustomed as she was to a large establishment of servants with the Queen at Windsor, found the constant presence of mute and deferential servants an aspect of Indian life difficult to live with. Lady Charlotte Stuart Canning confided to her diary:

> I am not sure that I do not regret creaking footmen. These gliding people come and stand by one and will wait an hour with their eye fixed on one, and their hands joined as if to say their prayers, if you do not see them – and one is quite startled to find them patiently waiting when one looks round. I have such scruples to giving them so many journeys up and down, and it's indeed far pleasanter to have creaking footmen in livery.

Lieutenant Vivian Majendie, himself a relative newcomer to India, found like those before him, attendance upon the individual to be a little overwhelming. He wrote:

> There are few things more striking to a person just landed, than the native servants who, to use an un-classical expression, walk 'quite promiscuous like' in and out of one's room all day, noiselessly, certainly, for there are no shoes on their dusky feet to creak and disturb you, but the very presence of these white clad figures flitting about one prevented me for some time from feeling that placid sensation of 'at home' and retirement which every man at times must long for.

At that time, servants in India were obligatory for even the most junior administrator, and although wages were low, since each servant was forbidden by his caste to do another's work, the size of staff considered necessary for even a modest establishment surprised many a newcomer unfamiliar with the practice. Henry Addison's friend advised:

> A sirdar or principal servant to look after your clothes; a kitmutgar to wait behind your chair; a hooker burder to take care of your hooker ... eight bearers to carry you in your palanquin, a peon to convey your notes and messages, a dhobee, a durzee (tailor), a bheestee (water carrier), a bobachee (cook), three syces to take care of your three horses, a grass cutter to supply them with hay ... and a moonshee (interpreter) as long as you are ignorant of the language.

Poor Addison, once he had recovered from his astonishment, could only gasp, 'Then I'll be shot if I shan't be ruined.'

With the approach of the hot weather season most families made haste to exchange the sweltering heat of the central plains for the relatively cool and bracing climate of a hill station such as Simla, 7,000 feet above sea level, Mussoorie, or Darjeeling. There, in comfortable stone bungalows built in the 'Swiss cottage' style, the wives at least could profit from a welcome break until the monsoon brought a temporary halt to the rising temperature on the plains. For those obliged to remain in cantonments, there was little to do but seek refuge behind drawn blinds, gaze listlessly out over a compound swept by clouds of grit and dust, and idly watch the thermometer gradually climb to an energy sapping 120°F in the shade.

Writing from Cawnpore in April, Surgeon Francis Collins could complain with some justification that 'The wind blows hotter every day, it is impossible to stir out with safety between 8.00 am and 6.00 pm. The very birds disappear at 9.00 am and we see nothing more of them till sunset . . . In the morning we see them with their beaks wide open panting for breath.' In a climate such as this, the practice of over-indulgence at meals by some may well have eased the path to promotion for others in both military and civil circles, by lowering their resistance to the many virulent fevers common to India.

One such dinner, which even by Victorian standards seems to have been a massive affair, was attended by William Howard Russell, the correspondent of *The Times*, who found:

> the incense of savoury meats hanging about like a fog. The soup is served, as it only can be in India – hot as the sun, thick with bones and meat – a veritable warm jelly. Then comes the fish – roach, or some cognate Cyprinus, hateful to me as Ganges fed; then joints of grain fed mutton, commissariat beef, curries of fish, fowl, and mutton, stews and ragouts, sweets of an intensely saccharine character, with sherry, beer, and soda water, and now and then a pop of Simpkin or champagne.

A chaplain in the service of the East India Company remembered both the delights and the discomforts of the occasion:

> There was a blaze of uniforms, most of the ladies looked pale. A hot climate and late hours soon bleach the English complexion. At such a gathering in such weather as this, one is oppressed with the

misery of woollen clothes. It would move your compassion to see men buttoned up to the chin in tight fitting scarlet or blue coats, and melting away like snowballs at a kitchen fire.

There was precious little relief to be had when having excused himself, the diner could retire to his bungalow for a fitful sleep – not without the risk of an encounter with a snake or a scorpion. 'We gaze at the punkha,' wrote Captain George Atkinson, 'we simmer and accidentally fall asleep just as it is the hour to get up.' Only in the relative cool of the evening, when he rose and dressed for the obligatory ride, was Atkinson released from what he described as 'a captivity enforced by the bars and fetters of a scorching sun and the blasts of a fiery furnace'.

Whilst the menfolk had specific tasks to occupy their time, there was little to relieve their wives from the long hours of boredom. Letter writing, receiving calling cards, engaging in needlework or supervising the household servants might be undertaken, but until the heat of the day was over, few outdoor activities were possible. Many women preferred to remain indoors, a restriction which undoubtedly contributed to the loathing of India expressed by many memsahibs in their letters home. The wife of a future Chief Commissioner of Oude found the dull routine of a military station stifling, and the sheer tedium of cantonment life is convincingly brought to life by Honoria Lawrence in a letter written four years before the Mutiny:

> the highlight of the day was reached when the married couples went out for the evening drive on the same dusty road where they had driven a thousand times, meeting the same faces they had met a hundred times. When they came in there is dinner, then coffee; then bed. So passes day after day till the corps or the civilian is removed, and then they settle down elsewhere to plod on the same eternal round.

The evening's parade of carriages along the main street excited the interest of *The Times* correspondent, then in Cawnpore. 'Whose buggy is that preceded by two native troopers and followed by five or six armed natives running on foot?' asked William Howard Russell.

'That is the magistrate and collector,' came the reply.

'What does he do?'

'He is the burra Sahib or big man of the station.'

'Who is that in the smart gharry with servants in livery?'

'That is the chaplain of the station who marries and baptises and performs service for the Europeans.'

'Does he go among the natives?'

'Not he; he leaves that to the missionaries.'

'Well, and who comes next along the drive, in the smart buggy with the bay mare?'

'That is the doctor of the station. He attends the sick Europeans. He also gets, under certain circumstances, head-money for every native soldier in garrison.'

'Does he attend them?'

'I should think not. Why on earth should he attend a lot of niggers?'

'But he is paid for them,' suggested Russell naively.

'Ah, that is another matter,' came the reply. 'You must understand our system a little better before you can comprehend things of this sort.'

'Who, then, is this jolly looking fellow on the grey Arab?'

'That is the judge of the station, a very good fellow. All judges are rather slow coaches, you know. They do the criminal business, and it is not much matter if they make mistakes, as they don't meddle with Europeans. When they can do nothing else with a fellow in the Civil Service, they make him a judge.'

Russell had to be content with this potted history of the station's hierarchy, but the inherent prejudice against the native population was not lost upon the Irish journalist when he wrote: 'The fact is, I fear, that the favourites of Heaven, the civilizers of the world, are naturally the most intolerant in the world.'

At Cawnpore, as with many other military stations, much of the evening's social activity took place around the bandstand. There, officers in tight-fitting uniforms and civilians in alpaca jackets would gossip and exchange pleasantries with ladies in sprigged muslin dresses to the accompaniment of a sepoy band playing distorted versions of popular tunes of the day. Families would gather beneath the spreading branches of a peepul tree whilst their offspring were led around the bandstand by an ayah, which, as one fond parent remarked, 'Would give the little things a decided taste or dislike for music in future years.'

Occasionally, an invitation to dine at a local rajah's palace made a welcome diversion, which Captain George Atkinson recalled in what might seem less than flattering terms:

The guests arrive, and are installed in velvet-cushioned chairs, and attar of roses is handed round with dried fruits and sweetmeats. Then come the dancing girls, gyrating on their heels, ogling and leering, and shaking their uplifted palms, with their idiotic contortions, indicative, in the eastern eye, of grace and dignity of motion. Lobsters and tart fruits commingled, whilst truffles, sausages, and sugared almonds share mutually the same dish. Nor is it for want of crockery as dishes and plates, and vessels even of the most domestic character, grace the board, side by side with silver plate and glittering ormolu, to the unsmotherable amusement of the guests.

To a recent arrival from Britain, there was something inappropriate in the way a local nawab displayed his devotion to Western table manners. John Lang, a barrister, after a visit to the palace of Nana Gorind Dondhu Pant, the Rajah of Bithur, better known as the Nana Sahib – Nana being a term of endearment – recorded his impressions:

> I sat down at a table twenty feet long ... which was covered by a damask tablecloth of European manufacture. But instead of a dinner napkin there was a bathroom towel. The soup – for the steward had everything ready – was served up in a trifle dish which had formed part of a dessert service belonging to the 9th Lancers – at events the arms of that regiment were upon it; but the plate to which I ladled it with a broken teacup was of the old willow pattern. The pilau which followed the soup was served upon a huge plated dish, but the plate from which I ate it was of the very commonest description. The knife was a bone handled affair, the fork and spoon were of silver and of Calcutta make. The plated side dishes containing vegetables were odd ones, one was round and the other was oval. The pudding was brought in upon a soup plate of blue and gold pattern, and the cheese was placed before me on a glass dish belonging to the dessert service. The cool claret I drank out of a richly cut champagne glass, and the beer out of an American tumbler of the very worst quality.

Apart from the few Britons who took pains to learn something of the native's culture, language and history there were many more who looked upon their service in India simply as an unavoidable step on the ladder towards self-aggrandizement. To many of those individuals the Indian was beneath ordinary notice. In reply to a question as to what she had seen of the country and its people since coming ashore, the wife of a newly appointed magistrate, replied: 'Oh, nothing, thank goodness. I know nothing at all about them, nor do I wish to. Really, I think the less one knows of them the better.' Comments such as these betrayed an unforgivable arrogance which was by no means confined to the newcomer, or griffin as he was known. Referring to the sepoys under his command, a major of a native regiment exclaimed to William Russell: 'By Jove, Sir! By Jove! Those niggers are such a confounded sensual lazy set, cramming themselves with ghee and sweet meats, and smoking their cursed chillumjees all day and night, that you might as well think to train pigs.'

That infantry major's attitude to his responsibilities would, however, have outraged many an earlier generation of Company officers. Writing some twenty-five years before the Mutiny, an enlightened Captain Albert Hervey advised the 'griffin' to divest himself of any notion that he was here to rule over an inferior race. He wrote:

> People come out to India with but very different ideas regarding the native. They think that because a man is black he is to be despised. The grand mistake on the part of the officers is their ignorance of, and their indifference to, the feelings of their men. As long as they look upon them with prejudiced eyes ... the poor soldier will be maltreated until his meek and humble spirit becomes roused, his pride hurt, and the consequence attended with fearful results.

Hervey of course, was referring to an earlier age when it was common for an officer to learn the language and customs of the people from his Indian mistress, and before the proselytizing by missionaries worked to the disadvantage of the East India Company. Sita Ram Pande, of the Bengal Native Infantry, recalled:

> In those days the sahibs could speak our language much better than they do now and they mixed more with us. The sahibs often used to give nautches for the regiment, and they attended all the men's games. Nowadays they seldom attend nautches because their padre sahibs have told them that it is wrong. The sahibs have done, and are still doing, many things to estrange the British officers from the sepoys.

No doubt the work of missionaries was much resented by the sepoys but the incompetence of many of the Company's officers was certainly a factor in the poor morale and lack of discipline prevailing among the lower ranks. Many of the British officers in the Native Infantry (NI) were the younger sons of minor English gentry who had been sent out to make something of themselves, but had been deemed unsuitable to fill the growing number of well-paid posts in Administration. Resentful, and with low self-esteem, they only occasionally exposed themselves to the stifling heat of the day to appear on parade, preferring to remain in the shuttered gloom of their bungalow, frustrated, bored and often drunk. John Lang, who was travelling through Oude, was told of a certain major commanding a native regiment. 'He knows nothing whatever of soldiering. All the sepoys as well as the Company officers, laugh at him when he comes on the parade ground and attempts to handle the regiment. For thirty years he was employed on commissariat duties. At the expiration of that period, he became a major; and then, according to the rules of the service, he was appointed to command a corps.'

'Surely you are jesting,' exclaimed an incredulous John Lang.

'On my honour, I am serious,' came the reply, 'that is part of our military system, sir.'

When the time came for Sita Ram to retire on a subadar's pension, the religious practices, which for centuries had formed an integral part of the Hindu or Moslem way of life, were already under serious threat from European missionaries. Fired with evangelical enthusiasm, these early Victorians looked upon the religions of India as 'one grand abomination' and their efforts to convert the natives to Christianity was to become a decisive factor which alienated both Hindu and Muslim who preferred their own established customs and religious practices to those being introduced by foreigners.

Queen Victoria readily appreciated the fears of her Indian subjects and in a letter to the Governor General's wife made clear her concern:

> There is a dangerous spirit among the native troops ... a fear of their religion being tampered with is at the bottom of it. I think the greatest care ought to be taken not to interfere with their religion – as once a cry of that kind is raised among a fanatical people – very strictly attached to their religion – there is no knowing what it may lead to & where it may end.

William Russell came close to an understanding of the sepoys' fears when he advised his readers:

It is hard to bear the rule of an alien at any time, but when that alien is haughty, imperious, and sometimes insolent and offensive, his authority is only endured till the moment has arrived to destroy it, or at least to rise in rebellion, hopeless or successful, against a Government which has violated all the conditions of possibility.

The growing number of young ladies of marriageable age who, now that an overland route via Egypt had supplanted the long and expensive voyage round the Cape, began to arrive from England in search of husbands, was a further factor in the isolation of the Company officers from their native charges. 'The arrival of a cargo of young damsels from England is one of the exciting events that mark the advent of the cold season,' wrote Lady Falkland to a friend. 'It can be well imagined that their age, height, features, dress, and manners become topics of conversation and as they bring the latest fashions from Europe, they are objects of interest even to their own sex'.

Among the most sought-after marriage partners were the Haileybury men employed in the covenanted Civil Service, which as John Beames explained 'was in those days an aristocracy in India'. These Company employees, who enjoyed a subsistence allowance in addition to their salary of £300 a year, were also obliged to contribute to a fund which guaranteed a pension of £300 per annum to their widow – an arrangement which earned for them the sobriquet of 'the three hundred dead or alive men', and of course, numerous invitations from the mothers of marriageable daughters. Because of the pecuniary advantage enjoyed by the civil employees, competition between them and the military for female attention usually ended in favour of the former despite the attraction of a smart uniform, and was naturally much resented by the officers of the station. At a dinner in Madras, an officer was heard to remark, perhaps rather ungallantly, to his female neighbour: 'Now I know very well Mrs ——— you despise us all from the bottom of your heart, you think no one worth speaking to in reality but the Civil Service. Whatever people may really be you just class them all as civil or military – civil or military, and you know no other distinction. Is it not so?'

'No', came the icy rejoiner. 'I sometimes class them as civil or uncivil.'

The conquest of the Punjab which followed General Gough's victory at Gurerat in 1849 was also a factor in the subsequent unrest, for it had serious consequences for the sepoys who comprised nine tenths of the Company's army. The pay of a native soldier was seven rupees a month, which could be supplemented by an additional allowance should he be asked to serve outside the Company's territory. Now that the Punjab was administered by the Government, duty there no longer qualified for extra pay, despite the fact that the sepoy was far from home among a people he feared and despised.

Worse was to follow. The Sikh who, according to some accounts paid scant attention to the personal hygiene so important to the high-caste Hindu, was being recruited for the Company's regiments.

'This annoyed the sepoys exceedingly,' recalled Sita Ram. 'They were never as smart as we were on parade and their practice of using curds to clean their long hair gave them an extremely disagreeable odour.'

The changes brought about by Dalhousie's annexation of the Punjab, and particularly that of the kingdom of Oudh in 1856, generated widespread discontent among the natives of the Company's regiments, who in addition to the loss of their foreign service allowance, found that they were no longer entitled to the concessions which were once their right in the Civil Courts. As a consequence, the prestige a sepoy had enjoyed among the elders of his village had diminished and he was becoming increasingly despondent. 'I used to be a great man when I went home,' complained a *sowar* of Native Cavalry to Sir Henry Lawrence. 'The best of the village rose as I approached, now the lowest puff their pipes in my face.'

Towards the end of February 1857 the first sign of general unrest had manifested itself in a mysterious but open distribution of chapattis – small flat cakes made of flour, water and salt. It was not known with any certainty where the chapattis had originated – some thought from Barrackpore – but they were carried in an east-west direction by village watchmen in batches, the *chaukidar*, or watchman, receiving them being requested to retain two and bake four more for distribution to nearby villages with the same message. So rapid was their progress throughout the North-West Provinces from Rohilkand in the north to

Allahabad in the south-east, that in ten days, almost every village had received its allotment.

Various theories were put forward to account for the phenomenon; some Indians thought that the chapattis were meant to draw the people's attention to some forthcoming event, or were even a spell against one of the many diseases – cholera was, in fact, prevalent at the time. Others recalled a similar occurrence some fifty years before, which was followed by a mutiny at Vellor in which fourteen officers and more than 100 British troops had perished. 'They think it is an order from Government,' wrote Lady Canning on 8 April 1857, 'and no one can discover any meaning in it.' To Mrs Elizabeth Sneyd, it savoured much of 'Gunpowder, Treason, and Plot' than anything else, and in a letter to her son she wrote: 'I fully now believe that something terrible was at hand, & would soon burst forth.'

The native police were equally mystified and in reply to a question from the magistrate of Delhi, the *thanadar*, or chief police officer, replied that his father had once told him that 'upon the downfall of the Mahratta power, a sprig of millet and a morsel of bread had passed from village to village, and that it was more than probable that the distribution of this bread was significant of some great disturbance which would follow immediately.'

No satisfactory explanation was ever recorded and it was left to a Calcutta newspaper to make light of the incident. 'Are all the chaukidars about to strike for increased wages?' the *Friend of India* asked its readers. 'Or is it someone trying out a new scheme for a parcel dawk? Is it treason or is it jest? Is the chapatti a fiery cross or only an indigestible substitute for a hot cross bun, a cause for revolt or only of colic?'

The affair was soon forgotten by most Europeans except for those in the up-country stations, but for the simple villagers it had the effect of instilling feelings of deep unease.

Chapter 2

THE GATHERING STORM

In January 1856, Lord Dalhousie had annexed the powerful kingdom of Oudh, resulting in the removal of Wajid Ali Shah, the king of Lucknow, who, in the opinion of the Governor General, had done nothing to reform his corrupt administration. Dalhousie's action, no doubt well intended, was followed by further measures in which landowners or *talukdars* as they were known, had their estates confiscated. This was done on the premise that they were unable to produce a title deed, or proof of ownership, a requirement previously unknown in Oudh.

'The truth was that so many people in Oudh had acquired property by methods which the Government would never recognize, that they began to fear an enquiry,' commented Sita Ram Pande. 'Since all these people had large numbers of relations, retainers and servants living with them who were all interested parties, it explained the great excitement prevailing in Oudh at that time.'

The unrest to which he referred was zealously exploited by the *talukdars* whose only means of regaining their confiscated possessions lay in the overthrow of British rule, and by the Muslim holy men who worked upon the feelings of the sepoys still smarting from the removal of their king. Sita Ram Pande was firm in his opinion that the 'seizing of Oudh filled the minds of the sepoys with distrust and led them to plot against the Government,' adding, 'They [the agents of the king] worked upon the feelings of the sepoys, telling them how treacherously the feringhees had behaved towards their king.'

Wild rumours were also fed to the credulous villagers to the effect that the *feringhees* were intent upon putting an end to caste by dropping pieces of beef and pork into drinking wells at night. It was also believed by many Hindus that flour bought by their wives in the Sudda Bazaar had been contaminated with the ground bones of cows.

The East India Company officials, who were certainly aware of these rumours, were not inclined to place any reliance on them, confident that the majority of Indians were satisfied with the peaceful era brought about by a firm but honest administration. That the misinformation put about by the troublemakers was having its desired effect was readily apparent to a new arrival from Britain however. 'Just forty-one days since I bade adieu to the shores of merry England,' noted Charles North, 'and, although but a few hours have passed since I landed, it is nevertheless apparent to me that the native portion of the community is in an unwholesome state of ferment. Where will it all end?'

Mrs Elizabeth Sneyd came close to sharing his disquiet when complaining that 'My ayah would often stand before the looking glass while admiring herself instead of dressing me when I wanted her, with the taunt, "Ah! Your rule will soon come to an end, and we shall have our own king!"'

Taking courage from the Company's reluctance to act, the supporters of the ex-king went about their business of encouraging a rebellious mood with enthusiasm, informing the impressionable sepoys that the Russians had defeated the invincible English in the Crimea, and in India, with so few English troops to oppose them, it would be a simple matter for the sepoys to drive the infidels into the sea. The portents were good and they were told that a Fakir had once predicted the Raj of John Company would last just 100 years. Plassey had been fought in 1757 so this year must see the end of foreign rule.

To the knowledgable observer it seemed that the overthrow of the East India Company would indeed be a relatively easy task as the demands of the Crimean War had greatly reduced the strength of the Queen's forces in India. In the spring of 1857 the total number of white troops in the northern and southern provinces amounted to little more than 22,000, against which could be ranged some 277,000 native troops, armed and trained by British officers, causing Major North to comment with justifiable exasperation: 'According to the favourite system, European troops have been generally dispersed with Cawnpore being garrisoned by a miserable detachment of Her Majesty's 32nd and all the stations on the Grand Trunk Road held by sepoys.'

He was not alone in harbouring misgivings concerning the gravity of the situation for early in March the commander of native forces in Madras was sufficiently alarmed to draw the attention of the authorities to 'a widespread feeling of sullen disaffection ... human endurance has a limit and I emphatically warn the Government that the limit has been reached in the army.' Despite his concern, it must be said that the Madras Army remained true to the Raj.

In sharp contrast to the apprehension felt by certain military personnel, most civilians continued to remain untroubled and in Calcutta no thought was given to cancelling the annual ball to be given in honour of Queen Victoria's 38th birthday. Commented a puzzled Major North: 'However much distrust is felt, none is expressed ... the inertness on the part of those Military Authorities who ought to make arrangements to meet every exigency is remarkable.'

About 6 miles north-west of Calcutta lay the artillery arsenal of Dum-Dum in an area described by an officer serving there 'as being surrounded by a salt water lake where it is not surrounded by jungle and paddy fields, and which has been specially selected as the headquarters of the artillery because it is the dampest place in India, and therefore eminently adapted to the purpose of carrying on experiments in gunpowder.' A depot had also been created there to instruct selected personnel in a new rifle drill and it was here in January 1857 that an approach to a sepoy by a native workman was to have far-reaching results in raising a 'Devil's Wind' which would eventually sweep across Bengal and Oude with terrifying fury.

At this time, in addition to the 'Brown Bess' musket, there were three other types of firearm currently in use in the Bengal Army. The Brunswick, the Minie – a rifled barrel version of the smooth-bore musket – and a carbine employed by the cavalry. Of these, the Brunswick was easily the worst. A report by a Select Committee in 1842 had discovered that 'at all distances above 400 yards the shooting was so wild as to be unrecorded ... the force required to ram down the cartridge being so great as to render any man's hand unsteady for accurate shooting.' All these weapons were muzzle loaders and charged by the simple act of biting off the end of a paper cartridge and pouring its black powder contents down the barrel. The rest of the cartridge containing the ball was then rammed home by a rod provided for the purpose.

In 1853, after successful trials, a new rifle was put into production at the Royal Small Arms Factory at Enfield having a calibre of 0.577 inch, smaller than the bore of the Minie, and with a barrel length of 39 inches. Weighing less than 9lb it had the advantage of a grooved barrel giving greater accuracy and a shorter loading time. Within months of the end of the Crimea War this new weapon was introduced to the 60th Rifles in Bengal, and every rifle range was soon echoing to the sharp crack of the Enfield rifle. The one controversy concerning the new cartridge was the fact that the it was a very tight fit and to smooth its passage down the barrel the lower half was coated in grease. But, whereas the cartridge for the Brown Bess musket had been impregnated with a mixture of wax and vegetable oil, the new paper cartridge was coated with tallow – a mixture of beef fat or pigs' lard – anathema to Hindu and Muslim alike. A low-caste *khalasi* at Dum-Dum was very much aware of this when he stopped a sepoy and insolently demanded a drink from the Brahmin's brass *lotar* or water bowl. The outraged Brahmin refused in no uncertain manner knowing that the *khalasi* would have defiled it with his touch. 'Today you are very particular,' sneered the labourer, 'but wait a little longer; the sahib logue will make you bite cartridges soaked in pig and cow fat and then where will your caste be?'

Filled with dread that such an act would destroy his caste and banish him from home and family, the sepoy hurried back to the lines with a message which horrified his fellow sepoys. Their concern was immediately brought to the attention of the officer in charge of rifle drill, and Captain J.A.Wright was sufficiently impressed to report to his superiors that 'There appears to be a very unpleasant feeling existing among the native soldiers who are here for instruction, regarding the grease used in preparing the cartridges, some evil disposed person having spread a report that it consists of a mixture of the fat of pigs and cows.'

Wright's letter was taken seriously by the Divisional Commander, Major General J.B. Hearsey, an officer with a comprehensive knowledge of native customs, who in turn recommended to Calcutta that the suspect ammunition should be replaced by cartridges impregnated with wax and oils, emphasizing a warning that 'here was a mine ready for explosion'.

In reply, the General was informed that the authorities had agreed to withdraw the existing stock of cartridges and allow the men to use coconut palm oil or any other mixture from the bazaar that they might think fit. This concession did little to allay the sepoys' suspicion that the Company had intended to put an end to caste. 'Without caste how could a man be rewarded for his acts in a previous incarnation?' asked a Hindu of his commanding officer.

The man's fears were readily appreciated by Charlotte Canning who in a letter to the Queen, pointed out that 'Sepoys are the most tractable good people, but any fear that religion or caste shall be tampered with, can always excite them to every possible folly.' Events were soon to prove the validity of the First Lady's comment for when rumour of the encounter between the *khalasi* and the Brahmin at Dum-Dum reached Berhampur, the sepoys of the 19th NI refused to accept an issue of the new cartridge despite a threat of being sent to Burma. In fact there had been nothing to fear for the cartridges issued by the storekeeper on this occasion were old stock, greased with tallow, which the sepoys had never previously refused to use. But they were in no mood to accept the assurances of their officers, and, sullen, suspicious and convinced that it was impossible to distinguish between the old and the new, they steadfastly refused to touch them, leaving the Colonel with no alternative but to report their mutinous behaviour to Calcutta. Eventually, after much consideration, the Governor General ordered that the regiment be marched 90 miles south to to the military station of Barrackpore, there to be disbanded in the presence of a battalion of British troops. On 31 March the sepoys of the 19th NI were paraded on a square dominated by the field guns of a European battery and ordered to pile their empty muskets. Then, after accepting their arrears of pay 'in a sullen and sluggish manner', they were allowed to return to their homes wearing their uniforms.

A further incident involving mutinous behaviour had occurred two days earlier when a sepoy of the 34th NI, armed and under the influence of hemp, strode up and down on the dust-covered parade ground, determined to demonsrate his defiance of the infidel's instructions. Mangal Pandey was a religious fanatic. The fear of losing caste was uppermost in his mind as he brandished his musket and screamed at the quarter guard to refuse the controversial cartridge. 'Come out, you *bhainchutes,* from biting these cartridges we shall become infidels!' The quarter guard, twenty tall men in scarlet jackets, white drill trousers and shining black shakos, fidgeted uneasily but the jemadah in charge of them made no attempt to obey an English sergeant major's order for him to arrest the sepoy. 'What can I do?' he replied. 'My naik is gone to the adjutant, the havildar is gone to the field officer. Am I to take him myself?'

It was not long before the disturbance attracted the attention of those off duty and as the crowd grew, so the excitement mounted until the drumming of hooves on the sun-baked parade ground turned a sea of faces in the direction of the officers' bungalows. Lieutenant Baugh, the adjutant, had been alerted by the naik and the un-accustomed noise which had disturbed the peace of his Sunday afternoon.

'Where is he? Baugh demanded of the sergeant major.

'To your left, Sir, but beware, the sepoy will fire at you', he warned.

In his drug-induced state, Mangal Pandey was not to be intimidated by the appearance of a single British officer, and whilst Baugh was still several yards away a shot from the sepoy's musket brought down his horse. In the struggle that followed, both Baugh and the sergeant major received several cuts from Pandey's *tulwar*, but before any further wounds could be inflicted Pandey was restrained by a courageous Muslim sepoy whilst the two Englishmen made their escape. Only then did the Muslim release the drug-crazed sepoy when members of the quarter guard threatened to shoot him if he had not.

Other Europeans were appearing on the scene, among them Colonel Wheler, the Commanding Officer of the 34th NI who, faced with this unexpected and potentially explosive situatioin, decided that the best course of action was to send for the Brigadier. The 66-year-old Brigadier General, Sir John Hearsey, assessed the gravity of the scene as his gaze took in the mob of excited sepoys, the sullen quarter guard and Mangal Pandey standing in a threatening attitude with levelled musket.

'Have a care, General,' came a voice from the crowd, 'his musket is loaded.'

'Damn his musket!' growled Hearsey and, turning to his son, he called, 'If I fall, John, rush in and put him to death.'

Sir John's swift reply, emphasized by a signifant wave of his pistol towards the jemadar, was enough to persuade Mangal Pandey that there could be no escape from the hangman's noose, and he turned the muzzle of the musket upon himself, touching the trigger with his toe. In doing so the musket moved and the ball simply grazed his chest. On 8 April, the 26-year-old sepoy was hanged in front of the assembled garrison despite his plea that he had been taking *bhang* and opium and was not aware of what he was doing. The jemadar survived him by just thirteen days before he too paid the penalty for his failure to arrest the mutinous Brahmin.

A young ensign of the 84th NI was a sympathetic witness to the execution of the jemadar, for on the previous day in the company of Lieutenant Pearson, George Blake had visited the prisoner in the guard tent. 'He was heavily ironed, and had four sentries posted,' remembered Blake. 'On our entering he got up, salaamed and seemed very civil. Next day the warrant came and we were formed up in a line facing the gallows ... At 4.00 pm we saw the procession coming, the prisoner sitting in the bullock cart escorted by detachments of the 53rd and the Governor General's bodyguard. He made a long speech which I believe exhorted the sepoys to take warning by his fate and was then swung off.'

Feelings in the native regiments were running high but to the astonishment of many Europeans, beyond the disbandment of the 19th and 34th NI, no further action was taken to meet the very real threat of insurrection about to sweep through the Bengal Army. Eighty-five *sowars* of the 3rd Light Cavalry at Meerut were the next body to demonstrate their unwillingness to accept the contraversial cartridges, despite assurances from their officers that this issue had not been greased with animal fat. It was said that the men would give no reason for refusing the order beyond saying that 'they would get a bad name'. This act of in-subordination was severely dealt with and at a subsequent court martial each man was sentenced to ten years imprisonment with the added disgrace of being publicly shackled. On 9 May, a day notable for dark low clouds and a scorching wind, 4,000 sepoys were drawn up to form three sides of a square, the fourth being reserved for the eighty-five *sowars* of the 3rd Light Cavalry.

'They were marched up in front of us and formed into close column,' reported Ensign Blake. 'The General then gave the orders: "Order arms. Pile arms, and Take off your belts", all of which were obeyed without the least hesitation. The General then made a long speech in their own language ... several old native officers broke down and cried like children.' It must have made for a depressing spectacle and reports had it that not a few present thought the punishment far too harsh for the offence.

'Ironing the 85 took a long time,' wrote Lieutenant Stubbs of the Bengal Artillery, 'after which they were marched down the line and off to goal, looking wicked. I felt relieved when it was all over.'

Many of the sepoys drawn up on parade had served in several campaigns, but unarmed and surrounded by British troops shouldering Enfield rifles, they were powerless to protest as their cavalry comrades were stripped of their uniforms and boots, and marched off to the local jail.

To an English officer of the 3rd Light Cavalry, the events of Saturday, 9 May seemed just as menacing as that of the dark mass of cumulus building up on the horizon, and when he went down to the jail later with his friend MacNabb, Cornet Hugh Gough felt deeply moved by the plight of the prisoners. 'Shall I ever forget the scene?' he wrote many years later. 'We found our men imprisoned in one large ward. Once they began to realise the terrible future before them, they broke down completely. Old soldiers, with many medals gained in desperately fought battles for their English masters, wept bitterly ... young soldiers too, joined in. It was very evident they, at any rate, knew but little of the events that would follow.'

That same evening, whilst sitting on the verandah of his bungalow, young Gough was approached by a native officer and warned that the men were planning to mutiny and that the sahib's own troop would join to free their comrades with the help of the native guard at the jail. Once that had been carried out they planned an outbreak of murder and arson. Gough was sufficiently alarmed to communicate his fears to the officers in the mess, only to be greeted with amused chuckles. When he had been in India a little longer, he was told, he would learn not to pay heed to rumour spread by the natives.

Gough was unconvinced and despite a snub from the Colonel, he nevertheless approached the Brigadier commanding the station. Brigadier General Archdale Wilson, however, proved to be just as disbelieving and Hugh Gough returned to his bungalow deeply troubled by the supine attitude of his superiors. 'Such was our ill judged confidence,' he recalled. 'But, indeed, few men would in those days have been inclined to believe in the treachery of our native soldiers.'

Around Gough's bungalow the earth was cracked and parched and what little remained of the grass was scorched to the colour of burnt straw. This was the hot weather season when the Commander-in-Chief, his staff and virtually the whole of the administration had hastily abandoned the central plains for the cooler region of the hill stations. For those whose duties kept them in cantonments, the topic of conversation that morning dwelt more on a speculation as to the probable rise of the thermometer and how soon they might be permitted to join their families in Simla, than with the threat of insurrection. Firm in the belief that no native power was strong enough to challenge their authority, most Britons felt secure and in Chinsurah, a few miles from Barrackpore, a young subaltern of the 84th of Foot, whose battalion had been brought back from Burma to maintain an armed presence at the disbandment of the 34th NI, began to fear that he would soon be returning to Rangoon, a place he detested. George Blake's concern was unfounded, however, for just as Lord Canning was on the point of ordering the 84th back to Rangoon, a report reached him of serious disturbances at Meerut and Delhi. The news that his battalion was to remain in Bengal delighted young Blake, for with the carefree attitude of youth, his thoughts were far removed from bloodshed and danger, but rather with the fact that at Barrackpore there were jackals to hunt.

About 400 miles to the north-west, another subaltern destined to win the Victoria Cross and eventually to become the most celebrated military figure of the Victorian age, sought out his kit for a hot-weather march, little thinking that he would never again return to Peshawar. Lieutenant Frederick Sleigh Roberts left his bungalow and everything in it, and made ready to join the movable column.

Elsewhere, European families continued to enjoy the comfortable if dull routine to which they had become accustomed. A newspaper correspondent writing from Delhi a few days before the incident at Barrackpore, admitted: 'as usual no news to give you. All quiet and dull.' At Cawnpore, the ever-popular Nana Sahib was staging yet another lavish party for the British residents and officers of the station. Early May in Meerut brought the usual proliferation of sporting events and social activities to occupy the attention of most of the residents and it began to appear that the warning Hugh Gough had received was, if anything, ill founded. 'There was little thought or apprehension of anything so serious as war breaking out,' he wrote. 'It was one of the pleasantest and most favourite stations in the Bengal Presidency.'

The fact that such rumours had been dismissed as being absurd was not surprising as Meerut boasted the largest force of European infantry, cavalry and artillery of any establishment in India. Unhappily, for many of the unsuspecting residents, such assurance was shortly to be disabused in the most brutal fashion.

Sunday, 10 May was a day of scorching heat and searing winds. Because of the heat, the evening service at the church of St John had been rearranged for 7.00 pm – a break with tradition that was undoubtedly welcomed by the ladies who would otherwise have been obliged to forfeit or cut short their siesta in order to complete their toilet and dress in the late afternoon. As she was dressing, an indication that the service might be interrupted was brought to the chaplain's wife by a tearful ayah. Nervously, the Indian woman begged Mrs Rotton not to go to church that evening because of the danger of a disturbance by the sepoys. The chaplain, busy with putting the final touches to his sermon, at first shrugged off the warning. Meerut, after all, was a popular posting with a full complement of British troops, but in deference to his wife's fears, he agreed that she and the children should be left in the care of the quarter guard provided by the 60th Rifles. It was a decision he was not to regret.

The European families, as they climbed into their carriages or strolled leisurely through a field of sugar cane towards the church, found the peal of bells comforting. In the foetid streets of the native bazaar that same sound was audible to the *sowars* of the 3rd Light Cavalry as they angrily discussed the shackling and imprisonment of their fellow troopers. The men were bitterly resentful of the humiliation which had been heaped upon their comrades, but although seething with discontent and taunted by the prostitutes in the bazaar – 'We have no kisses for cowards' was their cry – they were not yet ready to take the irrevocable step of releasing the men in the jail.

The trouble began when a *sowar* caught a glimpse of a detachment of the 60th Rifles falling in for church parade, and immediately rode for the native lines to spread a rumour that British troops were coming to relieve them of their arms. His report inflamed the already excited sepoys of the 11th and 20th NI who at once broke away from their assembly to run for their piled muskets intent upon releasing the eighty-five *sowars* and a motley collection of criminals from Meerut New Jail. The bond of loyalty to their British officers had been severed as had the religious differences between Muslim and Hindu in their shared interest of overthrowing British rule.

By nightfall, Meerut had become a place of horror. Earlier, when Gough had stepped out on to his verandah, he had been appalled to see the horizon turn into a sea of flame. Galloping for the cavalry lines he found 'a thousand sepoys dancing and leaping frantically about, calling and yelling to each other and blazing away with their muskets in all directions'.

Gough barely escaped with his life. His friend MacNabb was not so fortunate.

The ferocity and speed of the insurrection paralysed the senior British officers, many of whom were aged and confused, not having commanded men in action since their youth. The junior officers, Hugh Gough among them, tried to organize some resistance but without success, and the mutineers, followed by a mob from the bazaar, eventually departed for Delhi 40 miles to the south-west, unmolested by British troops.

Daylight revealed the rows of burnt and blackened bungalows, a scene of bleak desolation, while in the streets of the Sudder Bazaar, many mutilated and scorched corpses bore grim testimony to the fury of the mob. The night's horror had resulted in the deaths of some fifty European men, women and children. It also marked the beginning of a tragedy which would only end after more than a year's bitter fighting and further savage atrocities. But as the troops set about the grim task of laying out the bodies of the murdered Europeans, 250 miles to the south-east at Cawnpore, some 800 Britons and Eurasians, largely unaware of the horrors that had taken place in Meerut, were undisturbed by rumour, confident that they enjoyed the protection of the Nana Sahib.

Chapter 3

MISPLACED CONFIDENCE

Cawnpore, despite an unenviable reputation for its bazaars being the favoured resort of numerous thieves and hooligans, was a popular posting for the families of the European troops stationed in Oude, despite Caroline Lindsay's less than favourable first impressions. Having sailed from England she had journeyed up-country with her mother Kate, brother George, and sisters Alice and Fanny from Calcutta in late October 1856.

Still homesick for England, the eighteen year old made no attempt to disguise her disappointment when writing to her Aunt Jane in Rochester. 'The station is a very ugly one and dreadfully scattered. It is a distance of fully six miles from one end of the cantonment to the other and by no means pretty or inviting to look at ... I have often and often wished I could be transported back to England to all my friends.' Despite the allure of dinner parties and the occasional ball, like her sister Caroline, Alice too pined for the home they had left behind, and in a letter to their Aunt Jane she begged for news by return: 'and give an account of yourself. Do you still go to Mrs Webster's to be tortured?' she wondered. 'I hope you had a merry Christmas. I suppose it will be over by the time you get this letter'. It was, of course, and tragically had she but known it, Alice's young life was also drawing to a close.

With the prospect of cooler weather, Caroline, Alice and Fanny were at last able to put aside their feelings of nostalgia, for the European quarter between the town and the river had many facilities for social activity. Amateur theatricals were popular with both Europeans and Eurasians. There was a racquets court, a library, a race course marked out by 'inverted pots of white-washed crockery', a bandstand, together with regular dinner parties and dances in the spacious assembly rooms at which the Lindsay sisters were much in demand. Lieutenant Moorsom, in spite of his criticism of the regimental ball, where he found the 'floor very bad and the dancers fewer and not so good as those in Lucknow', he was more than pleased to dance 'some polkas and a Lancer's' with Alice and Caroline Lindsay.

Among its buildings Cawnpore boasted a church, whose tall white steeple rising above the surrounding trees was a recognized landmark, and if the town lacked the imposing architecture of Delhi, the broad expanse of the Ganges – almost 3 miles wide when in flood – was used by vessels of every shape and size carrying merchandise to places as far away as Calcutta 1,000 miles downstream.

About 13 miles to the north-west lay the town of Bithur. From 1819 the palace there had been the residence of the Peshwa Baji Rao, a Mahratta ruler who, following a defeat by the army of Brigadier General Sir John Malcom in June 1818, lived in considerable opulence on a pension of eight lakhs of rupees – equivalent to £80,000 – per annum. It had been a generous settlement by the East India Company who, given the Peshwa's dissolute lifestyle, could not have expected him to live beyond middle age. In fact Baji Rao II confounded them all by dying in 1851 at the ripe old age of seventy-six and with his death the pension terminated in accordance with Dalhousie's 'doctrine of lapse' which allowed the Governor General to take over the estate of a Hindu prince who had no natural heir.

According to Hindu belief, it was necessary for a son to perform the funeral rites in order to prevent his father's soul from hell after death and propitiate the souls of his ancestors. In the case of a Hindu having no male issue, Hindu law recognized an adopted son for that purpose. Therefore in 1827, with his astrologer's approval, Baji Rao took two young men as his adopted sons: Nana Govind Dondhu Pant, who took the household title of Nana Sahib, and Sadashur Rao, popularly known as Dada Sahib.

Nana Sahib was about thirty-six years old at the time of the Peshwa's death. A rather stout, pale-faced Brahmin, he enjoyed the reputation of being a much sort after benefactor and host, patronized by officers and memsahibs alike. John Lang had enjoyed the Nana's hospitality in his palace at Bithur a year before the Mutiny, and thought him 'not a man of ability but not a fool'. If Nana Sahib nursed a grievance against the Company for refusing to grant him part of his adoptive father's pension, he took care not to reveal it. A limited knowledge of English did not inhibit him from entertaining favoured Western visitors and he frequently gave parties which became the talk of Cawnpore.

The Nana seems to have shown a particular interest in the game of billiards. John Lang joined him in a game during his stay in Bithur and was impressed. 'I am not a bad billiard player,' he wrote, 'but it was quite evident to me that he suffered me to beat him as easily as I did, simply out of what he considered to be politeness.' Although outwardly a strict Hindu, Nana Sahib made no demands upon his guests in the matter of religion. Confessed Lang: 'If I preferred beef to any other kind of meat I had only to give the order.' In the interests of his host's religious belief, however, Lang was careful to request a vegetarian dish, although he was convinced that the Nana drank brandy and smoked hemp.

Despite his apparent good relationship with the British community, Dalhousie's refusal to grant him the right to use the title of Maharajah, or to allow him a salute of guns – an honour Baji Rao II enjoyed up to his death – was undoubtedly a source of vexation to the Nana, who in 1854 had lodged an appeal, only for Dalhousie to dismiss it out of hand. Undeterred by this rebuff the Nana, who dared not take the risk of polluting his caste by crossing the ocean, decided to send a trusted agent to present his case to the East India Company's Board of Control in London, or even petition Parliament itself.

The emissary chosen by Nana Sahib was a clever young man who as a child had been educated at the Cawnpore Free School, and after becoming a house steward in the Nana's service had risen rapidly to the position of a valued advisor. Azimulla Khan was undoubtedly gifted, possessing an extensive knowledge of both French and English. He was, according to Mowbray Thomson, able to converse, read and write fluently in both languages. Well supplied with money, Azimulla Khan set off for England with two companions, Raja Piraji and Mohamed Ali Khan, but when the ship eventually docked at Southampton, only two of them strode down the gangway. Raja Piraji, having succumbed to illness, had been buried at sea.

Azimulla's handsome appearance and polished manners charmed many ladies in London society, but singularly failed to win the favour of the Board of Directors with the Nana's petition, and the two Indians left England in June 1855 with their mission unfulfilled. Despite the Nana's insistence that

28

commitments to his father's pensioners had left him in reduced circumstances, it was a claim many would have found difficult to credit having visited his palace. As the visitor's gaze took in the sumptuous furnishings and tapestries, and as his feet sank into the luxurious carpets laid across the floors, he might be forgiven for believing that the Nana's pension from the Government was more than adequate.

Maharajah Dhondu Pant seldom left his palace in Bithur but in April 1857, accompanied by Azimullah, he paid a brief visit to Lucknow where he saw the Financial Commissioner, Martin Gubbins. The impression he made upon that worthy was less than favourable:

> His manner was arrogant and presuming. To make a show of dignity and importance, he brought six or seven followers with him into the room, for whom chairs were demanded. He appeared to be of middle age and height, and, as Hindoos of rank generally are in India, corpulent. Mahrattas of pure descent are usually fair in complexion, but the Nana is darker than they generally are.

Nana Sahib fared better in his dealings with the Commissioner for Oudh. Sir Henry Lawrence received him cordially and requested 'the authorities of the city to show him every attention'. The Nana, however, for reasons best known to himself, cut short his visit protesting that his presence in Cawnpore was urgently required. This excuse did not satisfy Martin Gubbins who suspected that he had used the occasion to secretly conspire with other discontented princes. He thought the Nana's conduct to be highly suspicious and with the approval of the High Commissioner, immediately conveyed his fears to Major General Sir Hugh Wheeler, the officer commanding the Cawnpore garrison. Wheeler, whose Indian wife was of the same caste as that of the Nana, and who had always found him to be agreeable, refused to believe that either he or his armed retainers posed a threat to the garrison. In fact, so confident was Wheeler of obtaining the Nana's co-operation in the event of trouble with the sepoys, that he invited him to take over the protection of the Treasury 5 miles away at Nawabganj, using the Nana's own household troops.

Since the late eighteenth century, when Cawnpore had been chosen as the base for an advanced British garrison by Warren Hastings, the town's importance as a military station had fallen away and now, although still the military headquarters of the

Bengal Presidency by virtue of the Grand Trunk Road which ran past its barracks, Cawnpore could not boast of a single British Army regiment. The 32nd of Foot was at Lucknow, and Cawnpore's military strength of 3,300 was made up largely of native troops from the 1st, 53rd and 56th NI, the 2nd Light Cavalry and a company of artillerymen. The only European troops available to General Wheeler were seventy-four invalids from the 32nd of Foot, sixty men of the 84th of Foot, fifteen men from the Madras Fusiliers and fifty-nine artillerymen. These, together with the British officers of the native regiments, brought the total number of Europeans to less than 300.

The officer commanding, Major General Sir Hugh Massey Wheeler, was a slightly built Irishman who, despite his sixty-eight years, carried himself as erect as any young soldier. He had served with native troops in India for more than fifty years and had led the 48th NI with distinction in the Afghan campaign. No one had a greater affection, or a firmer belief in the loyalty of his troops, than Sir Hugh Massey Wheeler.

In April, a party of rebellious troops from the disbanded 19th NI passed through the town spreading tales of the controversial cartridges, and it did not escape the notice of the more suspicious British residents that the malcontents were lavishly entertained by the Nana. When news of the mutinies which had over-whelmed Meerut and Delhi reached Cawnpore on 14 May it created little apprehension among the Europeans perhaps because of the distance involved – Meerut was almost 300 miles from Cawnpore – but the excitement in the ranks of the sepoys and among the native traders in the bazaar, grew appreciably. Several of the Eurasian merchants were sufficiently alarmed to arrange for boats to carry their families to Allahabad.

Despite the rising tension in the native quarters, Wheeler's trust in the Nana's integrity remained unshaken. The wife of at least one high-ranking officer on his staff shared his confidence. In a letter to her sister in England, Mrs Emma Sophia Ewart wrote on 18 May:

> My dearest Fanny. We are in the midst of surprising events. You will learn a great deal from the papers I dare say. As yet we are quiet here and the native troops have shown no disaffection at this place ... people here are for the most part in great terror, but my husband thinks needlessly so. The General, Sir Hugh Wheeler, is on the qui vive, and is said to be equal to the difficulties of his

position: cool and determined ... If this storm blows over, the events will at least open the eyes of the Government to the necessity of keeping a stronger European force in this country.

Mrs Kate Lindsay who had recently arrived in India with her family, was not so easily comforted. 'Oh Jane,' she wrote on 19 May, 'such a day ... I hope never to pass again ... Willie [Major Lindsay] said I must go with the girls & he was anxious for Lilly to go with me [to Calcutta] and also Mrs Bissel.'

Kate Lindsay's fears were assuaged somewhat when later that day, the telegraph reported that the rebels had marched on Delhi. Major Lindsay reassured his sister by telling her that Queen's troops were marching on Cawnpore as fast as they could. 'This gave me a more cheering feeling,' she continued, 'and we all went to church at ½ past 6 in the evening, and I think we all felt our minds calmed and comforted, and trusted in God, who is a good God, wd [sic] not quite forsake us.'

General Wheeler, despite the reports from Meerut, never wavered in his view that providing the Europeans and Eurasians – some 800 in a native population of 150, 000 – remained calm, the sepoys in Cawnpore would in all probability not mutiny. Nevertheless he was sympathetic to the fears of the civilians and should the worst happen, the General made it known that shelter would be provided in two barracks south of the canal currently used by the invalids and families of the 32nd of Foot. In the event of a mutiny, he pointed out, it was to be hoped that the sepoys would follow the example set by the Meerut rebels and immediately depart for Delhi. A telegram Wheeler sent to the Governor General in Calcutta on 18 May certainly reflected the confidence he felt: 'All well at Cawnpore ... the insurgents can only be about 3,000 in number, and are said to cling to the walls of Delhi, where they have put up a puppet king. Calm and expert policy will soon reassure the public mind ... the plague is, in truth, stayed.'

Whether his confidence was shared by Mrs MacMahon, the Eurasian wife of an English sergeant major in the 53rd NI is questionable. Shopping in the native bazaar, she was accosted by a sepoy of her husband's regiment out of uniform. 'You will none of you come here much oftener,' he told her with quiet menace, 'you will not be alive in another week.' Mrs MacMahon later

31

reported the threat but her tale was quietly put to one side in the interest of maintaining good relations with the sepoys.

The Collector's 21-year-old pregnant wife, Mrs Lydia Hillersdon, expressed her concern on the turn of events in typical fashion when writing to a relative in England. 'Fancy us, the governor of the country, obliged to shelter ourselves behind guns.' Then in an abrupt change of mood, she added:

> Oh! How I wish we were with you, and out of this horrid country. May God spare us and may we live to see each other again ... I send you some of the dear children's hair. We trust to our Father who governs all. Tell dearest G——— to keep the two little books Bishop Wilson gave me for my sake, and never forget that in the midst of life we are in death ... Oh, it is a hard trial to bear.

A week later, that same lady was writing with obvious relief: 'with God's blessing, one might say, the storm has now blown over and things are mending.'

It was not a belief held by Mrs Elizabeth Sneyd. On her way to visit her sister in Calcutta, she was obliged to spend the night in Cawnpore. Accommodation was difficult to find, for the one good hotel had been taken over by the Nana Sahib's retainers, but she did secure 'a most dirty room' normally occupied by the manager's clerk, for herself and her daughter-in-law. The meal put in front of them was no better, in her opinion, than the 'stale left overs of the native soldiers'. The conduct of the sepoys in the compound, usually polite, she found 'very strange and uncourteous'. 'These men did nothing but point and laugh at me among themselves whilst talking a great deal together in an undertone.' Elizabeth Sneyd confessed that she felt a 'presentment of evil', and she and Lousia Sneyd lost no time in resuming their journey to Calcutta.

In the last weeks of May the probability of a major insurrection could no longer be discounted and an appeal was sent to Sir Henry Lawrence in Lucknow begging for a company of European soldiers. Despite the difficulty of sparing even a single man, Sir Henry responded by immediately despatching a Company of the 32nd and a squadron of Oudh Irregulars led by Captain Fletcher Hayes, his Military Secretary, with instructions for him to report on the situation as he found it.

The reinforcement reached Cawnpore during the evening of 20 May having covered the 48 miles in less than twelve hours.

Cawnpore remained in a state of uneasy calm but the grisly sight of two European corpses floating down the river was reason enough for the Eurasian head clerk of the Commissariat department to regret the decision which brought his wife and two daughters to Cawnpore. 'Alarming reports continued to fly about the station daily,' wrote William Shepherd, nicknamed 'Jonah' by his family, 'and we lived in perpetual anxiety and dread.'

Appreciating that the community's nerves were stretched to breaking point, General Wheeler sought to lessen their fears by inviting those that desired it, to enter the barrack buildings. A great crowd did so, bringing their bundles of possessions and looking for all the world 'like so many travellers bound for a far country', commented Amelia Horne. To the vivacious eighteen-year-old Eurasian girl, it seemed rather exciting, if perhaps a trifle uncomfortable, to be sleeping on the balcony of the barracks with so many other people. She could hardly believe that anything worse could happen. The 32-year-old William Shepherd decided to remain in the town, but although refusing to give way to panic, he was sufficiently concerned to arrange for Indian dresses to be supplied to his wife and children.

Mrs Kate Lindsay, in expressing the fear she felt for her three daughters in a letter to her sister Jane Drage, pointed out that 'if our 3 native corps were to rise, which I pray to God to avert, we must all I am afraid perish.' Then, perhaps recalling that she had returned to India against advice and the tearful wishes of Caroline, she ended by begging her sister: 'Pray for us my dear Jane. My hand shakes. I am hardly able to write.' She was not alone in anticipating the worst, for in a letter to her aunt, Caroline confided: 'I have often and often wished I could be transported back to England and all my friends, but we must hope it is all for the best.'

The concern felt by the civilians was not shared by Sir Hugh Wheeler for on 3 June, confident that he had averted an insurrection in Cawnpore, he returned a detachment of the 84th of Foot and Madras Fusiliers which had arrived from Benares six days before, to Lucknow. Fortunate indeed were these eighty soldiers for with the telegraph down and every road infested with rebels, the letters they carried with them were the last before the town fell into enemy hands.

In defence of the General's action, it must be said that his confidence had received a boost on 21 May when in response to an invitation from Charles Hillersdon, the Nana had agreed to take part in discussions relating to the defence of the community in the event of a sepoy rising. The decision to involve the Nana, however, was regarded with the deepest suspicion by many of Wheeler's junior officers. 'Always hitherto we have been fighting against open enemies,' complained a young ensign to his mother, 'now we cannot tell who are friends, who enemies.'

Nanak Chand, the agent for a banker in Cawnpore, also had serious doubts regarding the Nana's intention. 'The Nana will keep up appearances,' he wrote, 'for if the troops [the rebel sepoys] get defeated, he will get a good name and a chance of restoration of his pension; and if the troops prevail and the Government is removed, then he will be the master of the country … it is certain that the bad characters with him are bound to make trouble.'

Sir Hugh Wheeler may have been confident that the Nana's presence would have a restraining influence on the behaviour of the sepoys, but he was not unmindful of the responsibility he had for the safety of the civil community, and in response to their increasing anxiety, it was agreed that a common refuge should be made available to all those scattered the length and breadth of the station.

There were two possible locations. The Magazine, a building of sweltering heat with its high walls, was 3 miles upstream and would have to be occupied before the mutiny broke out if the garrison was to have any chance of reaching it without a costly engagement. The second, concerned a number of single-storey barrack blocks, some of which were still under construction. Of these, two of the largest were brick built with walls almost 2 feet thick, one of which housed the families of the invalid soldiers, and the other with a thatched roof contained the sick of the 32nd of Foot.

These buildings stood on an open-plain close to the Allahabad road and although Wheeler was later criticized for taking up such an exposed position, there is some evidence that he had been influenced by a statement from Lord Canning that reinforcements would reach him by 15 June. If this was so, then the position he selected would have been the nearest to the road along which the relief would have marched, but even so Wheeler's choice of a defensive position did not meet with universal approval. Amelia Horne, in her memoirs, writes:

It appears that more than one officer had attempted to disuade General Wheeler from taking up the position he did. Their opinion from the beginning was that the spot and buildings would never stand a siege. Even those who had little pretensions to military tactics perceived the utter insecurity of the place, and pointed out that the magazine was better adapted to defence. It stood on the river bank and had huge walls of substantial masonry.

The one redeeming feature of Wheeler's chosen position lay in the fact that the compound possessed an inexhaustible supply of water from a well, and the site itself was close enough to the General's residence to enable him to exercise control once labour had begun on the construction of the defence perimeter. Unfortunately, the earth had been baked by the sun to a hard clay and there was not the water to soften it. Despite strict supervision, the native workers were only able to excavate trenches 'deep enough to give shelter from high angle shrapnel, and narrow enough to minimise the chance of a common shell dropping into it'. The unfortunate artillerymen found that their positions beside mounds of round shot were without protection of any kind.

Days of frenzied activity were viewed with amusement by the Nana's agent.

'What do you call that place you are making out in the plain?' asked Amizullah Khan of Lieutenant Daniell who had been a frequent visitor to the Nana's palace.

'I am sure I don't know,' replied the young cavalry officer.

'I think you should call it the Fort of Despair,' suggested Azimullah.

'Oh, indeed not,' came the confident rejoinder. 'We will call it the Fort of Victory.'

The next few days were tinged with apprehension for the European and Eurasian families. The native labour had still to complete the defence works and whilst many officers demonstrated their trust in their men by sleeping in the native lines, the civilians hurried from their places of work to spend each night within the perimeter of the entrenchment. 'Oh, such a scene, dear Fanny,' wrote Emma Ewart on 27 May. 'No one can say how or where the trouble is to end. Men, officers, women and children, beds and chairs all mingled together inside & out of the barrack, some talking and even laughing, some very frightened, some defiant, others despairing.'

It was a display of panic which dismayed Captain Fletcher Hayes the Military Secretary from Lucknow, who wrote:

> Since I have been in India I have never witnessed so frightful a scene of confusion, fright, and bad management as the European barracks presented. Four guns were in position loaded, with European artillerymen in night caps, hanging on to the guns in groups looking like melodramatic buccaneers. People of all kinds, of every colour, sect and profession, were crowding into the barracks ... buggies, palki–gharrees, vehicles of all sorts drive up and discharge cargoes of writers, tradesmen, and a miscellaneous mob of every complexion, from white to tawny, all in terror of an imaginary foe. I saw quite enough to convince me that if any insurrection took or takes place, we shall have no one to thank but our selves, because we have now shown to the Natives how very easily we can become frightened, and when frightened, utterly helpless.

That he did not exaggerate is borne out in a letter from Caroline Lindsay to her aunt.

'You may imagine we were all rather in a fright, the scene of confusion and fright everybody was in was past description. We were all very glad when day dawned.'

The unfortunate Fletcher Hayes was to be treacherously murdered on the road to Fatehgarh, when on 1 June, with another Englishman, he rode to join the 2nd Oudh Irregulars. Attacked by the *sowars*, Hayes and Carey spurred their horses furiously away, but Captain Hayes, unlike the cavalryman, was far from being a skilled horse-man and he was quickly overtaken and cut down.

The festival of Eid had been celebrated by the Muslims on Friday, 22 May and the occasion passed without incident in Cawnpore, but beneath the surface ugly passions were stirring, and on the night of 4 June, a blaze of incendiarism and a tumult of sound from the lines of the 2nd Cavalry signalled the beginning of the long anticipated sepoy uprising. 'We slept undisturbed on the night of the 4th June until about two hours after midnight,' remembered William Shepherd, 'when a great bustle and collection of people roused me from my slumbers. A motion of the hand pointing towards the 2nd cavalry lines accompanied by the words "listen", was all the excplanation I could get.'

Despairingly, Colonel John Ewart, commanding the 1st NI, a regiment which had been raised as early as 1787, pleaded with his sepoys as they made a rush for the stack of muskets: 'My children! My children! This is not your way,' he pleaded. 'Do not do so great a wickedness.' Although a few did refuse to join the mutineers and remained to fight at the side of their British comrades, the time had passed when a moving appeal in fluent Hindostanee might have restrained them, and brushing aside Ewart but without molesting him, his men hurried after the cavalry to join Nana Sahib's followers in sacking the Treasury.

When the 53rd and 56th NI followed on the heels of the rebellious 1st NI it seemed to those civilians who had taken refuge in the entrenchment that they had been spared the worst. Consequently, where before an air of gloomy despondency had taken hold, people now reminded each other that the sepoys had singularly avoided spilling the blood of their British officers, and that in a little more than a week the river would be high enough to permit the passage of steamers from Allahabad. In a letter to her aunt, Alice Lindsay wrote: 'we are still quite in an uncertain state of mind as to what is to be our fate, we only hope and trust we may be defended from all evil.'

Indeed, Alice's hope seemed at the time, to have some foundation for, intent on plundering the Treasury and one or two buildings in the city, the mutineers had left the Europeans in Cawnpore largely undisturbed.

The rebels were disorganized and as yet leaderless, but like the mutineers in Meerut, they decided to march on Delhi and declare support for their king.

As the sepoys of the 53rd busied themselves with looting and setting fire to the abandoned bungalows, the Nana began to consider his own position. As yet he had done little to associate himself with the uprising, but Azimullah Khan was all too conscious that for the rebels to succeed, the British would have to be destroyed in their trenches, and in order to accomplish this before the garrison could be reinforced, the mutineers must be brought back from Delhi. His argument won the day and perhaps fearing that any decision to the contrary might end in his own death, Nana Sahib agreed. After securing the Magazine, he mounted his state elephant and hurried up the Grand Trunk Road to induce the mutineers to return to Cawnpore.

Two days later, rising columns of smoke from the European quarter of the city signalled the return of the rebellious sepoys who had marched no further than Kalyanpur, the first stage on the road to Delhi. News of the Nana's involvement – for it had been on the strength of his promise of extra pay and a gold bracelet that had brought about the return of the sepoys – was greeted with groans of despair by the Anglo-European community.

Leaving his room to take up a post in the entrenchment, William 'Jonah' Shepherd looked upon the anxious faces of his wife and children and reflected bitterly on his folly in not sending them earlier to a place of safety.

Equally conscious of their vulnerability, the soldiers crouching behind the spoils thrown up in exavating the shallow trench, cursing the position chosen for them by their Commanding Officer. Instead of brick walls and an abundant store of ammunition and weapons which would have been available in the Magazine, accommodation for a community of more than 800 was now to be provided by two barrack buildings, one of which had a roof of thatch, and the other of tiles.

The perimeter to be defended had little in the way of shelter apart from the barrack blocks. Surrounding this area of approximately 200 square yards was the trench having a parapet over which it was said, 'any cow could jump'. On the north side, facing the river, a small bastion referred to cynically as 'The Redan' was commanded by fifty-year-old Major Edward Vibart, assisted by Captain Jenkins. A battery consisting of a mortar and two 9-pounders, brought in from Lucknow by Lieutenant Ashe a few days after Fletcher Hayes's ill-fated departure, covered the section in front of the native lines, whilst in the south-east Lieutenants Delafosse and Burney were in charge of three 9-pounders with a field of fire across the plain separating the cantonment from the city. A small brass 3-pounder completed the garrison's artillery strength.

The community now considered itself under siege and the last letter to leave Cawnpore for Lucknow was dated 1 June. It had been written by Mrs Emma Ewart to her sister in England:

Dearest Fanny. You will scarcely be able to realise the fearful state we are in – we can scarcely do so ourselves. No one can say how or when the trouble is to end, Mrs H [Lydia Hillersdon] is a sweet and amiable companion in affliction – We shall stick close to each other as long as it pleases God to spare us. Last night after much fatigue of mental torture, and several nights of imperfect rest, I fell into a state of stupefaction. Body and mind alike refused to be longer active ... Such nights of anxiety I would never believes possible ... another fortnight we expect will decide our fate & whatever it may be I trust we shall be enabled to bear it ... If these are my last words to you dearest Fanny you will remember them lovingly and always bear in mind that your affection & the love we have ever had for each other is an ingredient of comfort in these bitter times.

For a few days the mutineers devoted the whole of their attention to plundering the city. Europeans and Eurasians were the obvious targets but even the dark-skinned natives were subjected to the unwelcome attention of the rebels. 'Sowars are wandering in the streets,' noted Nanak Chand, 'and are giving rifles at doors of houses and extracting money from people by threatening them.' Then, whilst the garrison strove to improve the state of their defences, General Wheeler received word from the Nana that he was about to attack.

Chapter 4

THE STORM BREAKS

Within an hour of receiving news of the Nana's intention General Wheeler ordered all the officers who had strayed from the entrenchment to return immediately and, wrote Lieutenant Mowbray Thomson, 'with such expedition was the summons obeyed, that we were compelled to leave all our goods and chattels to fall a prey to the ravages of the sepoys and after they had appropriated all movables, they set fire to the bungalows. Very few of our number had secured a single change of rainment; some like myself, were only partly dressed.'

The main objective of the rebel artillery was the destruction of the two barrack buildings and the entrenchment, which offered a rudimentary shelter to the 900 European and Eurasian men, women and children, of which only 210 were European soldiers, with a sprinkling of loyal native officers and sepoys. To achieve this, wagons loaded with shot and powder from the Magazine abandoned by General Wheeler were soon to be seen making their way across the sandy plain in a steady procession towards the rebel batteries.

Sir Hugh Wheeler lost no time in gathering the hundred or so able-bodied civilians and equipping them with weapons to take their place along the perimeter of the entrenchment under the command of the Company's officers. Like the others, William Shepherd accepted his orders without complaint. 'How vivid is the recollection to me of this night,' he wrote many years later, 'being the first time I was called upon to perform military duty.'

Among the more effective were a group of twenty-five railway workers led by Robert Garrett, an Anglo-Irish railway engineer who had been given the task of evaluating a proposed line of track in Oudh. Finding himself stranded in Cawnpore, he formed what became known as the Railway Rifle Corps. Armed with hunting rifles or shotguns, and each a proficient marksman, they took their places in three of the unfinished barrack blocks, and were to prove their value when keeping watch from the frameless windows of the outer barracks.

It was a railwayman by the name of Murphy who was to earn the dubious distinction of becoming the first European casualty of the uprising in Cawnpore, and the only one to be buried in a coffin surrounded by his 'friends and companions with the minister performing the usual ceremony'. Henceforth the dead would be disposed of in a much cruder fashion without even the dignity of a burial service.

Precisely at 10.30 am on 5 June, as recorded by the Commissary clerk, an explosion of noise from an 18-pounder cannon signalled the beginning of a period of torment for the besieged community scarcely to be imagined. The dreadful screech that accompanied the iron ball as it plummeted close to a group of women and children standing near the hospital barrack building gave rise to a chorus of screams and shrieks. 'The consternation caused among them was indescribable,' remembered Mowbray Thomson, 'and every man rushed off to his place on the trench's perimeter, many of us carrying in our ears, for the first time, the peculiar whizzing of the round shot, with which we were to become so familiar.'

'I had no idea before of the very great report a bursting shell makes, and when so close as only a wall between, it was dreadful,' wrote William Shepherd. 'I cannot forget the frightful stir it caused some.'

For the rest of that first day the defenders sat behind a pitifully shallow rampart of earth, exposed to a scorching wind and the burning rays of the sun, in the expectation of an attack by cavalry or infantry at any moment. 'Waiting for the assault,' wrote Lieutenant Mowbray Thomson, 'not a man closed his eyes in sleep, and throughout the whole siege snatches of troubled slumber under the cover of a wall, was all the relief the combatants could obtain.'

Just as great a cause for concern was the limited supply of food – gone were the luxuries which even the lowest military rank could enjoy. Delicacies such as tinned salmon and herring were nothing more than a memory. Most private soldiers and their families had to be content with a ration of flour and split peas made up into a passable imitation of porridge. It was barely sufficient to satisfy a gnawing hunger but civilians who were not part of the perimeter guard were left to fend for themselves – an oversight which the head Commissary clerk thought quite unfair, particularly so when he had been on sentry duty for several hours with barely an opportunity for providing a meal for himself or his family.

'We had no food from home as our servants could not bring us any,' complained William Shepherd, adding with resignation, 'but there was so much anxiety and fear that no-one felt like eating.'

Later, the monotonous diet would be varied by the introduction of horse soup, and on one memorable day, recalled by Mowbray Thomson: 'The entrenched people were so fortunate as to shoot down a Brahminee bull that came grazing within limits where his sanctity was not respected.' Before that welcome occasion, Lieutenant Thomson could write with honesty: 'We had not a single good meal since entering the entrenchment, from the first living on half rations.'

In spite of their hunger, the garrison gave no sign that they were prepared to negotiate and after several days of fruitless activity, the Nana's resolve to prosecute the siege was only strengthened by the knowledge that many other mutineers were on their way to join him.

To the few like Amelia Horne who dared to stand at the barrack's verandah and gaze out across the plain: 'The whole surrounding country seemed covered with men at arms, on horse and on foot, and they presented a most formidable appearance,' she wrote. 'They seemed such fearful odds to keep at bay from our Lilliputian defences.'

At first, the rebel guns were sited too far from their targets to permit of any degree of accuracy and did little more than terrify the women and children with the noise of bursting shells, but reinforced by the introduction of large-calibre guns from the Magazine, a destructive bombardment of Wheeler's entrenchment and barrack blocks began on 7 June.

The artillerymen serving the Nana's cannon were, in the main, pensioners of the East India Company, and as the heavier 24-pounders were dragged closer to their target, they were able to inflict considerable damage to the defence works. 'By noon on Sunday they got ready a cordon of seven batteries,' wrote Amelia Horne, 'which opened such a hot and incessant firing on us that captain Moore remarked that he had never known such heavy and continued cannonading.'

It was the European volunteers in their exposed positions who bore the brunt of these bombardments and in just seven days, as recorded by Mowbray Thomson, 'fifty-nine artillerymen had all been killed or wounded at their posts ... the howitzer was knocked completely off its carriage – one or two of them had their sides driven in, and one was without a muzzle.'

Within a few hours of the rebel artillerymen's concentrated fire, the greater part of the barricades had been beaten down and not a door or window frame in the two barrack blocks remained intact. Lying on the floor of his crowded room, William Shepherd was jolted out of a fitful sleep by the rush of air as an 18-pound cannonball crashed through the window, removed the hat from the head of a clerk in the Collector's office, hit the inner wall, rebounded into a corner and fell with dire consequence on an ayah dozing there. Miraculously the baby on her lap was unhurt but the legs of the unfortunate woman were shattered, and, related the Commissary clerk, 'She died within the hour from loss of blood and pain.'

'Every shot that struck the barracks was followed by the heart rending shrieks of the women and children who were either killed outright by the projectiles or crushed to death by the falling beams, masonry, and splinters,' reported Amelia Horne, 'windows and doors were soon shot off their sockets, and the shot and ball began to play freely through the denuded buildings.'

Considering the horrors they were experiencing, the conduct of the majority of the women was remarkably courageous. At first, the unaccustomed sights and sounds were too great to bear in silence and Mowbray Thomson recalled that a chorus of terrified screams from the women and shrieks from the children would greet the arrival of each round shot. But as the days passed most accepted the situation with resignation and strove to keep their fears to themselves. Indeed, during this period of the siege, only one person seems to have behaved in a less than credible manner. Thomson was openly contemptuous of the man and noted with disgust that 'while women and children were daily dying around him, not even the perils of his own wife could arouse this man to exertion.' He did not disclose the man's name, but it is generally believed to have been Deputy Judge Advocate General, Edwin Wiggins, whose wife had 'quite lost her reason from terror and excitement'.

About 250 yards to the west of the entrenchment there existed a partially completed building originally intended for an addition to the sepoys' barracks. It was here that the mutineers posted a number of matchlock men. They were all noted marksmen and from the roof and window openings at a height of some 40 feet, the snipers were able to command a great part of Wheeler's encampment. Such was the accuracy of their musket fire that few defenders dared move out of cover for an instant without running the risk of becoming a target.

Returning from a perilous expedition to the well, William 'Jonah' Shepherd was grateful for the shelter of a heap of sandbags. Crouching low, he suddenly felt a tremendous blow to the base of his spine, which stretched him senseless on the ground. A spent musket ball had cut through several layers of clothing to penetrate an inch deep into his flesh. Seeking help, he was relieved to find that the wound was not as serious as he had first thought, and he could afford to smile at the surgeon's observation that 'nobody ever lives after getting a bullet in the part you have got, and as you have escaped this, you will live very long indeed.' 'Jonah' Shepherd was probably no less thankful to find that he was to be spared trench duty for a time, enabling him to spend a few days with his family. Lieutenant Swynfen Jervis of the Bengal Engineers was not so fortunate. Scorning to run through a hail of musketry, he walked 'with his back straight and his head held high' across the compound as musket balls kicked up the dust around his feet. 'Run! Jervis, Run!' Came the anxious shouts from a group of his fellow officers. The young subaltern, however, scornful of the sepoys' aim, ignored their advice and, commented Mowbray Thomson, 'suffered the consequence of his own foolishness with a bullet through the heart'.

Thomson himself very nearly became a casualty when, while assisting a comrade to hobble across an exposed stretch of ground, he was also truck by a spent ball. Fortunately, the injury proved to be nothing worse than an ugly spreading bruise and he was spared a protracted spell in hospital where the chance of being crushed by falling masonry was almost as great a risk as facing a rebel sniper.

Unable to silence the mutineer's guns with their own ineffectual artillery, the besieged accepted the hopelessness of the situation with resignation. The women in particular bore their discomfort with a degree of fortitude typical of the early Victorians.

44

It was always possible for their menfolk to involve themselves in the excitement of battle, but for the women there was neither privacy nor relief from the terrible heat of a tropical sun, nor could they obtain a moment's respite from the torment of a myriad of flies or the acrid smell of urine and body odour. The suffering of their kin was bound to effect even the most hardened of military veterans. The spectacle of small children sucking strips torn from goatskin water carriers, in an attempt to moisten their parched and swollen mouths, was one which Lieutenant Mowbray Thomson never quite forgot. Whilst the sight of his five-year-old daughter Polly, struggling within herself to 'smother the emotions that arose from feelings of hunger, thirst, and fear', caused William Shepherd's heart to 'bleed often to the core'.

Some, like the Collector's wife, Lydia Hillersdon, had the horrifying experience of seeing their husband killed in front of them. On 7 June Charles Hillersdon was conversing with his wife when a round shot struck him full in the body and his eviscerated remains collapsed at the feet of his horrified wife. Lydia herself survived just two nights before a ball brought down the ceiling of her refuge and buried her beneath an avalanche of rubble.

The greater part of the unfinished barracks beyond the entrenchment had been in the possession of the rebels since the beginning of the siege. After several determined sorties, however, the nest of snipers was dislodged and two of the buildings were occupied by detachments from the garrison. Number 4 block was held by a dozen young men from the Railway Rifle Corps with no experience of soldiering, but they made such good use of their breech-loading rifles that for three days every rebel attack was repulsed without supervision from a professional soldier until the arrival of Lieutenant George Glanville of the 2nd Bengal Fusiliers.

Their comrades in block No. 2 were equally effective in the defence of a room just large enough for the deployment of seventeen men, first under the command of Captain Jenkins, and after he was wounded, Lieutenant Mowbray Thomson.

Constantly raked with musketry and subjected to the occasional cannon shot, the men who made up the numbers in barrack blocks 2 and 4, fought on a killing ground where prisoners were despatched 'without reference to headquarters'. The defenders of the block commanded by Mowbray Thomson were particularly hard pressed, losing three quarters of their strength in the first few days. One of the early casualties was Robert Garrett. The circumstance of his death is unclear, but it is likely that he fell victim to either a shell or one of the snipers who crept up at night shielded by the heaps of bricks that littered the unfinished barrack blocks. Such was the importance of these barrack blocks to Wheeler that daily casualties there were immediately made good by volunteers, some of whom had a good knowledge of military weapons, although most of them were civilians whose only experience had been sniping at wildfowl.

To supply these positions with food and ammunition was a highly dangerous business, but there was no lack of volunteers prepared to run the gauntlet by taking advantage of whatever cover there was between the entrenchment and the barrack block. 'Two men of the picket, who acted as cooks, performed this dangerous journey daily when they went for our miserable dole of food,' recorded Mowbray Thomson. 'If ever men deserved the Victoria Cross these poor fellows did.'

The surgeons who sometimes accompanied them seldom lacked employment, for every stretch of ground or pile of bricks not covered by the defender's field of fire was occupied by mutineers who kept up a continuous musketry from doors, windows and even the ditches which faced the half-built barrack blocks. Occasionally, when the 'Pandies' became too troublesome, a party of some thirty powder-blackened desperadoes, armed with the new Enfield rifle, would sally forth to drive the rebels into the open where Delafosse's artillery swept them with grape.

In these operations no one worked harder than the thirty-year-old Captain John Moore of the 32nd of Foot. Mowbray Thomson described him as being a 'soldier of commanding presence, light haired, and blue eyed, whom no toil could weary, no danger could daunt'. Despite the handicap of having one arm in a sling, the result of a broken collarbone sustained in a fall from his horse, the tall Irish captain led many sorties against the mutineers, and when not venturing out with a party of volunteers, made sure that the weaker links in the garrison's chain of defences were suitably strengthened. 'His never-say-die disposition served many a sinking heart to the conflict,' enthused Lieutenant Thomson, 'and his affable and tender sympathy imparted fresh patience to the suffering women.'

Following on from one encounter with the sepoys, Lieutenants Daniell and Thomson heard the sounds of a desperate struggle in an adjoining room. Rushing in, they were confronted with the sight of Captain Moore pinned to the ground by a powerful sepoy who was on the point of cutting the officer's throat. Without pausing in his stride, Daniell immediately transfixed the sepoy with his bayonet, to earn the grateful thanks of the Irish captain who, but for his timely intervention, would certainly have died. 'In the manifold deaths which surrounded us in those terrific times,' wrote Thomson later, 'such hair breadth escapes were little remarked upon.'

Commenting on the garrison's desperate efforts to defend their entrenchments, Mowbray Thomson was convinced that if the rebels had only shown more enterprise or determination, 'we could not have held the place for four and twenty hours'.

On 9 June, the green flag of the emperor of Delhi was raised by a Muslim butcher who soon gathered a crowd about him to listen to a tirade of abuse against the infidels, whilst the Nana raised a red Hindu flag and distributed leaflets warning that every Hindu who did not 'join in this righteous cause, is an outcast; may he eat the flesh of cows'. Despite the rhetoric used by both religious factions, it was not until two days later that the first mass attack against Wheeler's entrenchment was launched. It was led by the *sowars* of the 2nd Cavalry – on foot on this occasion – supported by sepoys and malcontents from the city's jail, in a screaming mob which streamed across the plain towards the perimeter defences.

From his post near the hospital block Shepherd watched apprehensively as, in his words:

> some thousands of armed men spread about under every cover available, their muskets and bayonets only perceptible, and they fired as fast as they could load. Their batteries also threw in shot, shell and grape, and bullets came pouring in ... tearing away tents and pillars of the barracks on every side. The din of this fearful cannonading resembled continuous claps of thunder in a tremendous storm.

The assault was met with grim determination by men anxious to avail themselves of an opportunity to assuage their pent-up fury against the mutineers for the suffering of their womenfolk. Crouched behind the breastworks at an interval of fifteen paces, they wreaked such destruction that not one rebel succeeded in breaching the defences. For the rest of that evening and the whole of the following day, Nana Sahib's followers were content to use the safer option of artillery fire which filled Wheeler's entrenchment with choking clouds of black smoke and the whistle of iron fragments mixed with flying pieces of stone. Sheltering as best he could among the bricks which littered the floor of his barrack room, and expecting death at any moment, William Shepherd scrawled a pencilled comment on the wall:

> Should this meet the eyes of any who were acquainted with us, in case we are all destroyed, be it known to them that we occupied this room for eight days under circumstances so distressing as have no precedent. The destruction of Jerusalem could not have been attended with distress so severe as we have experienced in so short a time.

It was at this stage of the siege that the garrison welcomed its one and only reinforcement in the person of Lieutenant Boulton of the 7th Native Cavalry. He had been engaged upon district duty in Lucknow to keep open the road from Fatehgarh and was the only English officer to escape with his life when the 48th NI mutinied. Uncertain of Wheeler's position, he had waited for daylight before galloping madly through Nawabgunj, past the Nana's cannons, before going on to clear the parapet of the entrenchment watched by an astonished sentry in one tremendous leap. 'He joined the out picket and although a great sufferer from a gash in his cheek,' reported Thomson, 'he proved a valuable addition to our strength.'

Of the garrison's artillerymen, only a handful of the original crew were still alive but the volunteers serving the 12-pounders struck back as best they could, always exposed to a punishing ordeal from the enemy's mortars and small-arms fire. Cannons were knocked from their carriages and in the south-east corner of the compound the tinder-dry wood of an ammunition limber took fire, threatening to blow that section of the works and its occupants to eternity. Showing remarkable coolness Lieutenant Henry George Delafosse crawled beneath the limber and, ignoring the shellfire, worked steadily to pull away the burning splinters whilst two redcoats hurried to his assistance with buckets of water to finally extinguish the fire.

The thatched roof of the hospital building had long been regarded a hazard and at 5.00 pm on Sunday, 13 June, the worst fears of the wounded were realized when an incendiary projectile fell upon the thatch and assisted by a stiff breeze, set fire to the rafters. The ensuing conflagration, punctuated at intervals by thunderous explosions, cause panic among the helpless patients, and the women and children who had taken refuge there. So traumatic was the incident that a young Eurasian girl remembered it forty years later when, as Amelia Bennett, she published her memoirs of the siege. 'The cries of the sick and wounded to be saved from the flames and the falling building were heart rending. The rebels guided in their firing by the blazing pile, poured a continual volley of shot and shell into the building, and the occupants were dragged out without regard to the excruciating pain of their wounds.'

There was no help forthcoming from Wheeler's entrenchments, for as William Shepherd later confessed:

> It was perfectly impracticable to save any of the wounded or the medicine in consequence of the insurgents collecting in very large bodies in the adjacent compounds and buildings, with their muskets and swords, ready every moment to pounce down on us, and the men were compelled to keep their places under the walls of the entrenchment, and could not bear a helping hand to those in the barracks.

It was thanks to the prompt action described by Amelia, that just four people perished in the conflagration – the schoolmaster and his wife, and two artillerymen.

As the rebels rushed forward to mount their assault against the trenches, Lieutenant Ashe made ready with his battery and directed 'a most destructive charge of grape,' remarked Mowbray Thomson. 'Ashe was a great scourge to our enemies, in consequence of the surprising celerity and accuracy of the firing from his battery.' The rebel attack was successfully beaten off following half an hour of furious gunfire which left the sandy plain littered with sepoy dead and wounded.

The destruction of the hospital was a serious blow to the besieged for among the items lost were medical supplies vital to the well-being of the sick and wounded. 'All that the surgeons could save,' lamented Lieutenant Thomson, 'was a box or two of surgical instruments and a small chest of medicine.' Once that supply became exhausted, the plight of the sick became acute, and, 'from the utter impossibility of extracting bullets, or dressing mutilations,' he added, 'casualties were increased in their fatality.'

'It was now that our skirts were in demand,' confessed Amelia Horne. 'We tore every vestige, even to our sleeves, to supply bandages for the wounded.'

To the ordinary ranker, however, the loss of medical supplies was of secondary importance to the loss of his campaign medals and when the ashes of the barrack rooms had cooled sufficiently, the men of the 32nd 'raked them over with bayonets and swords, making diligent search for their lost medals'. Gone now was the shelter the building had afforded against a summer temperature rising, in the trenches, to 120 degrees, which baked the stocks of muskets making them too hot for use. Sixty years later, an underground chamber was discovered beneath the site of the barracks which, had it been available, would have afforded a cool and bomb-proof shelter for the whole community.

In the stifling heat, the women with their offspring who had previously availed themselves of the shade afforded by the hospital, now crouched together in the shallow trench, a sheet of canvas draped across a rude framework of splintered wood to serve as a canopy against the scorching rays of the sun. Eventually, even this crude shelter was torn away and to add to the mounting toll of casualties were those from heatstroke. 'Those who all their lifetime had been accustomed to enjoy the coolness provided by the khus tatties and punkhas during the hot weather, or had never ventured out in the hot winds,' observed Mowbray Thomson, 'were thus pitilessly exposed a whole day, to the powerful heat of the sun.'

'There was no shelter for the men now anywhere during the day,' wrote Lieutenant Delafosse, 'and from this date we lost five or six men daily from heatstroke.'

At night the temperature plunged and although no doubt the change was welcome, the steaming ground added to the discomfort of the shivering refugees.

'As the days passed, faces that had been beautiful became chiselled with deep furrows, haggard despair seated itself where there had been a month before only smiles,' remembered Mowbray Thomson. 'Some were slowly sinking into the settled vacancy of look which marked insanity.'

Amelia Horne's mother, who was seven months pregnant, was one such teetering on the edge of madness. 'I used to sit and listen to her ravings, muttered in broken sentences,' wrote Amelia. 'Her one theme was her mother whom she wanted to see. At one moment she would be calling for a conveyance to take her to her mother, and the next her mind would wander away to something else.' As she listened to her mother, Amelia could be forgiven for wondering: 'Great God, how was it possible that human beings could endure so much.'

Each day brought more deaths. Captain Jenkins, his jaw shattered by a musket ball, 'lived for two or three days in excruciating agony', reported Mowbray Thomson, 'and died from exhaustion.' Few women could have suffered more than Emma Haliday. Tortured by an insatiable thirst brought on by smallpox, her once fair skin erupting in ugly pustules leaving it scarred and pitted. Grieving for her husband and child, she lingered until the siege was brought to an end when death probably came as a merciful relief. The grim business of disposing of the dead posed a problem for the community. 'Not one of our killed was sewn in a bag,' reported Thomson, 'we had neither materials nor time for such labour. At nightfall each day the slain were buried as decently as circumstances would permit.'

'It was a difficult matter to dig graves for the dead on account of the hardness of the earth,' admitted William Shepherd. 'So that with few exceptions the bodies had to be put in a well outside the entrenchment.' The well in question, close to barrack block No. 4, which had been empty of water even at the beginning, was by the end of the siege to receive the remains of 250 men, women and children.

Many believed that the threat posed by the proselytizing of Christian missionaries to the Muslim and Hindu faiths had led to the sepoy revolt, but when faced with the consequence of their missionary zeal, no one responded with greater courage than Edward Theophilus Moncrieff, the station chaplain. Ignoring the iron fragments from bursting shells and the musketry directed at him, Moncrieff went from post to post reading prayers and giving what little comfort he could to the wounded and the dying.

'Short and interrupted as these services were,' related Mowbray Thomson, 'they proved an invaluable privilege. Mr Moncrieff was held in high estimation by the whole garrison before the mutiny, his self denial and constancy in the thickest of our perils made him yet more greatly beloved by us all.'

Following eighteen days of physical and mental torment which few could ever have imagined, the situation facing the besieged had now reached a critical stage. Years later, William Shepherd

51

could write with considerable understatement 'Nothing could surpass the awful miseries, and the horrible privations experienced by the besieged garrison. The stench arising from the dead bodies of horses ... and the unusually great influx of flies rendered the place extremely disagreeable.'

The serious shortage of food and water, coupled with the nauseous stench arising from animal and human remains which lay rotting in the sun, posed a threat of disease which the overworked medical staff could do little to mitigate. The well in use as a sepulchre was almost full and it was only through the gruesome activities of the vultures, which gorged upon the putrefying remains, that the risk to health was to some degree lessened.

A message carried to Martin Gubbins in Lucknow, by a native fortunate enough to slip through the rebel lines undetected, reflected the despair of a commander on the brink of abandoning hope. 'We have no instruments, no medicines, provisions for 8 or 10 days at farthest, and no possibility of getting any as all communication with the town is cut off,' wrote General Wheeler. 'The enemy have two 24-pounders and several other guns. We have only eight 9-pounders. We want aid, aid, aid.'

But Sir Henry Lawrence was powerless to help however. On 16 June he replied to General Wheeler's plea, pointing out that 'with the enemy's command of the river, we could not possibly get a single man into your entrenchment.' He added, 'we are strong in our entrenchment but by attempting the passage of the river, we should be sacrificing a large detachment without a prospect of helping you. Pray do not think me selfish. I would run much risk could I see commensurate prospect of success. In the present scheme I see none.'

On the 24th, General Wheeler replied in what was to be his last message: 'All our carriages more or less disabled, ammunition short; British spirit alone remains, but it cannot last for ever ... We have lost everything belonging to us, and have not even a change of linen ... we have been cruelly deserted and left to our fate. Surely we are not to die like rats in a cage.'

Three days later Wheeler's cry for help was answered by Sir Henry, assuring him that reinforcements were on their way from Calcutta and urging him not to enter into negotiations with the Nana Sahib. The General was never to see the letter, for by then the fighting was over and the next tragic episode in the saga of Cawnpore was about to begin.

Chapter 5

MISPLACED HOPES

Although failing light afforded a respite from sniper activity, darkness brought no relief from the constant artillery fire. There was scarcely a corner of the compound which offered shelter from the jagged pieces of metal thrown out by bursting shells, or the lethal ricocheting round shot. A shell fragmented with fatal consequence to a group of soldiers' wives huddled together for mutual comfort behind a sandbagged parapet, whilst a private of the 32nd, seeking a resting place for the night with his family, was struck by a ball which, passing through his body, broke both elbows of his wife and wounded one of the two babies she was holding. She was seen a few days afterwards by Mowbray Thomson in the main guard room, 'lying upon her back, with the two children, twins, one at each breast, while the mother's bosom refused not what her arms had no power to administer'. Both she and the twins died shortly afterwards.

In this nightmare of choking dust and swirling smoke, only the very young were blissfully ignorant of their perilous position. At the tender age of three most children barely noticed the absence of an ayah and many youngsters played with spent musket balls, completely indifferent to the missiles which sailed past 'with a noise like giant bees'.

Some of the older children faced their situation with as much patience as the calmest adult. William Shepherd's 5½-year-old daughter, Polly, was just such an example. 'I have often caught her eyes swollen with suppressed tears, fixed sometimes upon her mother's features and sometimes upon mine, yet the desire not to pain us was self-evident,' wrote the Commissary clerk. 'She would sometimes whisper her desires to our servant Thakooranee, at the same time begging her in a most pitiful manner not to mention to papa and mamma, as they would be grieved.'

William Shepherd was to suffer additional anguish when on 17 June, as his wife sat nursing their two-year-old daughter, a ricocheting musket ball lodged in the child's neck. A surgeon removed the bullet but within twenty-four hours 'she faded away,' wrote Shepherd, 'until she resembled the bud of a delicate flower.'

Some 500 yards to the south-east of Wheeler's entrenchment stood the barracks built to house the Company's sepoys, and in one, a group of fifty, all loyal to their British officers, were defying every attempt by the rebels to drive them from the block. For three days they had exchanged fire with the mutineers, but during the afternoon of the 9th an incendiary set fire to the thatched roof and as smoke and flames swept through the building, Havildar Ram Buksh ran across 500 yards of open ground to beg the officer in charge of that part of the entrenchment to allow his sepoys to join the garrison troops. 'The Major then told us that he could do nothing for us, there being an order of General Wheeler preventing any native from entering the entrenchment,' recalled Havildar Ram Buksh. All that the Major was prepared to do was to reward the sepoys with a few rupees and provide a certificate attesting to their loyalty, with the advice to look to their own safety. At nightfall the sepoys, a few from the 1st and 56th NI, but the majority from the 53rd NI, made their escape. Some sought refuge in a mango grove, others like Ram Buksh, after confronting roving bands of peasants, reached their villages without mishap. A few were apprehended by rebels and taken back to Cawnpore. Fortunately for them, after being relieved of their weapons and anything else of value, they were released after undergoing a beating.

Although food stocks were a cause for concern, the most pressing problem given the stifling heat was a need to satisfy the garrison's insatiable demand for water. The native water carriers had long since fled, and it was left to each family to fetch water for themselves and their dependants. The only available well had from the beginning of the siege been a favourite target of the rebel artillerymen. Within a matter of days the parapet, framework and hoist machinery had been demolished by round shot, and each bucket had to be hauled up from a depth of 60 feet by hand, whilst subject to musketry and shellfire. Even at night, the creaking of the windlass was sufficient to bring a hail of grapeshot directed at the well head.

'The sufferings of the women and children from thirst were intense,' wrote Mowbray Thomson, 'and the men could scarcely endure the cries for drink which were almost perpetual from the poor little babes, terribly unconscious they were, most of them, of the great, great cost at which only it could be procured.'

'We had to practise great economy in respect of our water ration,' emphasized Amelia Horne, 'and had to drink it in sips, not knowing when the next supply would be forthcoming. Notwithstanding the danger, cheerfully would the men go and draw it rather than see us perish from thirst.'

As Amy Horne pointed out, despite its hazards the task of drawing water from the well never lacked for volunteers and Lieutenant Thomson takes especial pride in citing the example of John McKillop, the joint magistrate of Cawnpore, who although no military man, was determined to make his contribution whatever the cost. In furtherance of what he considered to be his duty towards the more vulnerable in the community, he undertook the dangerous business of drawing water for the women and children. This brave thirty-year-old Bengal civil servant survived a week before sustaining a mortal wound, and, recorded Thomson, 'with his last breath requested that somebody would go and draw water for a lady to whom he had promised it'.

The drawing of water and the loss of medical supplies were not the only problems facing the garrison – the store of provisions was also rapidly declining. 'My poor little brothers and sisters, wee little things as they were, felt the want of food dreadfully,' wrote a young Eurasian girl, 'and would have eaten the most loathsome thing had it been served up as an article of diet.'

By the third week in June the deteriorating situation in Cawnpore was giving rise to anxiety among government circles in Calcutta. Lady Canning entered in her diary:

> Cawnpore is now the most anxious position, but everyone speaks alike of Sir Hugh Wheeler and his brave spirit. There is not a better soldier, & all say, if anyone can hold it he will. But all the civilians & women & children have taken refuge there, & he has very few troops even now. We know that the native troops have turned and left him, & fired the town, & he is shut up & probably short of provisions, so there is great reason for anxiety, & it will be some time before he can be relieved from Allahabad, about 130 miles off.

Back in the entrenchment, unwilling to accept that there was little hope of relief, attempts were made to contact the outside world through the efforts of trusted natives willing to act as couriers for relatively large sums of money in rupees. Theirs was an extremely dangerous mission for if caught they invariably faced execution or were returned horribly mutilated having had 'boiling oil applied to their severed appendages'. An early volunteer had been Private Blenman, an Eurasian, 'but so dark in complexion as easily to have been taken for a native', who on 24 May had courageously left the trenches in the hope of reaching Allahabad with news of the garrison's desperate position. With considerable skill he succeeded in passing through the cordon of rebels, but was apprehended by villagers just as dawn was breaking. Fortunately for Blenman, his story of being a 'leather dresser' was believed and he was eventually able to slip back to the entrenchment none the worse for his adventure.

Although almost no one now believed in the speedy arrival of a relief force, hope still existed and each morning the powder-blackened and sweat-stained defenders would search the shimmering horizon for a glimpse of European troops marching along the Grand Trunk Road from Lucknow. Most were at a loss to understand why the relief force should be taking so long to reach them.

'Often we imagined that we heard the sound of distant cannonading,' commented Mowbray Thomson. 'At all hours of the day and night my men have asked me to listen. Their faces would gladden with the elusive hope of a relieving force close at hand, but only to sink back again presently into the old careworn aspect.' What they dreaded most, and refused to accept, was that Cawnpore might be cut off from the rest of the province, with the bridge of boats destroyed, and every ford closely guarded by the mutineers.

Whilst battle casualties and sickness was a serious threat to Wheeler's strength, the number of rebels available to the Nana increased with every influx from the surrounding district. The new arrivals stared in astonishment at the feeble defence works which sheltered the Europeans. That such a patently weak construction should have survived so long reflected badly on the Nana's tactics, and with much bravado they urged their fellow mutineers to take heart – after a short rest and an appeal to Allah, they would storm the entrenchment and send the infidels to hell. Stung by the criticism, the Nana was determined to mark the

23rd of June – the anniversary of Plassey – by nothing less than the overthrow of the Cawnpore garrison.

Preparations were thorough, the Muslims turning to Mecca and swearing on the Koran to destroy the infidel or die in the attempt. Field guns harnessed to teams of bullocks were dragged to within a few hundred yards of Wheeler's entrenchment and for most of the night his pickets were kept on the alert by more than the usual amount of activity behind the rebel lines, where 4,000 mutineers were massing to attack the 250 able-bodied men of Wheeler's garrison.

As the sun rose on the morning of the 23rd with its customary brilliance, the rebel artillery erupted in a rolling cloud of black smoke pierced by stabs of flame. Summoned by the call of a bugle, *sowars* of the 2nd Cavalry, many of them high on drugs, spurred their mounts furiously towards the entrenchment brandishing their *tulwars* to cries of 'Deen! Deen!' followed at a distance by sepoys of the 1st NI. William Shepherd at his post in the north-east corner of the entrenchment was struck by the diversity of the rebels' attire. 'Some few had on their jackets and caps,' he wrote, 'others were without the former, and nearly the whole dressed like recruits with dhotis.'

With deafening reports of the artillery ringing in his ears, Sir Hugh Massey Wheeler left his wounded son Gordon in the care of his mother and sisters and hurried to the battery where Lieutenant Ashe commanded two 9-pounder guns. Wheeler held the gunners' fire until the enemy was within 50 yards before ordering Ashe to discharge a volley of grape which brought down the leading files in a struggling mass of men and horses, forcing those behind to rein in. The survivors, wheeling sharply, turned away in a body across the plain to the accompaniment of jeers from the garrison, who now turned their attention to the sepoys emerging from a cloud of dust. William Shepherd recalled:

> The insurgents in the rear gave a fearful shout and springing up on the walls made a charge, led on by the Subadar-major, who was a powerful looking man, but the first shots from our musketry caught him, he took a bound and fell down dead, a few rounds of canister then properly directed amongst them did good execution, causing a general dispersion.

The garrison now turned its attention to where a further body was advancing slowly across the sandy plain behind bales of cotton. The sepoys came to within 100 yards of the entrenchment before a further discharge of grape set fire to some of the bales and left more than a score of dead and wounded on the ground. A second fusillade of musketry caused many more to hesitate before making for the rear, leaving their wounded comrades to crawl towards the cover of the brick kilns. The bales of cotton untouched by the flames were quickly retrieved by the garrison troops and used to plug holes in their defence works.

Another rebel attack against an unfinished barrack block failed just as miserably in the face of the deadly marksmanship of Mowbray Thomson and his team. 'Mainwaring's revolver despatched two or three,' wrote Mowbray Thomson later. 'Stirling with an Enfield rifle, shot one and bayoneted another ... both charges of my double barrelled gun were emptied and not in vain. We were seventeen of us inside that barrack, and they left eighteen corpses lying outside the doorway.' In the fierce exchange of musketry which had ensued, Thomson was struck in the fleshy part of his thigh, bringing forth the comment: 'A ball ploughed up the flesh, but happily, though narrowly, escaped the bone.'

By midday most of the attackers had melted away and the relieved garrison looked at each other in astonishment mixed with relief. Wheeler's troops had survived the attack prompted by the anniversary of Plassey with remarkably few casualties. Brushing aside his men's congratulations, General Wheeler left the powder-blackened defenders and hurried back to his room, only to find his wife and daughters sobbing over the decapitated body of his favourite son, Gordon. In the artillery barrage preceding the rebel assault, a 9-pound round shot had crashed through the wall and taken off his head as his mother and sisters were attending to his wound.

This personal tragedy took its toll of Sir Hugh Massey Wheeler, but then practically every member of the community had suffered in one way or another. William Shepherd was fortunate to have survived the rebel attack without so much as a scratch, much to the relief of his wife Ellen. But, her joy was short lived when he announced to her that it was his intention to leave the entrenchment and pass through the rebel lines to gather intelligence. Shepherd's plan was to slip by the unfinished barracks at midday when the mutineers were taking their meals, and make for the city.

It was an audacious idea and at first his superiors refused to sanction the attempt, but persuaded by his enthusiasm and anxious to learn what he could gather about the condition of the rebel army, and the prospect of relief, Wheeler finally agreed to the plan after Jonah Shepherd convinced him that he did not intend to desert the camp.

Finally, after bidding his friends and family a tearful farewell, William Shepherd, wearing a sepoy's loin cloth, turban and a grease-smeared cook's coat, set off on 24 June fortified by a generous tot of rum from a sympathetic soldier. All went well until he had passed the first of the unfinished barracks when he was stopped by a native orderly from the Nana's headquarters. Realizing that he had been seen coming from the direction of the entrenchment, Shepherd decided to bluff it out. 'If you spare my life,' he told his captor, 'I will tell you the truth.' He had indeed escaped from Wheeler's entrenchment, he said, but only to escape being killed by the shot and shell. 'So do not kill me,' he begged, 'but let me go on my way.'

'You will not be killed,' replied the orderly, 'but come along with me. You must give all the information about the entrenchment to the Raja Sahib.'

William Shepherd's mission had come to an untimely end in less than hour of leaving his family. He was now a prisoner of the Nana Sahib.

In the rebel circles repeated failure to overrun the European's entrenchment had bred an indifference to the prosecution of the siege and a growing anger against the man who had brought them back from the rich pickings to be found in Delhi. Even the Nana's own artillerymen now preferred to spend more time at the stalls selling sweetmeats and sherbert, than in servicing their cannon. Confidence in the Nana's ability to drive out the English was rapidly waning among the Muslims and to a lesser degree with the Hindus. Muslim disaffection came to a head when two Muslem butchers were brought before the Nana's older brother, Baba Bhutt, accused of slaughtering a cow in the city's bazaar. They were tried and sentenced to amputation according to Hindu law, but the operation to sever their hands was bungled and the unfortunate butchers bled to death. The Muslim community, and in particular the *sowars* of the 2nd Cavalry, were outraged. 'By whose authority did the Nana act?' was the cry. 'Is he not a creature of our own hands and can we not appoint anyone else we like?' It took all of Azimullah's skill to appease the Muslim faction, but even so, it left the cavalrymen with a bitter resentment of the Nana Sahib's rule.

Faced with a growing threat of the Muslims turning against him, the Nana began to despair of defeating Sir Hugh Wheeler by force of arm; it remained a source of astonishment to him and to many of his advisors that a comparatively small number of Europeans, many of them women and children, could exist for so long under the most appalling circumstances and still show defiance. Ignorant of the real state of affairs within Wheeler's entrenchment, which was becoming ever more grave with each passing hour, Nana Sahib began to wonder whether the garrison might agree to evacuate the cantonment if they were given the promise of a safe conduct to Allahabad.

Late that afternoon, William Shepherd whilst in custody, overheard two sepoys discussing a rumour that 'an old lady from among the Christian prisoners' was to be sent with a message to the garrison offering safe passage to Allahabad providing they surrendered the entrenchment. He was overjoyed. There seemed to be hope yet for Ellen and Polly.

South-west of Wheeler's position beside the Grand Trunk Road stood a large house known as the Savada Koti. It had once been a charitable institution before being taken over by the rebels as their headquarters, and it also served as a prison for those captured and awaiting execution. On the evening of the 24th a woman was seen by a sentry in Thomson's block to be walking across the parade ground towards the entrenchment. As she neared the earthworks she was recognized by Amelia Horne as Mrs Jacobi, the widow of a watchmaker in the city. The letter she brought was addressed to 'The subjects of Her Most Gracious Majesty Queen Victoria', and offered a ray of hope to the beleaguered men and women who had courageously resisted every attempt during the last twenty-one days to batter them into submission.

Although unsigned, it was recognized to be the handwriting of Azimullah Khan and read as follows:

All those who are in no way connected with the acts of Lord Dalhousie, and are willing to lay down their arms, shall receive a safe passage to Allahabad. It is far better for you who are still alive to go at once to Allahabad, unless you wish to continue fighting;

if so you can do so. Let Cawnpore be given up, and you shall be saved.

It was an offer that at first General Wheeler did not feel inclined to accept, since it did not bear the signature of Nana Sahib. However, he had little choice in the matter.

The garrison had rations for three days at the most, their ammunition was almost exhausted, and their numbers were being reduced each day. At a hurriedly convened meeting of the officers it was agreed that the alternative of fighting their way through the ring of mutineers was hopeless. The act of capitulation was anathema to many, for as Amelia Horne suggested, 'The thought of white men surrendering to the blacks was most abhorrent to British prestige.' Nevertheless, however distasteful, it offered a chance of survival for the women and children. Captain Moore also pointed out that in the rains which were daily expected, the trench would quickly fill with water and there was every likelihood of the barrack walls collapsing from the battering they had undergone. It was his persuasive argument that finally won the day.

The women in the community, some of whom, wrote Amelia, 'looked old, haggard, desperate, and imbecile', were of course less concerned with honour but rather with the survival of their children, and they breathed a sigh of relief when Mrs Jacobi, who had spent the whole day in the entrenchment whilst the issue was debated, returned to the Savada Koti with the garrison's agreement.

Despite the doubts held by a few of the officers as to the genuineness of the offer, there was little else the garrison could have done, for as Amelia pointed out: 'Our ammunition was coming to an end and our food supply had run out. With starvation staring us in the face and black despair at our hearts, who could blame the wisdom of the decision?'

The next day it seemed that the prayers of many had been answered for a flag of truce was hoisted and an hour after midday Azimullah Khan and Jawala Prasad, the Commander of Nana's cavalry, approached the entrenchment with an escort of the 2nd Cavalry, to be met by Captains Moore and Whiting, who notified them of the terms on which General Wheeler was prepared to evacuate the defence works. In return for giving up their artillery, Wheeler's men were to be allowed to march out under arms with sixty rounds of ball ammunition. Carriages were to be provided for the women and children, and *doolies* for the sick. Covered boats were to be at the river landing stage, provisioned for the journey to Allahabad.

Later that afternoon, a *sowar* returned bearing a message to the effect that the Nana Sahib raised no objection to Wheeler's proposals but requested that the cantonment be abandoned that very night. Captain Moore thought that was an unreasonable demand and could not possibly be carried out until the following day, which brought a threat from the Nana that a further week of bombardment would leave no one alive to dispute the matter.

It was an ultimatum which left the British negotiators un-moved and with his Irish temper rising, Moore retorted that if the Nana wanted the entrenchment he had only to come and take it, his soldiers knew the way to it and were even more familiar with the way back. In that event, Moore pointed out, Wheeler had a man posted at each of the magazines which held enough powder to blow themselves and the mutineers to eternity should they manage to storm the parapets. The messenger returned once again to the Nana's headquarters, 'and by and by he came out to us again,' wrote Lieutenant Thomson, 'with the verbal consent that we should delay the embarkation until morning.'

Although that night the garrison rested unmolested for the first time in twenty-one days, Mowbray Thomson found sleep diffi-cult to come by. 'After such an acclimation of the brain to incessant bombardment,' he confessed, 'the stillness was actually quite painful.'

Many of the women could not believe that the nightmare was over. 'It was such happiness to quit a place so fraught with misery and so fearfully haunted with the groans of those death had snatched away,' observed a relieved Amy Horne.

A mile to the south, William Shepherd was also spending a sleepless night, languishing in a prison cell without the least notion of how his family was faring. The Eurasian clerk crouched in a corner tormented by the possibility that he would never see them again.

In the entrenchment, the survivors washed down a breakfast of boiled lentils and perhaps a chapatti, with copious amounts of water from the well. 'Draught after draught was swallowed, and although the debris of mortar and bricks had made the water cloudy,' wrote Thomson, 'it was more delicious than nectar.'

As the morning drew on, crowds of townspeople and natives from nearby villages, drawn by a rumour that the English were leaving Cawnpore, swarmed down to the Satichaura Ghat, where a flotilla of barges lay beached in the shallows – even the less observant among them could not fail to see that both banks of the river were lined with sepoys. In the early afternoon of the 26th a delegation of officers from the garrison, headed by Lieutenant Delafosse, were taken down to the ghat where they inspected the boats for their river worthiness. 'They found about forty boats moored and appearing ready for departure,' wrote Thomson. 'Some of them roofed and others undergoing the process.' The boats, most of them grounded in the mud, were the usual eight-oared budgerows, 30 feet long and 10 feet in the beam, roofed over with bamboo and straw to give some protection from the sun, and open at each end for the helmsman and the oarsmen.

A mile from the landing stage, a few of the redcoats in the entrenchments occupied themselves by beating out marching tunes on wooden casks accompanied by tunes on a penny whistle, for the amusement of the children, in an attempt to banish memories of their recent suffering. Amelia Horne was struck with pity for the miserable state of those redcoats as they danced and sung in front of the children. Many of the soldiers were blistered by the sun and tormented with boils.

'Worked to death, underfed, and, in the later stages of the siege, starved, their uniforms rotting on their backs, their faces unwashed, their hands covered in grime from the guns, which dried and formed hard coatings; they were such a pitiable sight to see,' she wrote.

On 27 June, shortly after dawn, the 450 survivors of the siege made ready to leave. Many of the garrison paid a farewell visit to the 60-feet-deep sepulchral well to breathe a silent prayer over the bodies of their loved ones, and perhaps to drop a note of loving remembrance over the low brick wall. Little time was spent over gathering their scant possessions apart from personal treasures or mementoes. Mowbray Thomson took his father's Ghuznee medal and a miniature portrait of his mother, but was also careful to stuff his pockets with as many cartridges as he could carry. Others pinned identity notes to their children; many, with little more than memories of a loved one, lingered for a few grief-stricken moments of prayer at the well. The last to leave the area appears to have been Major Edward Vibart, his few belongings carried by a mutineer of his regiment, 'with the most profuse demonstrations of respect'.

Mowbray Thomson took the opportunity to ask one of the native officers of the 53rd to put a figure on the number of casualties the rebels had suffered.

'From 700 to 800,' the man told him.

'I believe this estimate to have been under, rather than over the mark,' commented a sceptical Thomson.

By 7.00 am the evacuation was well under way. Sixteen elephants and eighty palanquins and bullock carts had been provided for the women and children, and a particularly magnificent beast for Sir Hugh Wheeler and his family. In low spirits and close to tears, he is said to have declined the offer and instead rode down to the landing stage on 'a skinny Galloway, muttering that he had once again been duped'.

Slowly the long column wound its way past the roofless barrack blocks scarred by the impact of round shot, across the plain, on a mile-long journey to the river, escorted by *sowars* of the 2nd Cavalry. In the van trod the ponderous elephants, their trunks adorned with gleaming brass rings and with colourful howdahs on their backs, one carrying Lady Wheeler and her daughters. It was followed by a train of bullock carts and palanquins with their wretched burdens of emaciated women and children, scorched and blistered by the sun. In the rear marched the surviving members of the 32nd of Foot in threadbare uniforms led by Captain Moore. The *doolies* bearing the sick and wounded, were even further behind with Major Vibart.

'Never, surely, was there such an emaciated, ghostly party of human beings as we,' thought Mowbray Thomson, an opinion surely endorsed by Amelia Horne when she wrote: 'Behold us as we then appeared, like so many ghosts, tattered, emaciated, and begrimed ... destitute of all the finery so dear to the heart of a woman.'

Lieutenant Thomson was taken aback by the women's state of undress, when he wrote:

> There were women who had been beautiful, now stripped of every personal charm, some with, some without gowns; fragments of finery were made available no longer for decoration, but decorum; officers in tarnished uniforms, rent and wretched, and with nondescript mixtures of apparel, more or less insufficient in all there

were few shoes, fewer stockings, and scarcely any shirts; these had all gone on bandages for the wounded.

At length the white-painted rails of the wooden bridge were reached and, watched by Azimullah Khan, Bala Sahib, Tatya Tope and a vast silent crowd, the refugees made their way down the steps into the muddy shallows of the Ganges. As Mowbray Thomson looked about him, the frightening thought that they were now at the mercy of the sepoy escort filled his mind. Lieutenant Delafosse approached his craft untroubled by any such misgiving. 'We got down to the boats, without being molested in the least,' he later reported.

The business of embarking began with the able bodied standing knee deep in the muddy water to assist the women and children and those less able, to board the budgerows as the native oarsmen looked on dispassionately. Amelia scrambled aboard with her stepfather John Cook and her younger stepsisters, to take her place under the awning, desperately hoping that the boat would be quickly freed from the grip of the mud and floated downstream away from what she regarded as a place of unforgettable horror.

In the stifling humidity of the pre-monsoon, a sinister silence was broken only by the occasional creak of timber, but the overloaded barges, some carrying as many as twenty people, were now ready to be poled out into midstream to take advantage of the deeper water and the fast-running current. 'We laid down our muskets and had taken off our coats in order to work easier at the boats,' remembered Henry Delafosse, 'but as the men put their shoulders to the stern of the clumsy craft, the shrill note of a bugle sliced through the air.'

Aboard the budgerows a chorus of terrified screams broke out as a thick cloud of greenish smoke and orange flame flared up from the straw canopies as the oarsmen thrust embers from their cooking stoves into the thatch of several of the boats.

Mowbray Thomson in his narrative paints a chilling picture of those desperate minutes which ended whatever hope the refugees might have entertained of reaching Allahabad:

At a signal from the shore, the native boatmen who numbered eight plus a steersman to each boat all jumped over and waded to the shore. We fired into them immediately, but the majority of them escaped. Before they quitted us these men had contrived to secrete burning charcoal in the thatch of most of our boats. Simultaneously with the departure of the boatmen, the identical troopers who had escorted Major Vibart to the ghat opened upon us with carbines. As well as the confusion caused by the burning of the boats would allow, we returned the fire of the horsemen who were about fifteen or sixteen in number, but they retired immediately after the volley they had given us. Those of us who were not disabled by wounds now jumped out of the boats and endeavoured to push them afloat; but alas! Most of these were utterly immovable. Now, from ambush in which they were concealed all along the banks, it seemed that thousands of men fired upon us; besides four 9-pounders, carefully masked and pointed towards the boats, every bush was filled with sepoys.

Those who survived the initial volley of musketry made frantic efforts to push the clumsy craft clear of the river bank but only three barges, one of which was afterwards swamped by the close fall of several cannon balls, gained the deeper water of midstream. The rest of the flotilla was raked by musketry as they remained firmly embedded in the mud. 'Some of the boats presented a broadside to the guns,' wrote Lieutenant Thomson, 'others were raked from stem to stern by shot.'

Passengers who were not immediately struck down were soon driven into the shallows by the collapsing masses of burning straw. A few sought the protection of the tall bowsprit, others waded out into deeper water in a vain attempt to escape the fire of the mutineers, but the rain of musket balls soon stained the surface of the Ganges with the blood of helpless victims. The Revd. Edward Moncrieff, a Bible in his hand, fell victim to a *sowar* who spurred his horse into the water towards him.

'If we English take prisoners, we do not put them to death,' he is alleged to have said to the cavalryman. 'Spare our lives and put us in prison.' His plea fell upon deaf ears and, struck across the neck by the *sowar*'s *tulwar*, the chaplain sank beneath the bloodstained surface.

'We had entered the boats joyfully, never for a moment expecting treachery,' wrote Amelia Horne, 'and were taken quite by surprise when we were fired on.'

An affidavit from a villager gives an eyewitness account of the ensuing slaughter:

Those who escaped the shots and the burning of the thatch, jumped into the water and tried to swim across but were picked off by the bullets of the sepoys, who followed them on shore. After a while the large guns ceased and the cavalry troopers entered the river on horseback and cut numbers down. The gentlemen and soldiers were hunted from one place to another and hacked to pieces.

Rising above the agonized screams of the women and children, and the crackle of burning timbers, were the desperate cries for help from those unable to free themselves from the threat of a blanket of burning straw. 'Mercifully,' commented Mowbray Thomson, 'volumes of smoke from the thatch somewhat veiled the horror of that morning.'

Of the two boats which had been freed from the shallows to gain the midstream current, one drifted to the Lucknow side of the river and the waiting sepoys, whilst the other, due in some measure to the frantic efforts of its compliment of twenty which included Major Vibart, Captains Moore and Whiting, Lieutenants Ashe, Glanville and Boulton, and also Private Blenman. Mowbray Thomson, having failed together with a few fellow officers to free their boat from the grip of the mudflats, saw through the veil of smoke Moore's vessel slowly drifting downstream and decided to make an effort to save his life by swimming for it. 'I threw into the Ganges my father's Ghuznee medal, and my mother's portrait, all the property I had left,' he later wrote, 'determined that they should have only my life as a prey' and, joined by a dozen others, he struck out in the wake of the drifting boat.

Most of the others, either struck by bullets or exhausted by their efforts, sank below the surface of the Ganges. Thanks to the swimming lessons he had taken at a baths in Holborn, Thompson reached Moore's vessel and was hauled aboard by the strong arms of Captain Whiting, together with one other survivor from the group of swimmers. Behind them a pall of black smoke hung above the ghat as a reminder of the frightful events being enacted there.

Chapter 6

'KUDA-KI-MIRZEE'

At the Satichaura Ghat most of the boats were ablaze or engulfed in smoke as the stiff breeze whipped the flames from one thatched canopy to the next. Among the sick and wounded who perished in the blaze were Amelia Horne's mother, and John MacKillop, the 'captain of the well'. Mercifully their agony was short lived. 'One mitigation only there was to their horrible fate,' recorded Mowbray Thomson. 'The flames were terrifically fierce, and their intense sufferings were not protracted.'

A horrified witness of the massacre was Mrs Letts, the Eurasian wife of a musician in the 56th NI, who explained:

> In the boat where I was to have gone was the school mistress and twenty-two missies. General Wheeler came last in a palkee. They carried him into the water near the boat. I stood by. He said 'Carry me a little further towards the boat,' but a trooper said, 'No, get out here.' As the General got out of the palkee head foremost, the trooper gave him a cut with his sword into the neck and he fell into the water. My son was killed near him. Some were stabbed with bayonets; others were cut down ... The school girls were burnt to death. I saw their clothes and hair on fire.

Mrs Letts together with a Mrs Bradshaw hid in the tall grass growing on the bank, waiting for nightfall when they could slip into the city, passing themselves off as beggars. The two women were among the fortunate few who were later liberated by Havelock's men when they recaptured Cawnpore.

Aware that the sepoys were approaching her boat, Amelia Horne pulled her little sister Florence down beside her, praying 'for mercy and help, my heart beat like a sledge hammer, and my temples throbbed with pain,' she wrote. 'But there I sat, gripping my little sister's hand, while the bullets fell like hail around me, praying fervently to God for mercy, and every second expecting to be in the presence of my Maker.' When the rebels reached her, one made a grab for her arm. 'My senses had very nearly forsaken me. I was in a sort of stupor,' she confessed. 'The search was made on my person while I was standing, but to speak more exactly I was made to stand while I was searched as a sepoy let off his gun over my head and shoulders in the most deliberate and cold blooded manner'. Amelia's trauma, however, was only just beginning. A *sowar*, riding waist deep in the water, commanded the two sepoys to throw her over the side. 'I was there upon brutally seized around the waist, and though I struggled and fought wildly, was quickly overcome and thrown into the river.'

She floated downstream for 200 yards before finding the strength to get to her feet in the shallows and collapse on the bank, haunted by the fading cries of Florence, calling; 'Oh, Amy, don't leave me!' Writing of the event many years later, it was still fresh in her memory. 'The cries of my poor little sister, imploring me wildly not to forsake her, still ring in my ears, and her look of anguish ... has haunted me ever since. That was the last I ever saw or heard of my family.'

Concealed by the lush growth Amelia was awakened from a fitful doze by the approach of another person – 'To my great relief, the well-known face and form of Miss Wheeler, the General's daughter'. Like Amelia Horne, Margaret Wheeler had been left to drown by 'men who perhaps thought she was not worth a bullet'. It was an hour before they were discovered by a party of rebels. Whilst Margaret Wheeler was hoisted onto a saddle and taken away by a *sowar*, Amelia was forced to join the surviving women and children after the Nana had given the order for their destruction to cease. By that time there were very few males left alive and only 125 women and children who were dragged from the river and herded together on a stretch of sand by the sepoys. 'Many of them were wounded with bullets and sword cuts, their dresses were wet and full of mud and blood,' testified Mrs Letts. 'They were ordered to give up whatever valuables they might have hidden on their persons.'

Amelia, in her words, was 'pushed and dragged along and subjected to every indignity. Occasionally, I felt the thrust of a bayonet, and on my protesting against such treatment with uplifted hands and appealing to their feelings as men, I was struck on my head, and was made to understand in language all too plain that I had not long to live.' Stumbling along half naked, and enduring the mocking jeers of the crowd of villagers, 'for my clothes had been torn to pieces when I had been dragged along by the men, and I had the mortification of being made a spectacle before these heartless and cruel wretches'. At length she was brought to a collection of huts where, thoroughly exhausted, she rested her aching head and fell fast asleep.

The prisoners in their bedraggled and half-drowned state – Kate Lindsay suffering from a wound in her back, Caroline, Fanny and Alice among them – were escorted along the ravine they had left an hour or two before, no doubt grateful to have escaped the slaughter, but all the time wondering what the future might hold. The frightened women and children stumbled along past the bazaar and the battered entrenchments until they were brought to a halt before the Nana's headquarters where the Peshwa emerged from Savada House and surveyed the wretched survivors before ordering their removal to the Savada Kothi. Amelia Horne, who had been kept apart from the prisoners, wrote:

> Whilst in my hut I heard the rebels around me talking of some of the unfortunate ladies who had been removed from the boats and the ghat. They were such pitiful objects to look at that even the black hearts of some of the monsters were moved with compassion, and they declared that it was a crime to put to the sword such fair and tender creatures.

On 26 June, Lady Charlotte Canning added a footnote to the day's entry in her journal. 'There have been horrors in Cawnpore, if we must believe a native's story. I think he exaggerates, so I will not repeat them.' A week later, Lady Canning, hoping against hope for better news, was writing: 'A horrid report that Cawnpore has been abandoned, & Sir H.Wheeler & everybody massacred, came yesterday ... A great doubt seems to exist about Cawnpore. A great many people do not believe it.'

By mid-July there could no longer be any doubt. Viscount Canning the Governor General, unable to sleep, paced his room tormented by thoughts that had he not reduced the number of troops in Oudh, the disaster might have been averted. His wife Charlotte, equally affected by events, attempted to explain the circumstances to Queen Victoria:

> The sad news of the fall of Cawnpore after the sad death of Sir H. Wheeler and the massacre of the garrison has proved true but no details are known. I believe it is possible without too much

delay, the Nana will be again attacked at his home at Bithur about 9 miles from Cawnpore. He is a small Rajah who used to pretend and delight in everything English and used to entertain the officers and go out shooting with them. The horrors committed by this man are too dreadful to relate. He has murdered every fugitive that passed thro' his country & his treachery & wickedness appear incredible.

The survival of those imprisoned in the Savada Koti now rested solely upon the speed of the advance of a small column of European soldiers fighting their way north along the Grand Trunk Road from Allahabad, led by Major Sydenham Renaud whose primary objective next to rescuing the Nana's prisoners was to 'reassert British authority and exact revenge'.

Meanwhile, deprived of the oars which had been thrown overboard by the native boatmen and the rudder which was shot away, the budgerow carrying Lieutenants Delafosse, Thomson and others of note, drifted downstream with the current on an erratic course between the sandbanks, which in the summer months made the Ganges such a navigable hazard. Its original complement of twenty had been swollen considerably by Major Vibart's act in rescuing the passengers of a sinking vessel struck by round shot and now, more than sixty men, women and children, some severely wounded, crowded into a space intended for less than a third of that number. 'We had no food in the boat,' recalled Mowbray Thomson, 'the waters of the Ganges was all that passed our lips.'

With only one or two spars available for steering the unwieldy craft, it was difficult to maintain a steady course in midstream, so that it frequently drifted close to the Oudh bank and the sepoys of the 17th NI who were following its progress downriver.

'We were often within 100 yards of the guns on the Oudh side of the river,' wrote Lieutenant Thomson, 'and saw them load, prime, and fire into our midst.'

Fortunately for the passengers, the deep loose sand on the bank prevented the sepoys from siting a cannon with any degree of accuracy, but one cannon ball raised a fountain of water close to the stern knocking over a female relative of Lieutenant Jarvis. A child, whose age Thomson thought could be no more than six or seven, came up to him sobbing bitterly. 'Mama has fallen overboard,' he told the Lieutenant tearfully and as Thomson attempted to comfort him, added, 'Oh why are they firing on us? Did they not promise to leave off.'

'I never saw the child after that,' recalled Mowbray Thomson, 'and suspect that he soon shared his mother's death.'

As Thomson and Delafosse jumped from the boat to free it from yet another sandbank, the sepoys who had followed along the bank began to fire at will, and the dead soon began to outnumber the living. Captain Moore, despite the injury to his shoulder, put his back to the stern of the budgerow in an attempt to shift it from the sand's grip, but he quickly collapsed into the shallows when a bullet pierced his heart. The same fusillade killed Lieutenants Ashe and Boulton as they jumped down to assist Moore, whilst a round shot slew both Burney and Glanville. A musket ball struck Major Vibart's arm as he struggled to help Thomson, whilst another round shot reduced Lieutenant Fagan's leg to splintered bone and sinews.

Through all this, nothing could persuade Major Edwin Wiggins to leave his place of refuge in the hold. 'No expostulation could make him quit the shelter of the bulwarks,' noted Mowbray Thomson, 'though we were adopting every possible expedient to lighten her burden. It was positively a relief to us when we found that his cowardice was unavailing; and a bullet through the boat's side that dispatched him caused the only death that we regarded with complacency.' Wiggins's corpse, with others, was committed to the muddy waters of the Ganges and the alligators that frequented its banks, and at last the budgerow floated free of the sandbar.

With the dead and wounded inextricably tangled together in the bottom of the boat, it had been a difficult and unpleasant task to extricate the dead from the living as Mowbray Thomson explained. 'It was a work of extreme difficulty though imperatively necessary from the dreaded consequences of the extreme heat, and the importance of lightening the boat as much as possible.'

Such was the frequency of the craft grounding on a sandbank or becoming entangled with branches in the shallows that it was likely that more than one body was heaved over the side without first checking the victim's pulse. Mowbray Thomson himself was rendered unconscious from a bullet which grazed his head. Fortunately, he regained his senses just as two of his comrades were reaching for his arms and legs. 'We were just about to throw you overboard,' one said as he began to stir.

Later that afternoon, despite everything that had been done to lighten the craft, it again grounded heavily on a sandbar, but it was decided to remain where they were until darkness fell before disembarking most of the passengers. That done, and once more on their way downstream, they were quickly faced with an unexpected hazard in the shape of a fire raft launched by hostile villagers. Carried by the swift-flowing current, the blazing mass of straw and bamboo passed within a few feet of the budgerow to be followed by a flight of flaming arrows of which a few lodged in the thatched roof of the canopy. The ensuing conflagration was quickly extinguished by the simple expedient of cutting the frame loose and toppling the blazing mass into the river, but for the rest of the night few people slept.

Morning came and with it the knowledge that a little more than 10 miles had been covered in a matter of twenty-four hours. Such disappointing progress cast an air of gloom over the whole party and when shortly after midday the barge grounded on yet another sandbar near the village of Najafgarh, their chagrin deepened into a mood of black despair. Najafgarh was the domain of a petty landlord who had sworn to return every fugitive to the Nana Sahib and within minutes the river bank became thronged with his armed retainers. When a brass cannon was dragged to within easy range it seemed to the refugees that they had reached journey's end.

Fortunately, before the cannon could be primed and loaded, the dark mass of cloud which heralded the approach of the monsoon shed a heavy downpour which soaked the sacks of powder and rendered the cannon virtually inoperable. Although spared a discharge of grape, a volley of musketry from both sides of the river took a disproportional toll of the boat's more notable occupants. 'Major Vibart had been shot through the arm on the preceding day,' recorded Mowbray Thomson. 'Nevertheless, he got out, and while helping to push off the boat, was shot through the other arm.' Captain Turner had his leg smashed, Captain Whiting and Lieutenant Harrison were both shot dead as they struggled to free the craft, whilst Private Blenman, who had bravely attempted to breach the enemy's lines at Cawnpore, was so badly injured in the groin that he implored an officer to make an end to his sufferings. His plea was refused.

Towards evening the wind freshened and through the mist rising from the river, a second vessel crammed with an assortment of villagers and sepoys was to be seen bearing down upon the stranded barge. It had been sent by the Nana to follow and destroy the survivors of the massacre at the Satichaura Ghat, but before the rebels could close with the fugitives heavily laden boat, their craft too had grounded. The sixty or so mutineers had every reason to curse their luck for with angry shouts, a score of ragged figures led by Thomson and Delafosse splashed through the shallows intent on wreaking vengeance for the murder of their loved ones.

'Instead of waiting for them to attack us, eighteen or twenty of us charged them,' recalled Thomson, 'and few of their number escaped to tell the story.'

The determined sortie enabled the Europeans to replenish their stock of ammunition, but there was no food available to satisfy their gnawing hunger, and exhausted by events most fell asleep.

That night, the second they had spent on the river, those in the group who were not in a deep slumber discovered that the combination of a stiff breeze and rising water levels had succeeded where their efforts had failed, and the craft was once again on its journey downstream. The relief they must have felt was short lived, however, for with daylight on 29 June came the bitter realization that the craft had drifted into a backwater in the vicinity of Surajpur, from which there was no possibility of escape. In less than half an hour a crowd of hostile villagers were directing a punishing musket fire into the trapped vessel.

It was then that Major Vibart, lying helplessly in the bottom of the boat, gave instructions for a sortie to be made against the villagers in order to give others in the boat a chance to free it from the sandbank. Led by Lieutenants Thomson and Delafosse, closely followed by Sergeant Grady of the 84th, a small group of eleven soldiers from the 32nd and 84th of Foot splashed ashore to drive their furious opponents to the fringe of the jungle. In the general fracas Sergeant Grady fell dead from a shot to the head, and when the party returned to the river bank, the boat had gone. They were never to see either it or its occupants again.

At Surajpur, the budgerow which the gallant band had left in an attempt to drive off the hostile villagers, had come under attack from the sepoys massed on the river bank. The fugitives, heavily out numbered, were faced with an unenviable situation and after a brief exchange of fire in which five officers were killed and several wounded, Major Vibart decided to raise a white flag.

The surrender was accepted by the sepoys who seemed to have spent their aggressiveness in earlier attacks. Carts were brought from the village to convey the wounded, the women and four children, the 18 miles to Cawnpore. The men, including the wounded Major Vibart and Lieutenant Fagan were bound with rope. Major Vibart succumbed to his wounds en route and was abandoned at the roadside, leaving his wife and children to complete the journey with the others. Later that morning the prisoners were brought to Savada House where the Nana Sahib left his tent to congratulate their escort and order the execution of the male prisoners.

'The Nana ordered the Sahibs to be separated from the Mem Sahibs and shot,' a native witness later testified. 'The Sahibs were seated on the ground and two companies of the Nadiree Regiment [Irregulars] stood with their muskets ready to fire. Then said one of the Mem Sahibs, the doctor's wife [Mrs Harris], I will not leave my husband. If he must die, I will die with him. So she ran and sat down behind her husband, clasping him around the waist. Directly she said this, the other Mem Sahibs said: We will also die with our husbands, and they all sat down, each by her husband. Then their husbands said: Go back. But they would not. Whereupon the Nana ordered his soldiers and they going in, pulled them away forcibly. But they could not pull away the doctor's wife, who there remained.'

Captain Seppings asked the Nana for a few moments of prayer, to which he agreed; the Revd. Cockey's arms were untied and he reached for the Bible in his jacket pocket. The group knelt in prayer and then, as they attempted to shake hands, the sepoys opened fire.

'One Sahib rolled one way and one another as they sat,' continued the native witness. 'But they were not dead only wounded. So they went in and finished them off with swords.' The bodies were stripped of their clothes and dragged to a corner of the compound to be left for disposal by the beasts and birds of prey. The women and children were taken to the Savada Koti , there to join the survivors of the massacre of 3 June. A mile away, the Commissary head clerk lay on the earthen floor of his prison bathed in the clammy sweat of a fever, recalling with anguish the care that used to be taken of him on such an occasion by his wife Ellen. 'Where was she now, and the dear ones I had left behind in the entrenchment,' wondered William Shepherd. The very uncertainty of their fate somehow gave him hope, for he had learned from the conversations of his guards that a great many women and children were still alive.

Back at Surajpur, Lieutenant Mowbray Thomson, having given up 'seeing the boat or our doomed companions any more', realized that the task of forcing a way through the jungle to Allahabad was beyond the capability of his small force and with the agreement of the others, it was decided to retire along the river's edge and sell their lives as dearly as possible. Soaked in perspiration, the group of thirteen trudged with blistered feet over sharp rock and burning sand for a distance of 3 miles before stumbling upon a ruined temple partially concealed by vines some dozen yards from the river. The cool interior came as a welcome relief from the cloying heat of the jungle and although there was no food to satisfy their gnawing pangs of hunger, the pint or so of stagnant water was scooped out with as much relish as if it had been vintage champagne. Tired, but fired with a determination to hold the temple against every attack by villagers or sepoys, Mowbray Thomson and his band crowded into the restricted area to await the inevitable assault.

The attack when it came was a vicious affair of close-quarter fighting in which, as Thomson described it, 'bayonets dull with rust took on a brighter hue' and a rampart of bloody corpses quickly grew in front of the temple's single entrance to provide an additional shield for the defenders. A bid to smoke out the Europeans with bundles of faggots proved unavailing as did an attempt by the villagers to demolish part of the temple wall. It was not until bags of gunpowder were brought up by sepoys and thrown onto the smouldering embers to create dense clouds of suffocating smoke, that Thomson ordered his men to break out in the direction of the river.

In a sudden rush which took their opponents by surprise, the thirteen charged through the black smoke scattering in all directions. Seven swimmers among them dashed for the river while the remaining half dozen, surrounded by a screaming mob, fought a desperate running battle with clubbed muskets or bayonets, until dragged down by force of numbers, dying to a man from the rebels' knives or swords.

A fusillade of musket shots peppered the surface as the others plunged into the water killing two of the swimmers who sank below the surface. Mowbray Thomson turning on his back, noticed that the bank was thronged with villagers and sepoys, howling for their blood, whilst in the background he could see others rifling through the tunics of the slain for anything of value.

Diving frequently to avoid the matchlock men pursuing them along the river's bank, Thomson, Delafosse and two privates, Murphy of the 84th and Sullivan of the Madras Fusiliers, were the only ones to escape the attention of their pursuers as they were carried rapidly downstream until all but a solitary trooper on horseback had been outdistanced. Eventually even he gave up the chase and the four fugitives turned thankfully for a sandbank, experiencing a moment of alarm at the sight of a trio of long-nosed alligators basking in the sun on an adjacent sandbar. After resting from their exertions, the four took cautiously to the river once more, floating downstream some 3 miles before the sound of voices sent them diving beneath the surface. When Thomson and the others came up gasping for breath, instead of the whine and splash of a musket ball, they were greeted with a friendly shout. 'Sahib! Sahib! Why swim away? We are friends.'

'We have been deceived too often,' called Thomson, 'that we are not inclined to trust anybody.' It was only after the Rajput matchlock men offered to cast their weapons into the water as an act of good faith, and explained that they had been sent by their Raja to conduct them to safety, that the swimmers were persuaded that it was safe for them to swim for the river bank.

Astonishingly, their frightful ordeal was over for they were in the territory of an elderly Raja, one Dirigibijah Singh, who was friendly to the British, and willing hands were extended to help them ashore. Mowbray Thomson could hardly believe his good fortune and of the many thoughts that flitted through his mind at that moment, one predominated. 'How excellent an investment, had been that guinea spent at the baths in Holborn learning to swim.'

The fugitives were in a pitiful state. Exhausted and naked they possessed only one flannel shirt and a strip of linen cloth between them – exposure to the sun had raised huge blisters on their shoulders and only Delafosse bore no mark of a bullet wound.

After a short rest and their first meal in more than seventy hours, a mood of cheerful optimism sustained them in spite of their poor physical shape and Thomson could afford to joke about his shirt from Messrs Thresher & Glenny which had gone into the siege a bright pink, but was now such a deplorable colour that he admitted: 'If these very respectable vendors could see it now, they would never accredit it as being from their establishment.'

The fort at Moora Mhow, to which they were taken, was the property of one of the most powerful Rajputs in that part of Oudh who still favoured the British. The two officers found him to be an agreeable character, much interested in their account of the siege and full of astonishment at the circumstances of their escape. It was, he told them, 'Kuda-ki-Mirzee', the will of God, an opinion with which the two lieutenants were in full agreement.

During the three weeks they remained under his roof, their time passed in a pleasant cycle of eating, sleeping – on straw mattresses, for an infidel's touch would have defiled the Raja's bedding. The group was measured by the Raja's personal tailor for Indian clothes, and, commented Mowbray Thomson, 'when Hindustani shoes were added to our toilet, we felt quite respectable again.' It said much for the integrity of their host that although the territory was infested with mutineers, many of whom visited the fort at Moora Mhow, they were never allowed access to the Europeans unless in the presence of the Raja's personal bodyguard. These occasional confrontations were a source of great amusement to the two officers.

'We were told that the Muchee Bhowan [at Lucknow] had been blown up with two hundred Europeans in it,' wrote Thomson. 'One day the Punjab was lost, another day Madras and Bombay were gone into mutiny, then a hundred thousand Sikhs were said to be marching south to exterminate the English.'

Both Thomson and Delafosse could not restrain themselves from bursting out with laughter, but the rebels were convinced of the truth of the matter and every attempt by the Englishmen to explain the impossibility of such claims was received with total disbelief. The fact of the four Europeans being granted asylum by Dirigibijah Sing was a sore point with the Nana and he ordered that they be given up. In the face of mounting hostility the old Raja suggested that it might be safer for them if they were sent to a less troubled area. Accordingly, after a week spent in the seclusion of a river village, whilst awaiting a British-manned boat to pass, on 29 July, no boat having arrived, they crossed the Ganges in the care of a friendly *zemindar* who provided them with a hackery to make the journey to Allahabad.

It was a journey undertaken with every expectation of success and as they jolted over a little-used track in the springless carriage, the four looked forward with some anticipation to the cool taste of an English beer. Their goal was not reached without one further alarm, however, for after little more than an hour, the native driver halted the carriage and in a low agitated whisper, informed them that sepoys had been observed among the trees. Bitterly resentful that fate should play such an ugly trick and sick with apprehension, the four pushed warily through the long grass, fearful that at any moment a shout of 'Ferungee by, Maro! Maro!' would bring their hope of salvation to a savage and bloody end.

The cry never came, and in breasting an incline near a tope of banyan trees, Thomson was greeted by the welcome sight of a detachment of the 84th on its way to join the army of Major General Sir Henry Havelock. 'Our bronze countenances, grimy beards, huge turbans and "tout ensemble" caused them to take us for a party of Afghans,' confessed Mowbray Thomson. 'However, Murphy soon recognized one of his old comrades of the 84th, and they greeted us with a truly British cheer.' The four also received their long anticipated beer, for so pleased were the friends of Private Murphy by his unexpected appearance that they willingly contributed their allowance of porter to 'treat the men who had not tasted beer for eight summer months'.

'Never was the beer of our country more welcome,' enthused Mowbray Thomson, 'and that first meal, interspersed with a fire of cross questioning about the siege and our subsequent history, inquiries after lost comrades and relatives ... made a strangely mingled scene of congratulation, humour, lamentation, and good will.'

When the column eventually reached Cawnpore, the group of four were summoned by General Neill to give an account of their experiences. 'Thomson,' recalled John Sherer, who was to succeed the late Charles Hillersdon as Magistrate and Collector, 'had the bright face and laughing eyes of an undergraduate in his first term. Both he and Delafosse struck me very much in one way; they took the events which had happened to them, events almost surpassing the most romantic adventures of fiction, as if they were ordinary circumstances to be looked for in the day's work of life.'

Chapter 7

THE BIBIGARH MASSACRE

As the Nana Sahib relaxed at Bithur, some 12 miles from Cawnpore, on rising ground covered by sugar cane and brushwood, he savoured the prospect of becoming Peshwa with feelings of delicious anticipation. General Neill's small force, decimated by cholera, was still at Allahabad, Henry Lawrence was trapped with his garrison in Lucknow, the bulk of the British Army was immobile on a ridge outside Delhi, and in much of the Central Provinces sepoys were rising against their British officers. The mutiny successes were such that it was not beyond the bounds of possibility that the British would be driven back to the sea – and so thought many of the merchants previously loyal to the Raj – but what was beyond doubt was the fact that the Company's administration no longer held sway in Cawnpore, and the Nana's succession to the throne as the legitimate Peshwa was assured.

Astrologers had recommended 1 July as being the most favourable date for the consecration of Baji Rao's adopted heir, and to the accompaniment of a twenty-one-gun salute, the sacred ceremony was duly undertaken at his palace in Bithur. An additional salvo was authorized when, conscious of the homage he would enjoy as the Supreme Ruler of the Mahratta nation, the Nana announced that gold from the treasury would be melted down and distributed to his soldiers as bangles, in recognition of the part they had played in securing his kingdom.

As darkness fell, Bithur was illuminated by a lavish display of lanterns and flares, rivalled only by the rockets which lit up the night sky above the palace. In Cawnpore, as the Nana celebrated his success with a nautch, the European prisoners, including those from Fatehgar and Surajpur, were transferred from the Savada Koti to a bungalow around 21 miles away, originally intended for an English officer's native mistress. Known locally as the Bibigarh, or House of the Ladies, with its two small end rooms, a larger central room and an open courtyard, it was to become the venue for an act of infamy which changed the suppression of a mutiny into a savage act of reprisal every bit as brutal as the atrocities committed by the agents of the Nana. In these two small rooms, each no larger than 10 feet by 8 feet, divided by a central room 10 feet by 24 feet, four men and 206 women and children were imprisoned for fifteen days without a punkha to cool the air and nothing but bamboo matting to ease the discomfort of a clay baked earthen floor.

Little more than a month previously many of the European women would have enjoyed the luxuries common to the lifestyle of most Victorian memsahibs – the morning and evening baths, the frequent change into clean cotton gowns, the comfort of beds with mosquito nets, but above all, the privacy. These privileges were now little more than a memory. Circumstances had changed dramatically and womanly modesty had to be cast aside as they sat together trying in vain to pull the remnants of their attire about themselves. Perhaps the greatest indignity for some was the necessity of accepting a crude native diet of chapattis and lentil porridge, humiliatingly served up on pans bereft of the most basic utensils, by natives of the lowest caste.

Ragged, emaciated, infested with lice and tormented by flies, mosquitos and prickly heat, the weakest became easy victims to the twin scourges of dysentery and cholera, with Alice Lindsay already suffering from the initial stages of the latter. Inevitably in such cramped and airless quarters, many succumbed to infection, for the windows were shuttered against the possibility of escape, and the open courtyard measuring 40 feet by 16 feet was daily drenched by the monsoon rains. In the first week of their incarceration, as recorded by a Mahratta physician, there occurred thirty-six fatalities: eighteen women, seventeen children and a Hindu nurse. Each day brought further deaths until the Nana became so concerned by the diminishing number of hostages that he gave the order for them to be brought out twice a day, under guard, for air and exercise.

It made little difference for by 10 July, cholera had a firm grip on the community and that day Alice Lindsay was numbered among the fatalities recorded by a Bengali doctor. Her death was followed two days later by that of her mother Kate. Caroline and Fanny were left to face death in a more violent form but before that, the demise of their family was recorded by Caroline on a scrap of paper:

Mama died, 12th July
Alice died, 9th July [it had been recorded as the 10th by the doctor]
George died, 27th June
Entered the barracks, 21st May
Cavalry left, 5th June
First shot fired, 6th June
Uncle Willy died, 18th June
Aunt Lilly, 17th June
Left barracks 27th June

To a lesser degree the citizens of Cawnpore were also suffering from the new regime, and an increasing number of townspeople began to rue the change when English law was supplanted by anarchy. The depredation caused by 20,000 mercenaries in the Nana's camp not being paid was becoming intolerable. In addition, revenue which could not be raised by voluntary means was being exacted in a none-too-gentle manner by the Nana's tax collectors. A great deal of resentment was caused by a demand that all looted property be given up, and in searching the native quarters his agents thought nothing of breaking into the homes of the pensioned artillerymen and insulting their wives. So widespread did these violations become that a number of 'golundazes' confronted the Nana in Bithur with loaded muskets. They were eventually pacified by the Nana's promise that the men concerned would be punished and the practice of ransacking their homes ended.

Nevertheless, resentment among the Muslims in the Nana's court was growing, and to rally support Nana Sahib promoted a number of Muslim courtiers, notably Azimullah, who was appointed Collector of Nana's dominions. Leadership of his army however remained firmly in Hindu hands. Teeka Singh was left in overall command, Jwala Prasad was made a brigadier, and Tatya Tope appointed Head of Commissariat.

Arrears of pay remained a sore point with the bulk of the Muslim sepoys and, wrote William Shepherd: 'Mahomedans, calling themselves the descendants of the Prophet, wearing garments of the most extraordinary devices, and many covered over from head to foot with armour, laden with five or six different kinds of weapons, poured in from Oudh, and other parts of the country by hundreds.' The houses of the townspeople were subjected to pillage and in some instances the Muslims 'took forcible possession of their women'. Confusion was widespread among

82

the merchants, leading one traveller to comment: 'Since the day of my arrival I never found the bazaar open, unless it were a few poor shops. The shopkeepers and the citizens are extremely sorry for losing their safety and curse the mutineers from morning to evening. The people and the workmen starve, and the widows cry in their huts.'

However, factional quarrels between Muslim and Hindu were quickly put to one side by the Nana with the news on 9 July that a punitive force 700 strong and led by Major Sydenham Renaud – of whom it was said 'was rather inclined to hang all black creation' – had left Allahabad on 30 June and was advancing rapidly along the Grand Trunk Road leaving a trail of burning villages in his wake.

The destruction being wrought by Renaud's column was certainly against Lord Canning's policy of peaceful resettlement, for the Governor General had hoped that by attacking only those villages occupied by the enemy, the native community would be encouraged to return to their homes 'with every confidence in the restoration of British authority'. Renaud's methods, however, were anything but selective and the stories of his ruthless exploits were legend.

The Times correspondent with the column was a shocked eye-witness to his methods of punishment. 'In two days,' reported William Russell, 'forty-two men were hanged by the roadside, and a batch of twelve men were executed because their faces were turned the wrong way when they were met on the march.' In a letter to his parents, a subaltern in the 78th Highlanders, who were bringing up the rear of the column, describes a scene of desolation with every village burnt to the ground and numerous bodies hanging from the trees by the roadside. Lieutenant George Digby Barker ended his letter by stating: 'The bodies of the rebels hanging from the boughs of trees have now become so common that the soldiers call them acorns.'

It was the Major's practice to leave the corpses hanging a foot above the ground to provide food for the pigs and this, and no doubt similar atrocities, so horrified the people of Cawnpore that hundreds, fearful of the retribution to come, abandoned their homes and sought refuge in the countryside. Such panic was understandable for by early July, Havelock, with 1,200 European soldiers and six cannon, was also marching north from Allahabad with the intention of rescuing the hostages in

Cawnpore before advancing to the relief of the beleagured garrison at Lucknow. Following close upon the heels of Major Renaud's smaller column, Havelock's troops passed through a desolate area bereft of human habitation save for the corpses hanging from the occasional peepul tree. William Oliver Swanston, a civilian volunteer who had joined Havelock's movable column from Allahabad, wrote of the devastation caused by Renaud's column. 'The whole road was deserted, the villages empty and all in ruins, and every here and there bodies were to be seen hanging from the branches of trees. These had been executions carried out by Renaud's force.'

The croaking of frogs in the swamps on either side of the road, and the hum of a myriad of insects encouraged by the damp and the heat, contributed to a degree of discomfort few in Havelock's column ever forgot. The onset of the monsoon had given rise to conditions almost beyond endurance as the men trudged through an expanse of glutinous mud, subjected at one moment to a torrential downpour, followed by exposure to the glaring heat of a cloudless sky.

'Rain coming up now,' complained Lieutenant William Groom in a letter to his wife, 'we shall have a wet march. I don't expect to be dry again for a long time.'

Personal comfort was not an issue for Lieutenant Henry Moorsom, for the prospect of delivering the English prisoners from the custody of the Nana outweighed every other consideration. 'Oh! 'Tis a heartrending, humiliating thought to see our countrymen, women and children, perishing within 50 miles of us without stirring a finger to aid them,' he wrote. 'I would we had a Sir Charles Napier here rather than a General Havelock, to determine their fate.'

Almost as though he was aware of such criticism, the 62-year-old General began to drive his men from one bivouac to the next in a series of forced marches which left the camp followers far behind and often outdistanced the baggage train. Consequently, at the all-too-brief halts, there was seldom much to eat, but John Sherer remembered only the high humidity. 'We sat on our beds drenched as if in a vapour bath,' he recorded, an irritation endorsed by Captain Francis Cornwallis Maude, who noted: 'The steam from the wet ground and our sodden tents together with the myriad of insects, put both our valises and our patience to the severest tests.'

84

Speed of movement was essential to Havelock, for Renaud's detachment of a hundred irregular cavalry and 400 Madras Fusiliers was advancing along a different path unsupported by artillery, in danger of being overwhelmed by a stronger enemy. Eventually, on 12 July, three hours before dawn, the two columns met. Marching to the rousing tune of 'The Cambells are Coming', they entered the small village of Belanda, 4 miles from Fatehpur, where a cavalry patrol confirmed Havelock's suspicion that Teeka Singh's rebel army was massing for an attack.

Anxious to give his men a much-needed rest, the General reluctantly accepted the challenge, but any misgiving that his men were exhausted was misplaced, for, as a civilian volunteer confirmed later: 'Out they came eager for the fray, like so many bulldogs and as jolly as possible, although just off a long march.'

The rebels, who themselves had marched 50 miles to face what they assumed to be Renaud's small force, pushed forward, but within minutes of the beginning of the action shrapnel from Maude's field guns, and a rapid fire from the Fusiliers' Enfield rifles, whose accurate range of 900 yards gave Neill's 'Blue Caps' an enormous advantage, so decimated the ranks of mutineers that they retired in disarray beyond Fatehpur. 'Knock over that chap on the elephant,' an officer had called out to Captain Maude. The round shot which brought down the elephant sent Tatya Tope sprawling on the ground unhurt but with his dignity severely bruised. .

'Thus the battle of Futtehpore was decided by the intrepid advance of our guns and skirmishers,' commented Charles North. 'Up to this time the troops had marched for 24 miles without a meal to sustain their over taxed energies; yet at 11.00 am Futtehpore was ours.'

'This was my first experience in real warfare … the first time I had heard balls flying in earnest; and I must say, I did not like it,' William Swanston confessed later. 'I then thought I should never get accustomed to the whiz of a bullet, or the sing of a cannon ball; but I have learned that art and can now hear them all about me, and not even wink an eye'. The only casualty which could be attributed to the battle was Major North of the 60th Rifles when a bullock, consumed with fury by the pain of its wounds, 'dashed violently against me,' he wrote. Caught between its horns, he was flung some distance but was fortunate to escape with nothing more than severe bruising.

The troops now enjoyed a much-needed respite beneath a tope of mangos. 'Most grateful was their shade after recent exposure to the fiery sunbeams, which seemed literally to pierce and seeth the brain,' confessed Major North. 'The relief was unforgettable.'

The humiliating ease with which his men had been defeated infuriated the Nana. His proclamation that 'The yellow faced and narrow minded people have been sent to hell and Cawnpore has been conquered,' was exposed as nothing more than an idle boast, and to many of his followers, it seemed that they themselves were exposed to an uncomfortable threat from British vengeance.

The report of the action presented by Teeka Singh dismayed the Nana's advisors in Bithur. The problem now confronting them was to find a way of defeating Havelock's column whilst it was still some distance from Cawnpore. At the same time, a second defeat was unthinkable for it would certainly put the new Peshwa's reign in jeopardy. It was with this thought in mind that the Nana appointed Bala Rao, the younger of his two brothers, to lead a strengthened force into battle, telling him, 'Kill all those men in the dirty shirts and blue caps, for they kill all my men before they fire.'

On 15 July, Bala Rao deployed his forces at Aong, a village 20 miles south of Cawnpore, spreading his men across the road behind two cannon in a bid to halt the British advance. The rebels were seen by a mounted patrol who reported back to Havelock that they were ensconced in a fortified position with a cavalry screen hovering on both flanks. Brigadier General Henry Havelock, a fervent Baptist given to distributing temperance tracts, was a competent if cautious commander, and in view of the threat to his baggage train from Bala Rao's cavalry, he merely sent a third of his strength against Aong, whilst keeping the rest in reserve.

The walled gardens and trees in the village afforded excellent cover for the rebels who directed a heavy fire against the oncoming Highlanders and Madras Fusiliers.

Charging at the head of his beloved 'lambs', Major Renaud quickly cleared the village but in the fighting he was struck down and carried to the rear with a severe thigh wound. The musket ball which had buried itself in his thigh had also driven in a piece of his scabbard and he was soon to die from septicaemia. 'He sank rapidly after the amputation of his left leg,' reported Major North. 'I had gone to see him, and found him in cheerful spirits, hoped for his ultimate recovery and now he is not. Sad realities of ruthless war.' That incident proved to be the turning point in the battle, for roused to a high pitch of fury by the loss of their commander, the 'Blue Caps' swept the rebels from the village in a determined bayonet charge.

'I never saw anything so fine,' remarked John Sherer, 'they went on with sloped arms, like a wall, till within 100 yards, and not a shot was fired. At the word 'Charge!' they broke like a pack of eager hounds, and the village was taken in an instant.' Meanwhile, Maude's artillery had been blasting the mutineers on the road with a mixture of grape and shrapnel to such good effect that many of the rebel artillerymen abandoned their cannon and fled to the rear. Thus deprived of a sizeable portion of his artillery, Bala Rao was forced to retire to a second position a few miles beyond the village where a single bridge crossed the Pandu river.

About two hours after the battle at Aong, Havelock learned from a sympathetic native that the rebels were in strength behind the bridge and had mined one of its three stone arches. Knowing that the destruction of the bridge would delay his advance on Cawnpore by several days, Havelock roused his men for one last effort. Believing that the women and children were still alive he promised his men: 'With God's help, men, we will save them, or every man of us die in the attempt.'

The relief march was of some 16 miles under a fierce sun 'which glared down with intolerable radiance,' recalled North, 'till the brain reeled and the eyeballs ached', but Havelock's men responded magnificently even to the extent of missing their breakfast in their haste to get to grips with the rebels holding the Cawnpore prisoners.

At the village of Maharajpore, a little more than 6 miles from the Pandu river, many of Havelock's weary troops, whose only means of quenching their raging thirst had been a dubious pool of rain water which had given rise to an outbreak of diarrhoea, came across an unusual but welcome discovery.

'On the line of march this morning,' wrote Lieutenant Groom to his wife, 'we found in a village, twenty-five casks of porter, fancy that! It is the best thing we have done yet. Guns are all over the country, but porter is not.' However, the discovery of the ale proved to be too great a temptation to some. 'Immediately before we started, a supply of porter had been issued,' wrote Charles North, 'and the pernicious effects of this heavy drink were too speedily manifest for as the men advanced under a broiling sun, numbers fell out of the ranks and lay motionless upon the road-side, utterly insensible' – perhaps not altogether surprising considering that the men of the 78th Foot were wearing the traditional Highland dress of thick tartan kilt, woollen jacket and plumed bonnet. The Movable Column's loss that day amounted to twelve men from heatstroke.

Encouraged by Havelock's victory at Aong, villagers sympathetic to the British informed the General that the rebels had crossed the single bridge over the River Pandu and now held a position of strength. In fact, seven guns commanded the road and more than 5,000 mutineers were deployed in an arc behind a series of mud-walled river villages, to meet what their leaders believed would be a frontal assault along the Grand Trunk Road. But Havelock was a veteran of too many Indian campaigns to be caught in such an obvious fashion, and he decided instead to outflank the enemy position. It was a manoeuvre helped by an extensive grove of mango trees, and at 1.30 pm his troops advanced 'dreadfully tired and with the sun fearfully bright'. In the van were the Madras Fusiliers with two light field pieces, followed by the 78th of Foot, with the 64th, 84th and a battalion of Sikhs bringing up the rear with the artillery.

The movement which succeeded in turning the rebels left flank was executed with great precision and before the enemy became aware of the danger, the General had wheeled the columns into line. Ignoring the round shot which smashed through the trees, splintering the trunks and bringing down a shower of branches, the Highlanders advanced beneath a film of cloud which far from shielding them from the sun's rays, only seemed to reflect the heat more intensely. As they neared the enemy, grape and case shot began to take effect but the stirring sound of the pipes raised the Scots' fighting spirit and sent them 'bounding forward with rigid jaws and hearts as hard as stone'.

When the leading files had closed to within 80 yards, the bayonets came down and the sight of these terrifying, bearded, kilted, screaming banshees, utterly demoralized the mutineers who broke and fled. The 64th, not to be outdone, captured a howitzer that had been particularly destructive, and went on to overrun the village, sending more rebels scurrying to the rear. As the sound of firing died away and the Highlanders congratulated each other, a 24-pound shot screamed through the air, bringing the celebration to a premature end. The heavy iron ball hit the ground and skipped along on its lethal passage before rising to take the head off a Highlander close by General Havelock. In an attempt to reassure his horrified comrades, who were wiping his blood and brains from their tunics, the General observed, 'His had been a happy life, for he had died in the service of his country.'

An anonymous voice broke the silence. 'For mysel', Sir, gin ye've nae objection, I wad sunner bide alive i' the service o' ma cuntra.' The guffaw which followed this remark most surely eased the tension.

Half hidden in the rolling clouds of smoke, the rebels could be seen frantically preparing the powder charges with which to destroy the bridge. A worried Havelock, knowing that if they were successful his advance on Cawnpore would be delayed by several days, roused his men to one last effort. From a position which enfiladed the enemy the Fusiliers poured such a heavy fire upon the demolition party that the charge was detonated prematurely – the parapet was shattered but the span remained intact. 'General Havelock, who had just had his horse shot from under him, now appeared boldly riding a hack,' noted Major North, 'the only man who dared to raise his head – so close and thick was the fire.'

The 62-year-old General, popularly known as 'Holy Havelock' from his long white hair and rigid Baptist views, sensed that a crisis in the battle had arrived. Turning his back on the enemy fire, he addressed the powder-blackened veterans of the 64th in his high, shrill voice. 'The longer you look at it, men, the less you will like it! The brigade will advance – left battalion leading.' The 2/64th of Foot responded with a rousing cheer which emphasized the fact that their enthusiasm had not been dulled by fatigue or losses, as round shot and grape from the enemy guns began to take effect.

'The enemy sent round shot into our ranks, until we were within 300 yards,' wrote Havelock in his official report, 'and then poured in grape with such precision and determination as I have seldom witnessed.'

'Every regiment had its hands full,' remembered Lieutenant Swanston. 'The enemy had taken up several different positions, so that as fast as two guns were taken from them, we found two more open on us from another direction.'

For a few moments the outcome of the battle hung in the balance when Maude's field guns, galloping to the aid of the infantry, became bogged down in the soft sand. 'If the Nana's cavalry who were close to us had possessed one atom of dash,' he admitted, 'they could have taken the whole of our eight guns at that moment without losing a dozen men.'

A prompt response to the threat of enemy artillery fire could often minimize its effect, as Ensign Pearson was quick to point out in a letter to his parents in a far from convincing attempt to reassure them. 'For the first 400 yards of our advance if we threw ourselves down directly we heard the report we were in time to let most of it go over us,' wrote the young officer. 'But as we approached the gun of course the shot reached us sooner, and if we were not on our faces as the gunner applied his match, we were too late.'

Prominent in the assault against the gunners had been the General's son, and in an act which surely merited his award of the Victoria Cross, Harry Marsham Havelock deliberately drove his horse at the muzzle of a huge brass cannon moments before it erupted in a deadly discharge of grape. Men each side of Havelock stumbled and fell, but miraculously he survived unscathed, and with a shout of triumph the Redcoats he led carried the position at the point of the bayonet. 'The 84th gave out this awful yell,' reported Ensign Pearson, 'screeched out the word "Cawnpore!" and rushed like madmen at the gun.'

The remorseless advance of the British infantry which presented an unbroken line of naked steel, unnerved the mutineers and their fire became ever more erratic. Maude's guns had now arrived upon the scene and the shrapnel which burst over the sepoys' position from four of the field guns only added to their discomfort. When the leading battalion of the 64th, 'red in the face from the exertion of running fully laden', poured in several volleys of musketry before coming on with the bayonet, Nana Sahib's men broke and fled. The Nana could be seen riding to and fro trying to rally his men, but to no avail, and without waiting to see the end of the battle, he left, bitter in the knowledge that his brief reign as Peshwa was almost over.

90

The Nana's return to Cawnpore was noted by Nanak Chand. 'It became now a little dark when news came that Nana was coming running back, and this turned out to be true,' he wrote. 'The man I sent to see told me that Nana was standing haggard in looks and soaked in perspiration ... mounted on a chestnut horse, accompanied by Maratha sowars. If even fifty British soldiers had arrived there he would have been caught; Nana rode away at a rapid pace for Bithoor.'

Havelock's troops had followed at a more leisurely pace until they reached the outskirts of Cawnpore, where they halted to bivouac for the night on the open plain. 'We bivouacked as we stood,' remembered William Swanston. 'All our baggage, food and everything of that sort, were 5 miles behind. We had nothing to eat and a very little dirty water to drink, but we were all so tired that we were glad to lie down as we were, and sleep with our horses' bridles in our hands.'

'We had neither tents, rations, nor grog,' confirmed Charles North, 'but we had the commendation of our General and the glowing terms in which he addressed us, proved how truly he appreciated our ardour.' One other person who had good reason to express his relief at the news of Havelock's success was William Jonah Shepherd. Released from his jail with numerous other prisoners by a jailer who no longer believed in victory for the Nana, Shepherd now stood on the open plain near the abandoned lines of the 56th NI. In the early dawn light, he saw 'an immense army, as it appeared at dawn, covering the whole of the low ground in front ... Can these be the rebel sepoys?' he wondered. Then, as the appearance of the soldiers became more distinct, he saw to his relief that they were British and stumbled towards them holding his chains aloft and crying hoarsely, 'Hurrah! Hurrah! Thanks be to God, I am saved ... I am saved!' but the tale he related to his saviours was so dreadful that it horrified and dismayed every one of his listeners.

The extensive gardens of the Old Cawnpore Hotel resounded to angry voices as the Nana's lieutenants argued as to the best course of action. Some suggested a retreat to Bithur, whilst others were in favour of contesting the British once again on the Grand Trunk Road before Cawnpore. 'If it were not for the rescue of the women and children in confinement, the soldiers would not rush on with such impetuosity,' a voice was heard to say. It was then that Azimullah offered a piece of advice to the Nana which was to bear heavily on the fate of the four men and 206 women and children confined in the Bibigarh. 'Kill the maimes and baba logues and inform the English of it – you will find the Europeans will be discouraged and go back.' The Nana listened and was impressed – with no prisoners to free, the British would have no reason for advancing on Cawnpore.

The decision to kill the captives quickly became known to the women of the Nana's seraglio where many of them vehemently protested, even to the extent of threatening to throw themselves from the windows should any further murders be committed, none of which seemed to concern Hussaini Khanum, a favourite of the Nana. She was a tall, fair woman, aged about thirty, with a persona so imperious that she was known to the others as the Begum. She took a delight in humiliating the captive memsahibs as much as possible. Only one *bhisti*, or water carrier, was allowed to service the needs of the women; consequently there was never enough water and many of the captives were obliged to cut off each other's hair to avoid an infestation of lice.

On the 15th, shortly after Bala Rao had returned to announce the defeat at the Pandu river, the male prisoners were brought out from the Bibigarh with their arms pinioned. Little ceremony seems to have been accorded to this ragged group for at the gate which opened from the compound they were met by a levelled row of muskets, and the shots which so alarmed the ladies in the Bibigarh ended the life of Mr Thornhill, a judge from Fategarh, Colonels Smith and Goldie, and the late Edward Greenway's fourteen-year-old son.

Within the hour the women too learned that they were to be shot. The chilling news was broken to them by Hussaini Khanum, and received with some scepticism by many who were convinced that the sepoys were too much in dread of the sahibs' vengeance ever to consider raising their muskets against the female prisoners.

'Are we all to be murdered?' the wife of Captain Moore asked Yousef Khan, the guard commander. The jemadar shook his head. His men would never accept orders from a woman of the harem. Frustrated by the jemadar's refusal to comply with her instructions, the Begum then went off in search of a person of authority, returning with Tatya Tope, who threatened to have the sepoys shot if they did not carry out the Begum's order. Reluctantly the jemadar led his men to the double doors which the women had vainly tried to secure, and they were wrenched open.

The women refused the order to come out, and linked arms and waists to frustrate the sepoys' half-hearted attempt to pull them out. One woman had opened a book of prayer and began to recite from a passage in the Litany: 'From our enemies defend us, Oh Christ'. This incident can be presumed if not verified from the fact that Mowbray Thomson later found a prayer book sprinkled with blood and lying open at that page, 'where,' he wrote, 'I have but little doubt those poor dear creatures sought and found consolation, in that beautiful supplication.'

When the sepoys appeared at the windows and door with levelled muskets, the screaming women and children rushed frantically for the courtyard to seek the cover afforded by the columns and the one tree growing there, but the crush was too great and most managed only to crowd together against the verandah or crouch helplessly on the courtyard floor. At Yousef Khan's command twenty sepoys fired a volley into the crowd of women and children killing and wounding many, but when a second group of sepoys moved in to complete the executions, perhaps sickened by the sight, and disturbed by the hysterical cries of the women, they refused to obey the order from Tatya Tope. This infuriated the Begum who went in search of others who would not share the sepoys' scruples.

Darkness had descended on that July evening when she returned with five men. Four were clad in the loose cotton dress favoured by the Hindustan peasant, whilst the fifth wore the red uniform of the Nana's personal bodyguard. All were carrying *tulwars* and several bore aloft a flaming torch. A bystander noted that the one in uniform was a half-caste with 'hair on his hands'. The shrieks of terror which greeted the men as they carefully closed the door before beginning the slaughter were clearly heard by the townsfolk outside, crowding close to the walls.

The full horror of the work can only be imagined, but William Shepherd was later told by a villager; 'Some of the helpless creatures in their death agony fell down at the feet of their murderers, clasped their legs and begged in the most pitiful manner to spare their lives, but to no purpose.' Twice, apparently, the man in uniform emerged from the Bibigarh to obtain a sword, having perhaps broken the previous one in a misplaced swipe against a wall or column.

A thin haze obscured the moon when after little more than an hour, the five men, their arms and clothes heavily coated with blood, emerged for the last time, as the Begum waited to lock the door behind them. The awestruck crowd of townspeople could no longer hear the cries and screams which had previously chilled their blood, but just as disturbing was a macabre sound as of individuals dragging themselves across the floor, and a low moaning 'which continued through the night'.

Early the next morning the five murderers returned with several low-caste sweepers to begin the task of removing the bodies from the Bibigarh for disposal in a nearby well 9 feet wide by 50 feet deep. A native witness testified:

> The bodies were dragged out, mostly by the hair of the head. Those who had clothes worth taking were stripped. Some of the women were alive. I cannot say how many, but three could speak. They prayed for the sake of God that an end might be put to their sufferings. Yes, there was a great crowd looking on. Yes, there were also sepoys. Three boys were alive. They were fair children. The eldest I think, must have been six or seven and the youngest five years. They were running around the well and there was none to save them. No, none said a word or tried to save them.

After the children had been killed the crowd of spectators began to disperse and by midday the only living persons in the vicinity of the Bibigarh were the three sweepers who had been detailed to remove those corpses which had not been cast into the well, for disposal in the Ganges.

In the city, news that the British were closing on Cawnpore, together with the knowledge that the prisoners in the Bibighar had been murdered, drove the townspeople into a state close to hysteria. Even those merchants who remained loyal to the Company left their homes to flee from the advancing British column. Nanak Chand, who had occasionally advised the merchants on legal matters, asked one citizen why he was abandoning his home. Because, the merchant replied, the British 'would spare nobody in their desire to avenge the massacre at Cawnpore'.

'I thought to myself, this must be true,' wrote Nanak Chand. 'At a time like this the British were not likely to distinguish between friend and foe,' and with this disturbing thought he hurried back to his home in the city.

In the early hours of Friday, 17 July, a detachment of the 84th, powder stained and coated with the dust and sweat of battle, reached Wheeler's old cantonment. Later that day Havelock's men took possession of the stables and for the first time in three weeks the entrenchment resounded to the clamour of British troops, including the 93rd Highlanders. Sergeant William Forbes-Mitchell, looking at what remained of Wheeler's entrenchment, wondered how so small a force could have held out for so long. John Sherer, whilst not in disagreement, thought that:

> Wheeler's entrenchment, which seemed so miserable when we came to look at it, proved really enough for what he was guarding against, namely, the confusion incident on an outbreak. But the advisors of the Nana induced him to send messengers after the sepoys, and offer them ample monetary remuniation if they would return. They did return, and all the world knows with what result.

Forbes-Mitchell inspected the ruins of the barrack blocks with mixed feelings. 'In the rooms of the building were still lying strewn about the remains of articles of women's and children's clothing, broken toys, torn picture books, pieces of music, etc.,' he wrote. Also picked up was a New Testament printed in Gaelic, which Forbes-Mitchell decided to keep as a relic of the Mutiny.

There were many interested visitors to the town, prominent among whom was Mowbray Thomson, who discovered that the natives who remained had erected all manner of signs to establish their innocence. 'This house belongs to Mokerjea, very loyal subject,' proclaimed one, 'please do not molest.' In furtherance of these pleas, John Sherer was asked to endorse a number of talismans designed to protect the occupant from the wrath of the British soldier. 'Fortunately for all parties,' commented the magistrate, 'Atkins was not permitted to roam into the city, and my talismans were never put to the test.'

William Shepherd, who had ridden in with the 84th, wrote:

> The entire population was so panic stricken that, leaving house and property, every man that had a hand in the rebellion took to his heels. People deserted their families on the way to escape with their own lives. From noon till midnight nothing but immense mobs were seen rushing away as fast as possible towards the west, some crossed over to Lucknow from Bithoor ghat. Others went towards Delhi, and the most part of the city people hid themselves in the neighbouring villages when they were nicely robbed by the zemindars.

Despite Sherer's assertion that the bazaar and streets of Cawnpore were prohibited to the British soldier, Tommy Atkins was nevertheless able to partake of the available plunder. 'Cawn-pore is crammed full of every description of liquor from champagne to bottled beer,' a sergeant of the 84th regiment confided to a friend in England. 'Shawls, tulwars, gold embroidered coats, and rich elephant trappings were sold in our camp for a few rupees.' Order was soon restored, as the same NCO made abundantly clear when writing a few days later. 'We have a Provost Sergeant and his Staff here now, and they would hang a European if they found him plundering or give him a dozen on the spot if they caught him half-a-mile from his camp. But as for a native,' he added, 'it is quite a common thing to have a few swung up every day. The least thing will do it.'

Chapter 8

RETRIBUTION

Captain Ayton's company of the 85th, to which William Shepherd had attached himself, passed the splintered trees, the charred remains of the European bungalows and the battered walls of the barrack buildings, and were astonished by the devastation around them. Everything that had once been familiar to them had been destroyed – even much of the Church of St John lay in ruins, and Wheeler's old entrenchment had evidently been used by the natives 'as a *cloaca maxima*,' reported by Russell of *The Times*. 'The smells are revolting,' he added.

As Captain Ayton and Lieutenant Moorsom neared the compound, they were joined by Lieutenant McCrae and a group of Highlanders. As yet unaware of the horrors that had taken place the day before, their attention was drawn to the Bibighar by two villagers who approached them hesitantly exhibiting every sign of apprehension, pointing to the Bibighar and whispering, 'Sahib! Sahib!' As Ayton and McCrae dismounted and walked over the flattened grass towards the double doors, they were conscious of a repulsive odour which grew stronger with every step. William Shepherd watched as McCrae put his shoulder to the door which creaked open. Almost immediately, the officer staggered back, his boots slippery with blood. Sick with apprehension, Shepherd asked him whether the room contained any bodies. McCrae, his face ashen, shook his head in mute stupefaction.

Lieutenant Moorsom was the next to enter. 'I went through the rooms strewn with Bibles and prayer books, and other religious works,' he wrote, 'with shoes, some of little children, certainly not three inches long, and amidst all these fearful stains and pools of innocent English blood.' A few months earlier he had visited the Lindsay family in Cawnpore, and now, however unpleasant the task, he took time to search for any evidence of their fate. 'Each room I entered, I peered into, expecting to see their bodies,' he informed his sister, 'but thank God I was spared that sight, their butchers threw them into a well.'

Those who followed the two officers were confronted with a spectacle which caused some to stumble out, retching violently, and others to remain with faces contorted with rage. 'The smell of the still reeking human blood was dreadful,' confessed Captain Francis Maude, 'and a thing never to be forgotten.'

John Sherer, who was probably the first civilian to enter the Bibighar, found the scene 'so unspeakably horrible ... The whole of the pavement was thickly coated with blood, long tresses of hair glued with clotted blood to the ground.' A Bible discovered half hidden beneath a litter of clothing bore an inscription on the fly leaf: 'For darling Mama, from her affectionate daughter Isabella Ball. 27th June. Went to the boats 29th. Taken out of the boats 30th. Taken to Sevadah Kottri. Fatal day.'

Despite the absence of bodies, the evidence that remained angered many, and one grisly detail in particular sickened William Munro, a surgeon of the 93rd of Foot:

> About six feet from the floor, a large iron hook was fixed to the wall, which, on examining I found to be covered with congealed blood, and on the wall immediately around it were many marks of blood which on close inspection, I saw were the hand prints of a little child ... the poor thing must have struggled for a long time, perhaps in the sight of its helpless mother. This was horrible to think of or to look at, so I hurried from the room.

A little more than 40 feet from the Bibighar was the well. Looking down, the horrified viewers saw a tangled mass of naked flesh, human limbs and severed heads stacked to within a few feet of the well's lip. 'I looked down and saw such a sight as I hope never to see again,' wrote an anonymous Highlander. 'The whole of the bodies were naked, and the limbs had been separated.' 'I have faced death in every form,' another veteran remarked, 'but I could not look down that well again.'

It was a sight so ghastly that when Sherer sought out General Havelock to report the discovery, the General immediately requested, 'Please, at once procure coolies, and have it filled up with earth.' The order was duly carried out, 'Not a moment too soon,' observed Sherer, 'for the effluvia was becoming excessively bad.'

On that day the slogan 'Remember Cawnpore!' was born, and it was perhaps understandable that a soldier who had fought in the Crimea where he had been reluctant to kill a Russian, felt any compassion for the mutineers desert him. 'As I looked around, I could almost have cried with rage,' confessed Colonel John Alexander Ewart of the 93rd. Remembering his cousin and his family, he wrote: 'I felt that I had become a changed man. All feeling of mercy or consideration for the mutineers had left me. I was no longer a Christian, and all I wanted was revenge.'

In feeling this way, he was not alone. The bloodstained walls and the sword cuts on a tree over the well, with here and there a trace of human hair sticking to the bark, filled young Hugh Gough with just one desire: 'Vengeance, deep and sure'. Similar feelings possessed even the most liberal minded. 'If I am wrong,' mused Lieutenant Swanston, 'may God forgive me, but it is hard to think of what our unoffending women and children suffered, and not have feelings of revenge rise in one's heart.'

In his capacity as Magistrate in Cawnpore, John Sherer submitted an official report to the Commissioner after the Mutiny had been suppressed, in which he stated:

> It seems probable that the volleys were first fired into the doors and windows and then the executioners were sent in to do the rest with swords. If the work was anything like completed, it must have taken a considerable time. At length the doors were closed and night fell upon what had happened. The hotel, where Nana had his headquarters, was within fifty yards of this house and I am credibly informed that he ordered a nautch and passed the evening with singing and dancing. Early the next morning, orders were given for the Bebeegurh to be cleared. There must have been near upon 200 corpses, so many I do not think could have been thrown into the well. It seems probable that a portion was dragged down to the Ganges. Considering the smallness of the house, and the crowded conditions of the captives it is next to impossible that all can have been slaughtered the previous night. It is exercising therefore no morbid imagination and pondering to no prurient curiosity to say that I hold no doubt some of the living met a more terrible death than assassination, even by being plunged with their dead companions into the tainted waters of the well.

The retribution exacted by the enraged Fusiliers and Highlanders, encouraged by Brigadier General James Neill – he had recently been promoted from Colonel – was every bit as brutal and indiscriminate as that inflicted by the rebels upon the unfortunate women and children in the Bibigarh. The guilty had long since fled Cawnpore, but the mere suspicion of having been involved was sufficient to convict a mutineer, and Neill, who had arrived on the 20th from Allahabad to take command, was quick to ensure that in his eyes, at least, the punishment fitted the crime.

Accompanied by Captain Gordon, his aide-de-camp, Neill had visited the Bibighar and was taken aback by what Gordon termed 'the horrors of that human slaughter house'. James Neill, despite a strict Scottish Presbyterian schooling which had taught him to combine justice with mercy, found it impossible to control his feelings, and was led to remark, 'No one who has witnessed these scenes of murder, mutilation and massacre, can ever listen to the word mercy as applied to these fiends. I can never spare a sepoy again. All that fall into my hands will be dead men.'

Given the amount of alcohol freely available it was no surprise that restraint was cast aside by the enraged redcoats. The first two mutineers captured in Cawnpore had been so badly wounded that they had been unable to make their escape. One, a *sowar*, and the other a corporal in the 53rd NI, were laid out in the sun as a preliminary punishment, and they protested by heaping abuse and curses upon their tormentors. William Shepherd, who was a witness, wrote: 'The Europeans rewarded them with a kick or so for their pains.' The pair were subsequently hung.

The Provost's party made sure that the condemned knew beforehand that their souls were not about to go to paradise by taking steps to defile their religion or caste. Beef was forced down the throats of Hindus and pork fat was smeared on Muslims. Many were buried in graves that they had been forced to dig themselves. Every Brahmin, under pain of the lash, was made to clean a portion of the bloodstained floor, which to a high-caste Hindu was tantamount to condemning his soul to perdition.

After witnessing the punishment of one such victim, John Gordon recorded the event in his diary: 'When he became a little dilatory at his work he was brightened up by several good cuts across his back from a cat which a European soldier was standing alongside with for that purpose. This was repeated several times and he roared like a bull.' The prisoner was then taken out to a gallows which had been erected in the compound and hanged before he could indulge in any ceremony of purification. Forbes-Mitchell, who earlier had seen Surgeon Munro examining the hook with tears streaming down his face, was present at the execution of three sepoys captured the day before the arrival of General Neill. 'The dried blood on the floor was first moistened with water,' he observed, 'and the lash of the warder was applied till the wretches kneeled down and cleaned their square foot of flooring.'

Few of the hangmen paused to consider whether they were punishing the innocent, and when Captain Maude suggested that the method by which they were sent to their deaths was just a little too casual, and asked the Provost Sergeant whether he thought so, he was not altogether surprised by his reply: 'Well, I don't know, Sir; I 'ain't 'eard no complaints.' Very probably, thought Maude, 'he had not'.

Feelings were certainly running high, for even after the well had been filled it was not difficult to find gruesome evidence of the appalling massacres that had taken place. Major Anson wrote to his wife in Kussowlee:

> Yesterday I went to see the house where so many of our unfortunate women and children had been murdered. It is a villainous looking place, and will be more famous than the Black Hole of Calcutta. We saw lots of remnants of gowns, shoes, and garments dyed in blood and blood upon the walls in different places. Outside in the compound there was the skull of a woman, and hair about on the bushes.

Neill's bizarre method of punishment continued until 18 July when General Havelock ordered that all intoxicating liquor be confiscated and put under guard, for as he explained: 'It would require one half of my force to keep it from being drunk by the other half, and I should scarcely have a sober soldier in camp.'

Soldiers were banned from entering the native quarters and the General warned that any found guilty of plundering would be 'hung up in their uniform'. In the event it proved to be an idle threat, for as an anonymous soldier stated, 'We have had one European hung, but they are very loath to do anything to the Europeans.'

In his tour of Wheeler's entrenchment and the surrounding area, Major Anson found the magazine to be a complete ruin and he was convinced that the old General had made the correct decision in occupying the hospital barrack and digging the entrenchment. He was of the opinion that but for the failure of provisions and a shortage of ammunition, the garrison could have held out pending the arrival of General Havelock. Major Anson's view however would have brought little comfort to William Shepherd, for although he now had his freedom, the knowledge that his wife and daughter had perished at the Satichaura Ghat meant that he could no longer entertain fond hopes for the future, and felt quite alone.

Early in August Lady Canning was able to provide further details to Queen Victoria relating to the tragedy when she wrote:

> I cannot write to your Majesty all the horrors we have to mourn over. The Cawnpore massacres were the worst of all & little has yet come to light ... Poor little scraps of journal, one by a child & a letter from a lady to her mother with verses of 'Farewell' were picked up in that house where they were murdered. The sight of those rooms makes strong men faint – the bodies were never seen. All were already thrown down a well. I think the spot will be cleared & consecrated & a simple memorial put up to their memory. I hear of letters from a large party of merry happy girls there who at first thought Cawnpore 'so delightful'. They did not wish to be sent away, they feared nothing & the life was so pleasant, like a picnic every day. After the siege began what a cruel contrast! Their house was shelled & the roof gone. Many were wounded. A list of deaths by wounds and cholera up to the last dreadful day was found & it has given comfort to many to see the names of their friends on it.

It was said that when Lord Canning learned of the massacre, he walked the halls of Government House all through the night, tormented by thoughts that had he acted sooner, the women and children might have been saved.

Although the Nana and his army of 12,000 had been driven from Cawnpore, it was still a force to be reckoned with but Generals Neill and Havelock could not agree upon tactics. A potentially awkward situation was only avoided when General Havelock announced his intention of taking command of the Lucknow relief column, leaving Neill with a small force to defend Cawnpore. On 25 July, Havelock left to join the relief column which earlier that week had made a hazardous crossing of the fast-flowing Ganges, 1,500 strong and equipped with ten field guns. Coincident with the river crossing was the beginning of the monsoon period which added to the difficulties experienced by Havelock's troops, not least to their personal comforts. 'The heavy and frequent rain incident during this monsoon weather makes writing a matter of difficulty,' complained Charles North. 'The ploughed ground beneath one's feet is a regular swamp. Water, water, everywhere! A dry jacket is a luxury unknown to us for many days.'

Held back by the monsoon rains, the Madras Fusiliers had been among the last troops to cross. 'Here we are still and the rain falling in torrents', complained Lieutenant William Tate Groom in a letter to his wife. 'Nearly the whole force are now on the other side of the river without tents. They say that the Sikhs are to cross this morning and we cross this evening ... No tents or baggage to be taken to Lucknow, so you may fancy what a comfortable time we shall have of it.'

'Nothing would keep the water out, it seemed to soak up from the ground,' wrote William Swanston. 'This state of affairs could not last long; cholera broke out and the men weakened by exposure and hard work gave out one by one.'

For three days Havelock's troops remained on the Oude side of the river without shelter of any description before moving on to a small village where, as recorded by Ensign Blake, 'cholera broke out, taking men off by the score'.

Having warned Calcutta that General Neill had been left in Cawnpore with a small force in prepared positions north of the canal, General Havelock began his march upcountry, conscious of the opposition he could expect from the Nana's troops and the Oudh irregulars who had joined them. The difficulties they would face were not lost upon Major Charles North. 'The entire population of Oudh is against us', he wrote on 27 July, 'therefore we may anticipate the most stringent opposition.' Nevertheless, he was certainly relieved to march away from Cawnpore, leaving it 'literally alive with all sorts and sizes of flies, some of them sleek and others bloated, apparently gorged with putridity and thriving on this pestilential atmosphere, which swelters with mortality'.

General Havelock was not given to taking undue risks and was beginning to appreciate the enormity of the task which lay ahead. The strength of his column and the amount of supplies he had brought were barely adequate, furthermore the monsoon rains had turned the rough country tracks into quagmires threatening to bring his advance to a halt. Major Bingham reported:

We are marching in the middle of a monsoon at a time when no troops of any description are moved in this country. The rains are very heavy. The country on both sides of the road is almost a swamp, in parts it is entirely so. The sun at other times is so hot when it shines that many of the men have been killed by sunstroke.

After ten days of being drenched to the skin and floundering ankle deep through mud, sickness and exhaustion had reduced the 1,200 British contingent – already weakened by drink – to the extent that unless reinforcements were available, Havelock's attempt to relieve Lucknow must be abandoned. On 29 July, a day of such intense heat that it led Lieutenant Groom to admit that he felt 'as if all my bones were dried up', the General's men fought a successful if minor engagement on the Lucknow road near the town of Unao. 'Four hours of good hard fighting,' enthused Major Bingham. 'Having displaced the enemy and captured five guns, we made an advance to a tope of trees under which we bivouacked for three hours during the great heat, the insufferable heat of the day. We had breakfast, and afterwards fell asleep, how refreshing! ... Men and officers completely exhausted.'

Before the day ended Havelock had followed up this success with another at Bashiratgunj, a walled village some 6 miles beyond Unao. Here, the attackers met with stronger opposition in the form of a brisk cannonade and withering musketry from the loopholed houses. The flooded state of the roads prevented the use of mounted troops, but supported by the Madras Fusiliers and the 78th Highlanders, the 64th of Foot were able to force their way between an enemy strong point and a bridge, to turn the rebel's flank. By sunset Bashiratgunj was in British hands. Havelock's men were now within 30 miles of Lucknow but with their ranks decimated by sickness in addition to battle casualties, General Havelock recognized the folly of maintaining the advance. On the 31st he withdrew from the town after sending a telegraph to the acting C-in-C, Lieutenant General Sir Patrick Grant, in Calcutta:

My force is reduced by sickness and repeated combats to 1,364 rank and file with two ill equipped guns. I could not therefore move on against Lucknow with any prospect of success, especially as I have no means of crossing the Sye or the canal. I have therefore shortened my communication with Cawnpore, by falling back two short marches. If I am speedily reinforced by 1,000 more

British soldiers and Major Oliphant's battery complete, I might resume my march towards Lucknow or keep fast my foot in Oudh, or I might re-cross and hold the head of the Grand Trunk Road at Cawnpore.

Havelock's decision to pull back to Mangalwar puzzled Lieutenant General Sir Patrick Grant, and on 5 August he conveyed his misgivings to General Neill:

I have been astonished by a telegram from Havelock intimating that his force being reduced by sickness and repeated combats, he could not move on against Lucknow with any prospect of success, and that he had therefore fallen back within 6 miles of Cawnpore, but that if reinforced by 1,000 Europeans and Oliphant's battery he may yet obtain a good result. All this puzzles me inexpressibly.

Neill, having sent on a half battery and a detachment of the 84th on 1 August, followed Grant's telegraph with a letter to Havelock remarkable for its level of insubordination:

I deeply regret that you have fallen back one foot. The effect on our prestige is very bad indeed. It has been most unfortunate your not bringing any guns captured from the enemy. The natives will not believe that you have captured one ... When the iron guns are sent to you, also the half battery and the company of the 84th escorting it, you ought to advance again. As for the infantry they are not to be had, and if you wait for them Lucknow will follow the fate of Cawnpore ... Return here sharp, for there is much to be done.

This forthright communication brought a furious reply from the senior of the two Generals:

I do not want and will not receive any advice from an officer under my command, be his experience what it may. Understand this distinctly; and that a consideration of the obstruction that would arise to the public service at this moment alone prevents me from taking the stronger step of placing you under arrest. You now stand warned ... I alone am responsible for the course which I have pursued.

Commenting on the exchange of words between the two generals, John Sherer wrote of Neill; 'He sometimes said things which others would have kept to themselves. He would laugh and declare, not heeding who was present, that "the old gentleman [himself] looked upon himself as the heir-at-law, so he would not expect to be liked more than heirs-at-law usually are.'''

Brigadier General Henry Havelock's eventual decision to retire upon Cawnpore was not influenced in any way by Neill's demand, but rather by a report that the 4,000 sepoys who had occupied Bithur were a direct threat to Cawnpore. His reason for abandoning the attempt to relieve Lucknow had not been disclosed to the junior officers and caused dismay and disappointment to many. 'We are still in the dark about the General's intention,' noted Lieutenant William Tate Groom. 'Everybody is frightfully disgusted at his conduct, but he doubtless is acting on the best information and has very good reasons for his apparent want of energy.'

George Blake, however, was more sympathetic to the idea of falling back on the old camping ground of Mangalwar. 'It is true that in these actions we always licked them well,' he wrote, 'but we could not afford to lose nearly 100 men a day, and the enemy's strength being more in thousands than we in hundreds, they did not feel their losses.'

Now that he had made a decision to retire on Cawnpore, Henry Havelock had no desire to leave an impression that he was in fear of facing the many rebels who threatened the approaches to Lucknow, and with this in mind he decided to inflict a second defeat upon the sepoys who had returned to Bashiratganj.

The rebels were now well served by artillery and entrenched in a strong position in the village of Burhia-ka-Chauki. Once again the Highlanders braved a storm of grape to wade knee deep through fields inundated with water from the monsoon rains and mount a fierce bayonet charge to capture the rebel guns before turning them against the enemy. 'Oh! if you could have seen the Highlanders,' young Harry Havelock enthused to his cousin. 'A handful – 120 men – overwhelmed almost with shot, shell and grape – up to their middles in swamp – rush with a cheer on two guns defended by not less than 2,000 sepoys and wrest them from them without a second's check – you would have been proud of your countrymen for ever.'

Following the successful outcome of this encounter with the rebels at Bashiratganj, Havelock sent a telegraph to Sir Patrick Grant in Calcutta: 'This action has inspired much terror among the enemy and I trust will prevent him effectually opposing our embarkation at Cawnpore.' By 13 August he was across the Ganges and back in Cawnpore having lost a quarter of his force from battle casualties and sickness.

Because thousands of rebels were known to be regrouping at Bithur, Havelock's men were allowed to rest for just three days before being told that they were to engage with the sepoys of the 42nd NI who were deployed near the Nana's palace with two field guns. Other mutineers lay entrenched in two villages where on more than one occasion John Sherer had heard musket shots and 'the clatter of troops as of a body of horse on the road'.

In discussing the situation with General Neill, who had suggested that the steamer *Brahmaputra* be used as a transport whilst a second column proceeded by bullock train to cut the rebels' line of retreat, Henry Havelock took a different view and on the 15th a disgruntled Neill protested in his diary: 'General Havelock after a great deal of parade determines to move out tomorrow against Bithoor in one column, and will not employ the steamer. I only fear he will fatigue his men and will not strike the blow. We shall see however.'

Although it had been planned to make an early start, the sun was well above the horizon before the men, who were dispersed in various bivouacs, could be assembled in full. The punitive column of 1,400, complete with two batteries of light field guns, set off across a tract of smooth country interspersed with stunted trees and numerous thickets of sugar cane. 'It was a beautiful day,' remembered Lieutenant Swanston, 'the country all round was looking nice and green, and it was pleasantly cool with a fresh wind blowing.' The welcome breeze was to be short lived and as the sun climbed in the sky, the day proved to be one of intense heat, with Havelock's tired troops taking eight hours to cover a distance of just 6 miles. In order to enter Sheorajpur from the south, the column was obliged to face the fortified villages which Havelock acknowledged to be one of the strongest objectives he had yet encountered. The Madras Fusiliers and the Sikhs were ordered to lie flat on the ground whilst Maude's cannon pounded the rebels' earthworks to little effect. 'There was a severe conflict on both sides ... his artillery fire was very heavy,' admitted Major Bingham. 'The sound of a 24 pound shot going through the air and close to you is anything but pleasant.'

Havelock's troops were pitting themselves against what was said to be 'the flower of the mutinous soldiery', but undaunted,

Fusiliers, Highlanders and Sikhs advanced steadily towards their objective as hundreds of *sowars* massed on their left flank. One rebel troop, bolder than the rest, broke away from the main body and galloped down the road towards the 'Blue Caps', but finding themselves unsupported, reined to an ignominious halt after refusing to confront the jeering fusiliers.

A frantic struggle soon developed, however, with the sepoys of the 42nd, supported by the Gwalior contingent, meeting the Europeans with great determination and bravery, refusing to withdraw until many of their comrades had fallen. 'They stood to their guns to the last,' admitted Lieutenant Moorsom with grudging respect, 'and fought their two guns against our fourteen or fifteen right well.'

'They fought desperately,' confirmed General Havelock in drawing up his official report, 'otherwise they could not for a whole hour have held their own, even with much advantage of ground, against my powerful artillery fire, the stream prevented my turning there, and my troops were received in assaulting the position, by heavy rifle and musket fire.'

'"Cawnpore, my lads, remember Cawnpore!" was the battle cry,' related William Swanston. 'At least 250 must have been cut up before being driven back, their guns captured and infantry chased off the field in full retreat.'

The losses sustained by Havelock's column were not insignificant comprising fifty battle casualties plus another dozen from heat stroke. At the end of the engagement the General made a point of riding along the line of his exhausted soldiers to the accompaniment of their cheers. 'Don't cheer me, my men,' he exclaimed. 'You did it all yourselves.'

Pursuit had been out of the question for Havelock had no cavalry, and his infantry was in no condition to give chase. They returned to Cawnpore the next day in pouring rain having first, as Major North observed, 'blown up the buildings, the property of the Nana Sahib at Bithoor'.

The decision to abandon the relief of Lucknow and the effect it must have had upon that garrison was a cause for concern among Havelock's men, a point raised by Major G.W.F. Bingham. 'Their feelings can easily be conceived,' he wrote. 'We did our best but could not go to their relief owing to the vast numbers of the enemy around Lucknow and also to the large numbers of sick and wounded and having no carriage for them.'

108

On his return, Henry Havelock read in the Government *Gazette* that two important changes had taken place in his absence. Sir Patrick Grant had been replaced as Commander-in-Chief by Sir Colin Campbell, a veteran of fifty years distinguished service, stretching from the Peninsula War to the Crimea. Promotion had been slow in coming but Sir Colin enjoyed the reputation of being a 'fighting general' who at sixty-five retained the vigour of mind and body of a man half his age, and was adored by the men of the Highland Brigade he had commanded in the Crimea. Lady Canning, who had met him three months previously, held him in equally high regard. 'Very agreeable and cheerful,' she thought, 'if an endless talker and *raconteur*.' Secondly, the Dinapore and Cawnpore Divisions were to be combined under the leadership of Lieutenant General Sir James Outram, a man eight years younger than Havelock, who was expected to reach Cawnpore in early September. Disappointed Havelock may have been, but he at least had the satisfaction of knowing that he would be able to work in greater harmony with Outram than he had ever done with General James George Neill.

At Cawnpore the situation was generally peaceful and only a few thieves troubled the merchants in the bazaar. News of the Nana was scarce and there was only the occasional rumour to report on his movements. One had it that he was at Fatehpur Chaurasi preparing to cross the river and join Tatya Tope. Another that he had fled to Chandemagore in a bid to secure the assistance of the French, whose possession it was. Sir Colin Campbell, however, was more concerned with pacifying the country between Cawnpore and Lucknow than in chasing rumours, and on 3 November he arrived at Cawnpore from Allahabad with his staff.

The Bibighar had still not been cleaned after inspecting the rooms littered with pathetic reminders of the massacre, the men Campbell had brought with him departed thirsting for revenge. 'Here am I in the town of horrors, scarcely a soul visible and all the houses in ruins,' wrote Surgeon Francis Collins. 'Even now the traces of what happened on that fearful day of slaughter are only too visible ... the sight of all this makes, to say the least about it, one shudder.'

Forbes-Mitchell doubted whether those being punished for the crime were the guilty offenders, a view supported by Lieutenant Edward Hope Verney. 'We hear of reports circulated of the barbarities practised by the sepoys upon our countrymen and women, which we believe to be greatly exaggerated,' he explained in a letter to his sister. 'This is a war in which the worst passions are likely to be excited, but I have heard of great cruelties being perpetrated by our own people.'

It was left to Sir Colin Campbell to put a stop to these acts of vengeance, in particular that of licking portions of the blood-stained floor, which he described as being 'unworthy of the English name and a Christian Government', before leaving for Lucknow on 9 November, confident that an attack would not be made on Cawnpore before he returned. It was debatable whether Campbell's assurance was shared by many of his soldiers, for as Forbes-Mitchell observed:

When proceeding on our march to Lucknow it was as clear as noonday to the meanest capacity that we were in an enemy's country. None of the villages along the route were inhabited, the only visible signs of life about them being a few mangy dogs ... it needed no great powers of observation to fully understand that the whole population of Oude was against us.

Left in command of the garrison was 47-year-old Major General Charles Ashe Windham of Crimean fame, with 500 European troops and a battery of four field guns. His orders were to hold Cawnpore as a staging post for the Lucknow refugees Sir Colin expected to bring back with him now that the bridge of boats had been restored. Campbell's parting instructions had been clear and concise: under no circumstance was General Windham to engage the enemy unless it became necessary to protect the bridge of boats. He was to observe the movements of the Gwalior contingent, but British troops arriving in Cawnpore were not to be detained, merely redirected along the Grand Trunk Road to Lucknow.

Meanwhile, 46 miles south-west of Cawnpore, the Nana Sahib's most able commander, the thirty-year-old Tatya Tope, informed by his spies in Cawnpore that General Campbell had departed for Oudh with 3,400 men, including a Naval Brigade armed with heavy guns and rocket launchers, crossed the Jumma with the intention of cutting off Windham's communications with the north. The thousands of rebels who Tatya Tope had accumulated began to deploy along the banks of the Jumma until almost every town and village from Akbarpur to Sheorajpur,

20 miles north-west of Cawnpore, was occupied. Windham did what he could to improve his field of fire by demolishing houses and reducing groves of mango trees, but he could be forgiven for feeling that Campbell's departure for Lucknow had prejudiced his position in Cawnpore.

Chapter 9

THE GWALIOR CONTINGENT

Despite the improvements Lieutenant Mowbray Thomson had made to General Wheeler's earthworks, little had been done to minimize the danger facing Windham's garrison from a labyrinth of narrow streets in the old native quarter, no more than 100 yards distant, considerably limiting any early warning the garrison would have of the approach of the enemy. The threat facing Windham's small garrison was no idle one. Tatya Tope was known to have at least 9,000 sepoys, a strong force of cavalry and an artillery strength of thirty cannon.

Of some assurance to Windham, however, was the fact that since the end of October he had been able to detain troops from regiments bound for Lucknow, which had given him a further 1,700, considerably adding to his strength and raising the morale of the garrison. This change in circumstances had encouraged the General to consider taking punitive action against Tatya Tope's leading column, now on the banks of the Ganges Canal, 15 miles from the city.

Although Campbell's orders had strictly forbidden an attack unless absolutely necessary, General Windham felt confident that with his increase in manpower and artillery – on 14 November he had received Campbell's blessing to retain as many men as deemed necessary to defend Cawnpore – an assault against the two rebel-held villages before Tatya Tope could arrive with his main force was bound to be crowned with success.

Less than half a mile from Windham's position the canal ran north to where two villages, one on each side of the canal, were occupied by the mutineers from Oudh. It would be a boost to morale and no doubt a feather in his cap, reasoned Windham, if a detachment of 1,200 troops were to be floated down the canal at night and disembarked at dawn at a point close to the two villages. Supported by light field guns galloped along a parallel path, and fresh from their boat journey, the men would be able to

112

inflict a damaging blow against each of the two groups of mutineers, which might conceivably weaken an attack against the entrenchment.

So confident was Charles Ash Windham of success, that he quietly assembled a number of flat-bottomed native boats before requesting permission from Campbell's headquarters for the assault. The reply he received on the 19th was non-committal, Campbell's Chief of Staff merely suggesting that it would be advisable to wait for the Commander's approval before launching the operation. Shortly afterwards communication with Lucknow ceased and for several days nothing more was heard from Sir Colin's headquarters.

In the absence of further messages from Lucknow Major General Windham's anxiety increased, for the last report had confirmed that the Residency had been reached and for all that Windham knew, refugees might already be on their way to Cawnpore. On the 29th a message brought in by a native proved to be nothing more than a request for commissariat stores. The note caused Windham some alarm for it seemed to imply that Campbell was trapped in Lucknow and unable to return. He decided to ignore the request since transport and the provision of an escort to Lucknow was beyond his ability to provide.

After two days, Windham's native spies reported movements which indicated that the Gwalior contingent was being strengthened by groups of rebels from Oudh crossing the river at different points, signs which pointed to the fact that an attack against the bridge of boats was likely in the next few days. This intelligence altered the General's plans, for he dare not risk any part of his force in a separate engagement along the canal whilst the bridge of boats across the Ganges was under threat. Now that the majority of his force was positioned behind the brick fields on the city's outskirts, General Windham ordered his troops to advance to a point where the Kalpi Road crossed the canal. From there it would be possible to keep a watchful eye on the bridge, whilst in a position to proceed along the canal should Windham revert to his original plan.

By late November a large part of the Gwalior contingent had advanced to within 3 miles of Cawnpore, Windham's troops were put on full alert and the baggage train sent to the rear. Charles Windham and his staff, accompanied by a troop of the 9th Lancers, rode forward to reconnoitre and soon established the movements of the enemy from the cloud of dust which enveloped them in a thin brown haze. The rebels appeared to be in considerable strength but although it was desirable to prevent the native quarter from being overrun, Windham was nevertheless restricted in what he could do by virtue of his brief from Sir Colin Campbell.

At a later meeting with his staff, the General seems to have decided to act upon his own initiative, since the situation called for immediate action. 'These small engagements are awkward things, very little glory gained in winning them and perhaps some valuable life is lost,' he told Captain F.C. Maude. 'I am certainly not going to let these fellows think that we cannot act on the offensive.'

Leaving behind a token force to guard the baggage, Windham advanced with 1,200 men from the 34th, 82nd and 88th of Foot, plus the 2nd Battalion of the KRRC, supported by eight field guns from the Bengal Artillery, towards Tatya Tope's advance columns at Pandu Nadi.

The battle began in the early hours of 26 November with the Rifles advancing through high-standing corn, closely followed by the Connaught Rangers and four quick-firing guns. The 34th took up the left side of the road with four 9-pounder guns, whilst the men of the 82nd were kept back in reserve. The Riflemen and the Irishmen soon came under fire from six rebel cannon and musketry from 3,000 rebels occupying the dry bed of a stream, but in spite of the numerical disadvantage Windham's troops carried the position with a rush, driving the enemy through a nearby village and going on to capture two 8-inch howitzers and a 6-pounder cannon.

The engagement was over in less than an hour and although successful Windham's loss was appreciable considering the brief nature of the engagement, being sixteen killed and seventy-eight wounded. Despite their casualties, the troops returned to their former positions beside the Kalpi road in good heart, while Windham, on his return to headquarters, was relieved to find a message from Campbell announcing that he had broken through the mutineers' cordon around the Residency and was on his way back with the refugees from Lucknow.

Although General Windham had defeated one body of rebels, reliable intelligence was becoming increasingly difficult to obtain; what little information there was of Tatya Tope's movements ceased altogether after several of Windham's native spies returned to camp horribly mutilated at the hands of the fanatical Muslims. At 10.00 am the following day, a sudden cannonade on Windham's right flank and centre signalled the beginning of a sustained attack on the brickworks. It was the teenage naval cadet Edward Spencer Watson's first experience of artillery fire and it left an indelible impression upon his memory. 'It was a beautiful day, very hot, and the sky was quite blue,' he wrote. 'The shell burst very high and a long way off from where we were, and the white smoke oozing out from it against the bright blue sky looked beautiful. It was the first shell that I ever saw fired in real warfare, and I shall never forget it as long as I live.'

Taking advantage of whatever cover was available, the mutineers drove in the English pickets in a desperate attempt to carry the position. The attack was met by the 34th and a company of the 82nd on the flank, and by the 60th and the 88th in the centre, ably supported by large naval pieces known as 'cow guns', manned by seamen from HMS *Shannon* who soon came under fire themselves. 'The shot knocked up the dust about a hundred yards ahead of us,' wrote Watson, 'and came tearing along at a tremendous pace right between our two guns. Luckily no one was standing in the way, or they would have been eased of their legs very quickly.'

Unfortunately for Windham, after an hour the gun crews' ammunition began to run short when the frightened bullock drivers deserted their charges which, as Cadet Watson remarked, 'were quite dangerous to go near'. It was only with great difficulty that the heavy naval guns were dragged back to a position of safety.

Now that artillery support had been reduced, morale collapsed and the men on Windham's right flank began to fall back. Despite committing reinforcements which he could ill afford, the pressure from a numerically superior enemy proved too great to resist. The battle had already lasted several hours and when it was discovered to have largely been a feint to allow Tatya Tope to occupy the native part of the city, resistance crumbled altogether. Threatened on three sides by upwards of 25,000 mutineers equipped with forty cannon, General Windham was left with no choice but to abandon the brickworks and retire to the fort and the entrenchments. 'Then it was a case of everyone for himself,' confessed Edward Watson, 'a tremendous fire pouring in on every side all the while.' The withdrawal through the city was completed without sustaining a single casualty but in such haste that much of the soldiers' kit was left behind to be plundered by the victorious sepoys.

Mowbray Thomson wrote:

> The sound of the retreat threw a panic into the whole neighbourhood. From the native city came merchants with their families and treasure, seeking the protection of the fort; from the field, helter skelter, in dire confusion, broken companies of English regiments, guns, sailors, soldiers, camels, elephants, bullock hackeries with officers' baggage, all crowding at the gates for entrance.

The situation in which Windham's garrison now found itself was serious, for the enemy was in possession of the native quarter, a circumstance which Lieutenant Thomson had witnessed, precipitating a flood of refugees seeking the protection of the entrenchments. They were joined by groups of inexperienced young soldiers who thought nothing of discarding their weapons in their haste to reach a place of safety and promptly got drunk on wine stolen from the medical store. 'Among the stores were some casks of beer and wine ... some of the soldiers found this out, and by some means got at it and there were a great many cases of drunkenness among them,' explained Edward Spencer Watson, 'and the howling and noise they kept up through the night, as they were prisoners at the main guard, was enough to prevent anyone from sleeping.' The naval cadet was careful to add, 'The sailors remained very steady, not one case of drunkenness occurred among them.'

The Sikhs in the fort were astonished that British soldiers could behave in such a fashion. Some patted the redcoats on the back reassuringly as they streamed past in disorder telling them, 'Don't fear! Don't fear!' It was said that one old Sikh veteran standing by the gate exclaimed, 'You are not the brothers of the men who beat the khalsa.'

Such was the confusion that William Shepherd, who had returned to Wheeler's old entrenchment with the 84th, began to fear that he would find himself besieged for a second time. 'The confusion and panic which prevailed that evening in the entrenchment baffles description,' he wrote. 'It was perhaps fortunate that the enemy had not followed up their advantage ... our men were so harassed and knocked up with the day's work that they would have been unable to repulse them.'

116

Despite his difficulties, unencumbered with women and children and well stocked with provisions, 'very, very different was the position of General Windham from that of Sir Hugh Wheeler five months previously,' commented Mowbray Thomson.

General Windham's whole force was now concentrated behind the new defensive system which Thomson had so tirelessly supervised, and Windham felt certain that the position could be held pending Sir Colin Campbell's return. In his latest despatch the 48-year-old General took pains to reassure Campbell's headquarters staff: 'In retiring within the entrenchments, I followed the general instructions issued by your Excellency, conveyed through the Chief of Staff; namely, to preserve the safety of the bridge over the Ganges, and my communication with your force, so severely engaged in the important operation of the relief of Lucknow. As far as possible I strictly adhered to the defensive'.

Windham's troubles were not yet over for at noon the next day Tatya Tope launched two attacks which fortunately were met in equally determined fashion by troops led by Colonel Walpole and Brigadier Wilson, the latter sustaining a mortal wound in an attack on a battery of six guns. By nightfall the British were back in the fort having abandoned the civil station and suffered 315 casualties in an engagement many in the garrison referred to as 'Windham's Mess'. The General, however, looked upon the action as something of a triumph and wrote in his despatches:

> On the left advance, Colonel Walpole with the Rifles, supported by Captain Green's battery, and part of the 82nd Regiment, achieved a complete victory over the enemy, and captured two 18-pounder guns. The glory of this well-contested fight belongs entirely to the above-named companies and artillery. It was owing to the gallantry of the men and officers under the able leadership of Colonel Walpole and of my late lamented relation, Lt. Col. Woodford of the Rifle Brigade and of Lt. Col. Watson of the 82nd, and of Captain Greene of the Bengal Artillery, that this hard-contested fight was won and brought to a profitable end. I had nothing to do with it beyond sending them supports, and at the end, of bringing up some myself.

On 29 November a rain of shells fell upon the entrenchments heavier than any experienced by Mowbray Thomson and William Shepherd in the first siege. Fortunately it was of short duration, for once Peel's naval guns had the range, little time was lost in silencing Tatya Tope's artillery. After Windham's defeat on the 27th, the rebels had diligently searched Cawnpore for European and Sikh stragglers. One incident moved the soldiers of the 64th of Foot to impotent fury, when it was disclosed that two wounded officers of their regiment had been captured and hung from the same banyan tree that Neill had used to hang sepoys.

Nana Sahib and Azimullah Khan were no longer in the vicinity of Bithur, but Bala Rao, Jwala Prasad and Rao Sahib had returned to the European quarter of Cawnpore which was now little more than a smouldering ruin. Few shops were open and, wrote Nanak Chand, 'Low caste men looted the roti godown [bread stores]. Some servants marched about armed with match-locks, looting on behalf of their zemindars.'

Around 60 miles to the north-east of Cawnpore lies the city of Lucknow, the capital of Oudh. In 1858 William Russell wrote: 'There is a city more vast than Paris, as it seems, and more brilliant.' It did, however, possess a sprawling maze of narrow streets and alleys, the home of 600,000 people, occupying an area of 12 square miles; it was bordered on its northern side by the River Gumti, and on its southern face by a canal which encircled that part of the city. To the east, the Residency, a large impressive structure built on high ground overlooking the river and the city, had been the home of several residents appointed by the East India Company; in April 1857 it was occupied by Sir Henry Lawrence, the 51-year-old Chief Commissioner of Oudh.

To the south-west, on the road to Cawnpore, stood the Alambagh, a pleasure ground and former palace of the kings of Oudh, whilst on both sides of the city's walls was an accumu-lation of buildings the most prominent of which were the Kaiserbagh, the Sikanderbagh, and the Shah Najif. Beyond these edifices, south of the canal, were two other important buildings, the Martiniere a school for European and Eurasian children, and the Dilkusha, the palace of Wajid Ali Shah, who had been deposed by James Outram, the Company's representative in Oudh, in February of the previous year.

These limestone buildings, with their minarets and gilded domes, were among the most impressive in Lucknow and led William Russell of *The Times* to further praise when he wrote: 'Not Rome, not Athens, not Constantinople, not any city I have seen, appears to me so striking and so beautiful as this; and the more I gaze, the more its beauties grow upon me.'

1. 'Thomas Henry Kavanagh being disguised as a native'. Oil on canvas by Louis William Desanges.

2. 'Sir James Outram'. Engraving by V. Froer of a photograph taken by an unknown person.
(National Army Museum)

3. 'Gallant attack of Windham's force on the Gwalior contingent'. Chromolithograph by D. Sarsfield Greene.

(National Army Museum)

4. 'The chamber of blood'. Tinted lithograph by Vincent Brooks after Lieutenant C.W. Crump.

(National Army Museum)

5. 'The hero of Lucknow'. A coloured stipple engraving of Major General Henry Havelock by A.H. Ritchie. (National Army Museum)

6. 'Lieutenant T.A. Butler winning the VC at Lucknow, 9th March 1858'. Oil on canvas by Louis William Desanges.
(National Army Museum)

7. 'The house of the massacre'. Photograph after Lieutenant G.R. Miller, by Orlando Norie. (National Army Museum)

8. 'The battered barracks'. A tinted lithograph by Vincent Brooks after Lieutenant C.W. Crump.

(National Army Museum)

It was not a description which Amelia Horne would have subscribed to – she detested Lucknow and wrote:

> The place held out no inducements. It was so different from anything I had ever seen, the houses so strange, the streets so narrow and the people so unlike those in Bengal that I used to feel as if I had got into another world ... the streets are never known to be swept; and the flies abound in such numbers that sometimes the shops can only be opened at night.

Within two months of her arrival, the pretty seventeen-year-old Eurasian girl had been accosted by boisterous youths in a manner which infuriated her stepfather and he decided to leave Lucknow with his family for Cawnpore.

Signs of unrest began to surface in the city even before the uprising at Meerut and when a Doctor Wells of the 48th NI, feeling unwell, thoughtlessly sipped from a medicine bottle used by his Hindu patients, it was witnessed by a native apothecary who lost no time in informing the sepoys. Outraged by this slight to their caste, the sepoys took their revenge by burning down the doctor's bungalow from which his wife and children only narrowly escaped with their lives. Shortly afterwards a mutiny by the 7th Oudh Irregular Infantry was only prevented by Sir Henry Lawrence when he ordered up a detachment of the 32nd of Foot backed by a strong force of artillery.

Further indications of the widespread dissatisfaction prevailing came from posters exhibited in prominent parts of Lucknow urging all true Muslims to rise up and kill the infidels. At the Residency a sentry of the 32nd was approached by a fakir who after abusing him in a language the sentry did not understand, drew his hand across his throat, a piece of insolence which earned the punishment of a hundred lashes for the holy man. In what perhaps was something of an understatement, the Revd. Henry Polehampton, who had recently taken up employment there as Chaplain, wrote to his mother: 'The sepoys and natives generally are just now in rather a disagreeable state of feeling towards us.'

'It was considered unsafe for Europeans to visit the crowded parts of the city,' commented Mr L.E.R. Rees a Calcutta merchant, 'yet ... every evening I used to ride towards the Muchee Bhawn, armed of course, without however meeting with any accident. On one occasion, my pistol dropped, and a man

119

politely picked it up. Yet a lowering, sullen, obstinate look was discernible on almost every countenance.'

Following the uprisings at Meerut and Delhi, no one doubted that the current mood of disaffection would shortly spread throughout Oudh. Sir Henry Lawrence, for one, made sure that should the 'devil's wind' blow across Lucknow, he would not be caught unprepared. Families in the outlying stations were instructed to leave for their own safety and proceed to Lucknow, a move which did not at first find favour with Mrs Huxham, an officer's widow. 'We lived in a miserable state of suspense,' she wrote. 'The heat was terrible, but as the days passed on and the city was apparently tranquil, we began to think that we had been needlessly alarmed, and entertained hopes of being allowed to return to our own homes.'

It was a vain hope for preparations for a state of siege were already in place. Trenches had been dug in the immediate vicinity of the Residency, gun emplacements constructed, provisions stockpiled and ammunition suitably stored in protected magazines. Civilians were enrolled as armed militia and trained by NCOs from the 32nd. When these men were first brought together at the commencement of the siege, the chances of making them act in an efficient body was, wrote Captain Anderson, 'a hopeless task. There were men of all ages, sizes and figures . . . but had it not been for our volunteers, we should never have been able to garrison the place.'

That such measures had been taken none too soon was confirmed by a trusted sepoy, who confided to Captain Thomas Wilson of the 71st NI that the firing of the 9.00 pm gun on the last Saturday in May was to be the signal for the sepoys to burn their huts and murder their British officers. When that day dawned and the evening gun eventually sounded, Lawrence was at dinner with friends, and mindful of the sepoy's warning the diners around his table waited in expectation. The silence which followed the single report was broken by the voice of the Chief Commissioner. 'Wilson, it would seem that your friends are not punctual.' But before he or anyone else could reply, there arose a confused babble of voices intermixed with musket shots. All thoughts of dinner were cast aside and from the Commissioner's verandah his guests were alarmed to see that the customary velvet blackness of the night sky had been diminished by a lurid blood-red glare. Fortunately, the sepoys were too busily engaged in burning and looting the officers' bungalows to approach the Residency or the diners in Sir Henry's bungalow.

'At the Residency, we were all very anxious; all that we could see were bright flames rising up from the cantonments,' wrote Captain Anderson, 'and every now and then we heard the report of a gun, followed by a rather sharp musket fire.'

'The sight of the burning bungalows was awful,' echoed Mrs Case, 'and we could do nothing but watch the flames with beating hearts, and listen tremblingly to the booming of the cannon.'

Along the road halfway between the Residency and the city, Mr Rees, who had come to Lucknow on business, challenged the approach of a horseman from the vantage point of a terraced roof.

'Who are you?' he demanded, conscious of the uproar from the native lines.

'A friend,' came the answer. 'I carry a message to the Residency'.

'What news then?'

'Good news,' called the stranger.

'Well, what good news?'

'The bungalows are being burnt and the Europeans are everywhere being shot down.' With that the shadowy figure galloped off into the darkness, leaving an astonished Rees to speed his departure with a musket shot.

The next morning Sir Henry Lawrence rode out with 300 men of the 32nd and four guns towards the race course where the mutinous 71st were bivouacked at Mudkipur. A few rounds from his artillery were enough to disperse their camp and the sepoys were joined in their flight by most of the 7th Cavalry. In a pursuit of 10 miles, sixty prisoners were taken, and it was afterwards discovered that the entire native cavalry and almost the whole of the native Irregular troops had gone over to the mutineers.

By that afternoon, it was clear that the insurrection had been welcomed by the civilian populace when thousands of Muslims left the mosques to parade through the streets of Lucknow with banners proclaiming their faith, whilst the *budmash* of the city swarmed through the bazaar looting and ransacking, attacking Europeans and forcing merchants to close down their businesses.

Now that the period of uncertainty was over, work on the defences of the outbuildings commenced with an urgency which perhaps had previously been lacking. Captain R.F. Anderson of the 25th NI pulled down the garden wall of his house on the Cawnpore road which might have afforded shelter to rebels, and in its place dug a ditch with pointed bamboos at the bottom, and a wooden stockade. Even the contents of library shelves had their uses as Martin Gubbins, the Financial Commissioner, was to discover when a volume of *Lardner's Encyclopedia* stopped a musket ball in 128 pages.

Sir Henry was careful to ensure the safe passage of refugees by employing Sikh cavalry to patrol the roads around Lucknow, a measure which enabled families fleeing the rebels to reach the Residency in ever-increasing numbers.

Spread over an area of some 30 acres, the Residency site was certainly of a size to accommodate the flood of refugees. The building itself had ample living space in three storeys of lofty apartments, wide verandahs and high windows. It was well supplied with water and was not overlooked at all by buildings housing the mutineers.

Few of the original residents had given thought to the upheaval likely to accompany such an influx of refugees, and even those who had been obliged to leave the familiar comfort of their own home met a scene of utter confusion. Having survived a four-day journey from Gouda with a party of seven ladies, twelve children and four officers, Mrs Katherine Bartrum arrived on 9 June with little more than the clothes she wore, only to find that she was to share a room in the Begum Koti – 'a most uninviting looking place, so dirty' – with fifteen other women and children. Separated from her doctor husband and ignorant of what had become of him, the 23-year-old girl from Somerset found herself among strangers too concerned with problems of their own to pay much attention to her and the baby. 'We had to endure intense heat, mosquitoes and flies in swarms,' she complained. 'How great a change after the comforts of our own homes! And at the same time how great was our anxiety concerning the fate of our husbands.'

Like many of the refugees, the unaccustomed change to communal living was far from welcome. Mrs Adelaide Case felt compelled to enter her diary with the observation: 'There is not one hole or corner where one can enjoy an instant's privacy. The coming and going, the talking, the bustle and noise, inside as well as outside, the constant alarming reports, and at times the depressed expression on some of the countenances baffle all description.' She discovered one compensation, however, for as she freely admitted:

> The view from the top of the Residency is truly beyond description, and in the early morning when the sun begins to shine on the gilded mosques and minarets and towers, it is like a fairy scene. The whole of this vast city spread out before one, and on all sides surrounded by beautiful parks and magnificent trees, forms a panorama which it would be difficult to see equalled in any other part of the world.

As the days passed, the work of turning the Residency into a fortress continued at a feverish pace. Buildings skirting the outer defence works were half demolished to form a barrier against the impact of artillery fire, and where streets crossed the Residency boundary, barricades were erected. Mrs Huxham noted:

> We could see from our balconies the work of destruction going on around, for many handsome buildings and gateways surrounding the Residency were pulled down, so as to avoid giving our enemies commanding positions from which to open fire upon us in case of coming to close quarters with them. The trees and shrubs were dug up by the roots, the gardens destroyed, and treasure and ammunition buried in their place ... even large empty beer casks were filled with sand and put up as a sort of protection to do duty as walls ... Sir Henry Lawrence would sometimes go into the town outside the Residency in disguise to see how the work was progressing. He seemed to take no rest, actuated as he was by a high sense of his responsibility, and he won the love and admiration of all, high and low.

On 6 June news reached them of the mutiny at Cawnpore. The sufferings of that unfortunate garrison, and the fact that Lucknow could offer no assistance, cast an air of gloom over the whole community. When Sir Henry Lawrence heard of the massacre on the evening of the 28th, he realized that his own ordeal was merely a matter of days away.

Rebels in Oudh had been increasing in number and, mindful of the fact that a party had already reached Chinhat just 8 miles away, Martin Gubbins, the opinionated Financial Commissioner, repeatedly urged Sir Henry to sally out in strength to disperse them. He would not take 'no' for an answer, going so far as to suggest that 'we shall be branded at the bar of history as cowards.' Eventually, Lawrence much against his better judgement, agreed to mount an operation, which he hoped might confuse the rebels and delay an attack against the Residency.

On 29 June, a 600-strong column comprising 300 men of the 32nd of Foot, 230 loyal native troops, 100 Sikhs and a small detachment of volunteer cavalry, supported by ten guns and an 18-inch howitzer drawn by an elephant, was put into a state of readiness for a dawn march the next morning. From its inception the expedition proved to be an unmitigated disaster. Lack of staff planning meant that the sun was already high in the sky before the march commenced and, since food had not been prepared, the troops marched on empty stomachs. In the absence of breakfast, many of the Europeans had indulged rather too freely in liquor and it was with throbbing heads that many tramped along in a sullen frame of mind with the sun shining directly in their faces.

'We were given to understand that there were only 5,000 of the enemy,' lamented Henry Metcalfe, 'but we found out our mistake when we got [nearer] ... However our hopes were strong and we thought we could thrash all before us, but we were sadly taken in.'

Some 3 miles into the march a halt was made whilst Sir Henry Lawrence and his staff rode ahead to reconnoitre. On the way, a group of merchants were encountered who, when questioned, told them that the rebels had fallen back leaving only an advance guard in a nearby village. Sir Henry, who was concerned about his men's fatigued condition, considered returning to the Residency, but a majority of his officers were in favour of continuing the advance and the column set off once more, covered by the cavalry, with the artillery rumbling along in the rear. It was then that matters deteriorated rapidly for the native water carriers, perhaps sensing the presence of mutineers in the grove of trees ahead, deserted with this precious commodity, and the small force of Europeans had not proceeded very much further before it came under a heavy fire of musketry. Lieutenant Ludlow-Smith explained in a letter to his father:

The Europeans were dreadfully distressed and done up by the heat. We had scarcely formed up when the enemy opened fire. Their first round shot passed over those in front and just missed us in the rear ... the next hit one of the native artillerymen ... the scene that took place then amongst this native artillery is indescribable. They rushed their guns off the road down the side which like the side of

124

all the roads in India, was a mass of scoops, hollows and holes, out of which mud has been taken to make the road. It had rained so you can imagine what a condition the place was in.

The rebel force, led by a skilful General Barhat Ahmed, was in considerable strength – 5,500 infantry supported by ten guns – but, undeterred, the men of the 32nd quickly deployed to bring their own artillery into action and a fierce exchange of gunfire began. The first British shell, fired from a range of 1,300 yards, burst above the heads of the enemy gunners and was quickly followed by others equally destructive. The rebel sepoys began to move off the road and for a moment it appeared that they might even be retiring. Rees, who rode with the column as a volunteer, had no doubts and when Captain Wilson came riding up crying, 'That's it! There they go, keep it up!' he quite thought the day was won. In fact, the mutineers were merely changing front and although the howitzer, christened by the men of the 32nd as 'Turk', continued to tear great gaps in the enemy's ranks, it was the beginning of the end for Lawrence's punitive column.

An attack by the 32nd on the village of Ishmailganj petered out when Colonel William Case fell mortally wounded; weakened by hunger and suffering severely from the heat, his men refused to advance any further, merely lying down in the long grass to begin an exchange of musketry. The native artillerymen with Lawrence, seeing the strength of the opposition, cut the horses traces and deserted to the enemy; even the elephant which had been pulling the howitzer was driven off by its mahout. Shading his eyes against the glare of the sun, Rees saw that the plain between Ishmailganj and Chinhat was 'one moving mass of men ... the flanks covered with a foam of skirmishers, the light puffs of smoke from their muskets floating from every ravine and bunch of grass in our front'.

The enforced retreat of Lawrence's column soon took on the appearance of a rout as, buoyed by their success, the mutineers attacked on both flanks. A few loyal sepoys and the more deter-mined of the 32nd stood their ground with powder- blackened faces and throats parched from biting the ends off cartridges, but their stand was little more than an impotent gesture and beneath a hail of grape and canister the survivors fell back in confusion. 'Throughout the whole affair there had been mismanagement and mistakes,' wrote Ludlow-Smith, 'and now with the retreat, these were increased ten fold ... We had no earthly means of carrying them away [the wounded] and saw them cut up under our eyes.'

The few who refused to retire were seen 'fighting like bulldogs held at bay'. Those with flesh wounds were able to grasp a stirrup, some were laid across gun limbers, whilst others were removed on the backs of loyal sepoys, but for the rest left on the field, observed Rees, 'none asked for mercy, for none expected it.'

In full pursuit came the main body of the enemy, including a strong detachment of rebel horse who at one time threatened to cut Lawrence's line of retreat. They were clearly visible to the Calcutta merchant, who was astonished to see they were commanded by a 'handsome looking man, well built, fair, about twenty-five years of age, with light mustachios, and wearing the undress uniform of a European cavalry officer, with a blue and gold laced cap on his head'. Rees later recalled that a Russian had been arrested and then released just before the outbreak of unrest in Lucknow.

Possession of the bridge at Kokrail was essential and Sir Henry, with remarkable presence of mind, ordered one of the few remaining guns to be unlimbered and hauled to the middle of the bridge with a gunner standing over it, a lighted portfire in his hand although there was neither powder nor shot for the cannon. The ruse had its desired effect and whilst the mutineers held back fearing a discharge of grape, a squadron of volunteer cavalry rallied immediately to the trumpet call of Captain Radcliffe. Without a moment's hesitation, thirty-six horsemen set spurs to their mounts and dashed for the bridge as two rebel 9-pounders belched flame and smoke. As the round shot whirred harmlessly over their heads, the shrill notes of a bugle sounded the 'charge' and the group of volunteers, sabres flashing in the sun, broke from a gallop into a charge. Astonishingly, the rebel cavalry made no attempt to engage the oncoming horsemen but turned away and the infantry's line of retreat was secured. The men of the 32nd, too exhausted even to load their muskets, retired from the bridge as best they could, leaving the road strewn with the bodies of their fallen comrades.

This defeat and the losses suffered by his column troubled Sir Henry greatly. 'My God! My God!' a soldier heard him exclaim. 'And I brought them to this.'

Meanwhile, those in the Residency, as yet unaware of the debacle, continued to work at a pace. Men sweated over their charges or directed native prisoners and coolies in the work of demolition to create improved fields of fire. Then, as rumour of the disaster at Chinhat began to circulate, the natives began to steal away, taking with them the tools of their trade. Half an hour after the first group of redcoats had begun to stream into the Residency grounds, there was scarcely a native to be seen in the confines of the entrenchment. Henry Polehampton, who had seen the column march out of Lucknow, witnessed their return. 'By about 12 o'clock the whole of the remains of our small force had come in,' he noted in his diary, 'hard pressed by the enemy who had taken two howitzers and one 9-pounder. Colonel Case, Captain Stevens, Lieutenant Brackenbury and about 112 non-commissioned officers and men were left on the field.'

The return of the Chinhat expedition added to the despondency of the refugees quartered in the Residency. Mrs Julia Inglis, although suffering from an attack of smallpox, left her bed to peer out of a window. 'They [the soldiers] were struggling in by twos and threes, some riding, some on guns, some supported by their comrades,' she observed. 'All seemed thoroughly exhausted, I could see the flashes of the muskets, and on the opposite side of the river could distinguish large bodies of the enemy through the trees.'

A little later Mrs Case entered the room. 'Oh, Mrs Inglis, go to bed,' she urged. 'I have just heard that Colonel Inglis and William are both safe.'

'A few minutes afterwards John came in,' continued Mrs Inglis. 'He was crying; and after kissing me, turned to Mrs Case and said, "Poor Case!" Never shall I forget the shock his words gave me, or the cry of agony from the poor widow.'

Around the compound the women did their best to alleviate the suffering of the wounded, moving about them anxiously with fans and jars of iced water, 'for up to that time we had a good supply of ice,' explained Mrs Huxham, 'and this refreshed them in their exhausted condition'. As the last of the redcoats limped over the iron bridge, those mutineers who were not looting the bazaar could be seen through the trees, closing in on the Residency. Before the day was over they had taken possession of the houses surrounding the entrenchment and had begun work on the construction of gun emplacements. As night fell, watch fires were to be seen on every side. The siege of Lucknow had begun.

Chapter 10

BATTLE FOR THE RESIDENCY

On 1 July an intensive bombardment by rebel artillery began, using every kind of missile from conventional round shot to bundles of telegraph wire. One of the first fortified posts to be targeted by the rebels was captain R.P. Anderson's house on the Cawnpore road, when a round shot carried away one of its stone pillars and brought down the verandah, burying a volunteer – a Mr Capper – under 6 feet of masonry and timber. As the dust settled, a faint voice could be heard crying, 'I'm alive! Get me out! Give me air, for God's sake.'

It seemed to his rescuers, obliged to lie on their stomachs to avoid flying fragments of iron and stone, that the task was beyond them and the feelings of most was reflected in the view of one sweating civilian when he muttered, 'It's impossible to save him' as he struggled to shift a heavy piece of masonry. Capper's indignant reply came in a tone of sharp reproof: 'Nonsense! You damn well try.'

Fortunately for him, a beam had come down in such a way as to support most of the debris and after an hour's strenuous labour under a hail of musketry, a dazed but grateful volunteer was freed from what might otherwise have become his tomb, 'suffering merely from bruises and feeling a little faint'.

Darkness brought an end to the enemy's fire but although the night was relatively peaceful the stifling humidity brought little rest to the families with young children. The heat in the crowded rooms was almost unbearable and did much to add to the children's fretfulness. When at last they fell asleep, Mrs Bartrum admitted: 'We used to gather round a chair which formed our tea table sitting on the bedside, and drinking our tea by the light of a candle which was stuck in a bottle, that being our only candle-stick, and then we talked together of bye-gone days, of happy homes in England where our childhood had been spent.'

Daylight saw the resumption of the shelling and later that morning a determined rush by the rebels against the Water Gate which was only repulsed with difficulty. Again it was the women who suffered most from the uncertainty. Confined to their quarters, very often a cellar devoid of natural light, the noise of exploding shells, the rattle of musketry and the shouts of the combatants must have been little short of terrifying. Many, like Mrs Case mourning the death of her husband, sought refuge in prayer and for her at least 'the soothing effect of communing with God' brought comfort which eased her mind and made her feel a 'different person'.

The loss in manpower following the fateful encounter at Chinhat had meant that the defence perimeter around the Residency was now desperately in need of volunteers to man it, and it was decided to send for the garrison of the Machi Bhawan to make good the shortfall. Messages to and from the old fort had ceased with the desertion of the native runners, and it was not until a primitive semaphore had been constructed and operated from the Residency roof that instructions could be conveyed to Colonel Palmer in charge of the garrison. The signal was short and to the point: 'Spike the guns well. Blow up the fort and retire at midnight.'

At precisely that hour, when many of the rebels were fully engaged in plundering the city, a twenty-minute fuse was laid to the magazine and Colonel Palmer led his men out of the fort accompanied by a procession of carts bearing the sick and wounded, and the women and children of the garrison, on the three quarters of a mile journey to the Residency. It was completed in just fifteen minutes without a shot being fired and with only one absentee – a drunken Irishman of the 32nd who, having fallen asleep in a quiet corner, could not be found when the roll call was completed. As the last of the garrison passed through the Baillie Guard Gate, 240 barrels of gunpowder and 594,000 cartridges erupted with a thunderous roar which shook the Residency building to its foundations and spread a pall of dense smoke over the area. 'An immense black cloud enveloped even us in the Residency – darkness covering a bright starry firmament,' observed the Calcutta merchant. 'The shock resembled an earthquake.'

'The enemy thought they had done it by their incessant firing of shot and shell,' commented Private Metcalfe, 'and they gave such a yell of triumph that you would have thought, with Shakespeare, that hell had become uninhabited and that all the demons were transferred to Lucknow.'

No one had seen fit to warn the women and for a few terrifying moments many thought that a mine had exploded and that the sepoys had forced their way in. 'We were awoke by the most horrible explosion . . . it shattered every bit of glass in the house,' wrote Mrs Maria Germon. 'There were four doors to our tye khana, half glass, and the concussion covered us with the glass and shook one of the doors off its hinges, I believe we all thought our last hour was come.'

In the Begum Kothi, bricks and mortar fell from the ceiling and so thick was the fog of brick dust that when Mrs Brydon lit a candle the occupants of the room were barely able to recognize each other. 'It was such a tremendous shock that we all sprang up not knowing what had happened,' she wrote. 'The poor little children were screaming in terror.'

Early the next morning, a shout from outside the Baillie Guard Gate brought the duty guard to its feet. 'Arragh, be Jasus. Open the gate.' The sentries rubbed their eyes and burst into roars of laughter for, standing before them, was the naked and powder-blackened figure of the missing soldier, leading a pair of bullocks and an empty cart. Blown in the air and regaining consciousness to find himself alone, he had resumed his drunken slumber before coming to his senses and making his way to the Residency. His had been an experience guaranteed to have persuaded most alcoholics to a vow of total abstinence, but true to character, the Irishman lost no time in celebrating his miraculous escape with several glasses of grog.

The hilarity which greeted his return was soon to be overshadowed by an event which plunged the whole community into the deepest gloom. From his room in an upper storey, Sir Henry Lawrence enjoyed a wide field of view over the rebel positions. Even so, his was a position of some danger, particularly vulnerable to the enemy's artillery. A shell from the 8-inch howitzer captured by the rebels at Chinhat smashed through a window later that day as Sir Henry conversed with his secretary, fortunately without exploding, but nevertheless serving as a timely warning to the Commissioner that it would be advisable to change his quarters.

On the morning of 2 July Captain Wilson reminded him of his earlier promise to move to a safer part of the building, and was assured by Sir Henry that he had not forgotten but would rest for an hour before doing so. It was a fateful decision for as he rested on his bed another shell from the same howitzer exploded just after 8.00 am, filling the room with dust and smoke. Wilson was thrown to the floor. He lay there stunned for a few moments and then, rising to his feet, he called, 'Sir Henry! Sir Henry! Are you hurt?' There followed an ominous silence and Wilson called twice more before a low voice answered him: 'I am killed.' When the smoke cleared Wilson could see that the Commissioner's injury was indeed a frightful one. A fragment of shell had smashed the upper part of his thigh and fractured his pelvis. When Sir Henry Lawrence was removed to another room it was discovered that little could be done other than to apply a tourniquet. Both Doctors Fayrer and Hadow realized that the wound was mortal and when the Commissioner asked how long he had, Dr Fayrer replied with brutal honesty, 'Forty-eight hours, Sir.' The forecast proved remarkably accurate for Sir Henry died quietly at 8 o'clock on the morning of 4 July. He was buried that night in a shallow grave, as were several gunners who had been killed during the day.

When news of his death became generally known, even the most insensitive redcoat felt that he had lost a friend. 'His death cast a great shadow over the garrison, and at such a time was most depressing to all concerned,' observed Ensign Ruggles. 'His uprightness, unselfishness, and genial affectionate nature made us all feel that we had indeed lost a friend, and that in time of great need.'

Sir Henry Lawrence had inspired widespread confidence, but with his demise many began to question whether it had been right to attempt to defend a perimeter of more than a mile with a force of little more than 1,700, of which only 780 were professional soldiers. The defence ring around the Residency comprised a number of fortified houses, linked by mud walls and trenches taking the form of an irregular pentagon divided into seventeen posts, each having its own commander and a compliment of thirty British troops, plus civilian volunteers and sepoys who had remained loyal to the Company. Of the seventeen redoubts, the Redan battery mounting two 18-pounders and one 9-pounder was the most important and this was manned entirely by British soldiers under the command of Lieutenant Samuel Lawrence, the nephew of the late Commissioner. Facing the river, his battery overlooked the one area thought to be the most likely for a rebel mass attack. On the east face of the perimeter, next to the Water Gate, was the hospital and a battery of three mortars, and almost adjoining it the Baillie Guard Gate which had once been the grand entrance to the Residency. Here, Lieutenant Aitken of the 13th NI had charge of two 9-pounders and a howitzer. This section of the perimeter was close to the walled gardens and houses occupied by the mutineers, which in some instances were no more than 25 yards from the Residency; having loopholed the garden walls, they were eventually to make use of them to sink mine shafts unseen by the defenders.

Fortunately, the boundary wall facing the rebel position was a solid affair with several fortified houses possessing flat, castellated roofs. One was the property of Dr Fayrer, another was used by Martin Gubbins as an office and was commanded by Captain Saunders of the 13th NI. Among other notable buildings was the Brigade Mess, the high roof of which afforded an unobstructed field of fire for the marksmen among the community. In command here was Colonel Master of the 7th Light Cavalry, popularly known as 'the Admiral' from his habit of climbing to the uppermost part of the gabled roof and hailing the men in the surrounding posts.

Most exposed of all was the post commanded by Lieutenant Innes of the Engineers. Sited on a spur of high ground slightly proud of the main defence line, this single-storey house was overlooked by several buildings which had not been demolished and were now occupied by the rebels. Despite this shortcoming, Innes' command was important from its value as an observation post and as such was protected by a battery sited near the church, and by the heavy guns of the Redan.

Given that at least 8,000 mutineers were ranged against them, numbers which were increasing with each passing day, the defenders could not afford to relax their vigilance for an instant. Duty spells were of necessity continuous and the garrison of a post were rarely able to leave their position except at night when provisions were brought to them. In these circumstances rank could not exercise its usual privilege and guard duties were shared equally between officers and men. Should a person be fortunate enough to snatch a few hours of broken sleep, it was always in his clothes and with a loaded musket at his side. There were few instances of relief and the posts were rarely visited by a superior officer, save for an occasional inspection by Brigadier Inglis or a member of his staff.

Although each garrison was separated from its neighbour, the symbol of the Union flag floating above the Residency tower inspired every Englishman with a pride in his nationality and a determination to defend it with his life. The flag became an obvious target for the rebels and its halyards were frequently cut by musket shots, but it was lowered each day at sunset and the torn cloth patched. When the sun rose the following day, the first object to meet the enemy's eye would be this infuriating emblem of the British Raj hanging from a splintered flagpole.

When he lay dying, Sir Henry Lawrence – much to the chagrin of the Financial Commissioner, Martin Gubbins – had appointed Major Banks, the Commander of the Lucknow Division, to succeed him, and he quickly restored order to the Residency area. The Commissariat bullocks, some of which, crazed with thirst, had stumbled about and fallen into the wells, were securely penned, and numerous horses, many of which had chewed the tails of their neighbours to assuage their hunger, were now safely picketed.

In the early days of the siege the rebels had kept up a constant musketry rather than making extensive use of artillery to breach the walls, and this had accounted for most of the fifteen casualties per day in the first week. Warnings of potential rebel assaults were frequent, and on these occasions, wrote Mrs Bartrum, 'there would come the cry of all lights out; the children would cry at being in the dark and the women would be trembling in fear lest the enemy attack proved successful and the sepoys should get in.' The dreadful consequence of such an event provoked frequent discussions among them as to the legitimacy of suicide. Mrs Adelaide Case observed:

> Some of the ladies keep laudanum and prussic acid near them. I can scarcely think it right to have recourse to such intent, it appears to me that all we have to do is to endeavour, as far as we can, to be prepared for our own death, and leave the rest in the hands of Him who knows what is best for us.

A few of the more spirited ladies however, chose to demonstrate their defiance by remaining on the balcony verandah and singing popular songs.

Often it was the innocent who suffered the consequence of neglecting to seek shelter in the event of enemy activity. Mrs Bartrum, standing at the door of the Begum Kothi, smiled at a little girl playing with a spent musket ball. As she watched her at play, Katherine Bartrum was reminded of her own happy childhood. Then, as she was lost in thought, there came the sound of a musket shot and before Katherine's horrified gaze, the child's head was reduced to a bloody pulp from the impact of the heavy lead ball. The shock to Mrs Bartrum was so great that she collapsed in a faint and, as she later confessed: 'I could never afterwards think of that poor child without a shudder.'

Prominent among the rebel snipers was an African employee of the ex-King of Oude, who seldom failed to send a ball through the head of his selected target. So deadly was his aim that he earned for himself the soubriquet of 'Bob the Nailer'. His accustomed post was a turreted two-storey house across the street from the Cawnpore battery, and this commanding position gave the African a good view of Lieutenant Anderson's redoubt, which was sufficient cause for the defenders to single the African out for special attention. Shells lobbed into the building proved ineffectual and in a determined sortie against the house by the redcoats of the 32nd, he escaped the fate of most of his comrades. Not until many weeks later, when a mine was exploded beneath the African's chosen post, did the rebels' most effective sharpshooter meet his end in a singularly spectacular fashion.

The second week of the siege saw a noticeable reduction in the number of casualties from gunshot wounds. The soldiers and civilian volunteers were learning from experience the safest way to move between posts and were exercising a great deal of caution. But, although battle casualties had been reduced, the chance of contracting one of the many virulent fevers endemic to India was just as great and removal to the hospital, whether due to sickness or enemy action, was perhaps one of the community's greatest fears.

On 29 June, the group of women in the Begum Kothi suffered their first loss. 'A sudden blow has fallen upon us, the first of our little band has been taken away' 'wrote Mrs Bartrum. 'Poor Mrs Hale died today.' Before the incident of the little girl, Katherine Bartrum had never encountered death in any shape or form, but, as she subsequently confessed, 'mixed with feelings of sadness', came the thought that 'perhaps Mrs Hale was to be envied in that her sufferings were over'. In the weeks that followed the death of Mrs Hale, cholera, that scourge of the Victorian Age, was to strike with increasing frequency. Minor ailments were common and whilst not life threatening, were nevertheless an irritant. Mrs Germon wrote in early July of her health problems. 'Got up feeling wretched, my face is becoming covered with boils, but hardly anyone is without them.'

'About this time death began to be busy in our quarters,' confessed Mrs Huxham. 'Mrs Wells first lost her baby. Mrs Clarke died in the Begum Kothi, followed by both her children; Mrs Bruere's baby succumbed to fever; but my two children continued in pretty good health till the 24th July, when my baby was attacked by dysentery.' Mrs Huxham's baby was to die in the early hours of Sunday, 9 August.

The long Banqueting Hall in the Residency was now in use as a sick bay and although resistant against the impact of cannon balls, it was not considered safe. Since all the windows had been barricaded against sniper activity, the general atmosphere was stifling and the occasional blast of hot air from an open door merely added to the oppressive sultriness. There were few beds and practically no change of linen. The patients lay on makeshift mattresses in rows along the floor, or on sofas, more often than not tormented by swarms of flies. L.E.R. Rees paid a visit to the hospital in mid July and was appalled by the 'squalor and disagreeable, foetid smell which pervaded the long hall of the sick ... Everywhere cries of agony were heard,' he wrote, 'piteous exclamations for water or assistance.'

Ensign Ruggles was another deeply effected by what he observed. 'The distress among the wounded in hospital was most pitiable. They were terribly crowded; comforts were almost unobtainable; most of the invalid diet had been used. Needless to say great mortality was the result, even among those slightly wounded, gangrene being frequently one of the causes.'

The women did what they could for the sick, moving among them with dressings and iced water, and none worked harder than Mrs Emily Polehampton, the wife of an English pastor, who so impressed a sergeant of the 32nd of Foot that he felt justified in pointing out that 'any history of the defence of Lucknow would be incomplete if it did not contain a mention of that noble hearted woman, Mrs Polehampton.'

Following his visit to the hospital, Rees seems to have left with an unfavourable impression of the nursing, but since antiseptics and an effective anaesthetic had yet to be discovered, he was perhaps being unfair on the hard-working staff when he wrote: 'as practised by the garrison's surgeons, it is a law in medical science that death follows amputation as sure as night follows day.'

The deaths certainly could not be blamed on a lack of concern for the patients, for as William Swanston was quick to point out: 'Everything that could be done by the Medical Officers was done; but without medicines, or means of any sort, it was hard to fight against disease.'

With no sweepers to empty the latrines, the stench from these and the carcases of animals decomposing in the heat hung over the compound as a nauseous vapour. On occasion the garrison was forced to go to extraordinary lengths to remove injured animals from the vicinity of their outposts.

When his horse broke a leg, Captain Anderson, with the help of several loyal sepoys, risked his life by crawling outside the post and by dint of pulling on the head rope and pricking the animal's rump with a bayonet, forced the unfortunate beast to hop on three legs outside the entrenchment. Despite every effort of the fatigue parties to remove them, many putrid carcases could not be reached and the noxious smell was certainly a factor affecting the health of women and children, already weakened from the effects of a diet which, according to Mr Rees, had been reduced to 'an abomination which a Spartan dog would turn up his nose at'. Commenting on the shortage of supplies, Mrs Case admitted: 'Money has ceased to be of any value, and people are giving unheard of prices for stores of any kind.'

Although an attack had yet to be pressed home in a determined fashion by the rebels, numerous false alarms were having a disturbing affect on the beleaguered garrison, and the prolonged cries and screams from the nearby bazaar were certainly an irritant to the redcoats in Captain Anderson's post. 'I say, Bill, I'm blowed if these 'ere budmashes don't yell like so many cats,' was a typical remark from a long-suffering redcoat.

'Gawd, 'ow they do,' came the reply from his comrade, 'and I only wishes that I was behind 'em with a tin pot of bilin water as they opens their bleedin' mouths.'

Another soldier of the 32nd, driven frantic by the incessant noise from a mutineer's tin whistle, was heard to say, 'I only wish I 'ad 'old of the black rascal as plays that. I'd not kill the vagabond, I'd only break that infernal hinstrument over the bridge of 'is nose.'

The rebel's reluctance to mount an attack against the Residency was not a charge that could be levelled against their artillery and Anderson's post became such a favoured target that before long only the lower storey remained habitable. Captain Anderson found that he had to share one of the few remaining rooms with an Eurasian merchant and his wife who were overfond of the bottle. The husband invariably retired the worse for drink, whilst his wife took the opportunity to boast of the number of men who had made love to her before she had reached the age of forty. 'Had she remained,' wrote Anderson, 'she would probably have made every Seik desert from us, by reason of her gloomy conversation.' The Captain, who no doubt held the strict moral views of many early Victorians, deemed her quite disgusting.

On 8 July a rare assault on the Baillie Guard and the Cawnpore Battery was successfully repelled, despite the fact that many of the defenders were the worse for drink. An adjacent cellar in use as a wine store had been broken into despite the owner's precautions, and his last bottles of brandy and champagne had quickly disappeared. It was no consolation to Rees's friend, Mr Dupret, whose cellar it was, to discover that the clarets and Haute Sauternes had been ignored.

Drunkenness was an ever-present problem, sometimes leading to a heated exchange between officers and other ranks. Lieutenant McCabe, who had the reputation of being something of a disciplinarian, had occasion to reprimand a sentry for failing to challenge him. 'Why the devil didn't you challenge me?' he demanded of the Irish soldier.

'Because I knew it was you, sir, and that you would be coming this way.'

'You should have fired, sir. You are not supposed to know anyone outside your post, especially at night, sir'.

'Then be Jasus,' the angry sentry replied, 'the next time you come the same way at night I will accommodate you. I will shoot you right enough!'

The officer took no further notice,' reported Corporal Metcalfe, 'and never troubled that sentry again.' Lieutenant McCabe was later to suffer a mortal wound when leading a subsequent sortie against a rebel position.

It was during the assault of 8 July that Henry Polehampton was struck by a musket ball. 'At first I thought that it was a spent ball,' he wrote, 'but on looking, I saw a hole in the flesh.' An examination of the wound showed that it was not serious and on the 17th he was confident enough to write: 'Yesterday I walked the length of the ward for the first time. My wound going on very well, health very good.' Unfortunately, the improvement was not to continue – two days later the Revd. Polehampton contracted cholera and on Tuesday, 21 July, he died.

The artillery fire directed at the Residency, which had not ceased since the beginning of the siege, now showed signs of the rebels being short of ammunition. Missiles were now being used fabricated from bits of iron, bundles of stone and even blocks of wood as large as a metre in diameter. If the latter were largely ineffectual, they were at least a source of amusement to the battle-hardened veterans of the 32nd.

'Here comes another barrel of beer,' one would exclaim as he watched a balk of timber sail over the wall.

'Be Jasus! They must t'ink we're short of firewood,' another would remark.

On 10 July the garrison was to experience its first major assault when at 8.30 am an observer from a turret in the Residency noticed a massing of the enemy across the river, and at various other places in the vicinity of the perimeter defences which gave rise to great excitement. No immediate move was made by the rebels and a period of uneasy quiet was maintained until well after breakfast. Not a gun had been fired for almost two hours when a tremendous explosion shook plaster from the interior walls of the Residency building. The mine which had been planted to explode beneath the Redan Battery was, fortunately for the defenders, well short of its target – a miscalculation hidden from the mutineers by a thick cloud of sulphurous smoke.

The horde of rebels who rushed towards the anticipated breech was met by a murderous discharge of grape which scythed through their ranks as they emerged from the smoke of the crater, bringing the charge to an immediate halt. It proved to be a temporary reverse and it was not long before almost every defender was engaged, and as the ferocity of the fighting increased, even the wounded left their sick beds to take up a musket, whilst those who could do little else, busied themselves in loading them. Rees, full of admiration, commented: 'It was indeed heart rending to see these poor fellows staggering along to the scene of action. Pale, trembling with weakness, several of them bleeding from their wounds which had re-opened by the exertions they made.'

The Calcutta merchant, himself hurrying to his post at the Water Gate as musket balls kicked up the dust around his feet, felt that his last moments had come. He breathed a short prayer bidding a fond farewell to those he 'loved best in this world', before taking up his musket in preparation to meet the enemy. But, as the noise of battle increased, any fear that Rees may have had quickly gave way to a nervous excitement culminating in a compelling desire to kill which, when he did, as he freely admitted, gave him a 'strange feeling of joy'. 'This tremendous fire of musketry and cannon, both from out and in, rendered our position one mass of sulphurous smoke, so that we could scarcely see,' remembered Rees. 'I must confess that for some minutes I felt the fear of death predominate within me. I was certain, and I think most of our little handful of men too, that this was our last day upon earth.'

By this time the entire southern face of the Residency perimeter was under assault. Martin Gubbins's house had long been the target of the artillery, the fire being severe enough to cause the ladies who earlier had taken up residence to abandon the upper rooms. The shattered upper storey was the only building to which a few of the more determined sepoys now gained access. They were quickly bayoneted out before others could join them, but such was the ferocity of the close-quarter fighting that Lieutenant Grant, hurling grenades as fast as they were made available, had the misfortune to seize one with a short fuse – it exploded, blowing off his hand and severely wounding an officer standing close to him.

About 400 yards to the east, the rebels closed on the Cawnpore Battery with bugles blowing, drums beating and the green banner of Islam streaming in the breeze. Again and again a screaming horde of mutineers would surge against the redoubt, but each time they were met with dozens of bursting grenades and blister-ing volleys of musketry. Close by the Cawnpore Battery, at Lieu-tenant Anderson's outpost, several mutineers managed to force their way through the stockade to reach the front of the ditch. Mr Capper, the volunteer who had survived the alarming experience of being buried alive, heard one of the sepoys call to his comrades, 'The place is ours, there's no one here!' Outraged to think that a rebel could believe that the post could be left undefended, Capper yelled back, 'There are plenty of us here, you rascal,' and accompanied his shout with a musket shot which toppled the rebel into the ditch.

Three separate attacks were repelled, but Lieutenant Anderson was beset by fears that the volunteers manning the posts on either side of him might be overrun. 'We well knew what we had to expect if we were defeated, and therefore each individual fought for his life,' he wrote. 'Each loophole displayed a steady flash of musketry, as defeat would have been certain death to every soul in the garrison ... We dreaded that the other posts might have been further pressed than we were. At intervals I heard the cry: "More men this way!" and off would rush two or three ... and then the same cry was repeated in the opposite direction.'

Cowering in their rooms listening to the noise of battle, the women expected at any moment to hear that the sepoys had broken through, and the thought occurred to Mrs Case: 'What would be the feelings of any lady suddenly transported from quiet, peaceful England to this room, around which the bullets are whizzing, the round shot falling, and now and then a loud explosion, as if a mine was blowing up, which I think is almost worse than all the sharp and fast firing of the musketry?'

Equally alarmed was Mrs Georgina Harris, wife of the other Cawnpore chaplain.

'Huddled together in the underground room called the Tye Khana, damp, dark, and gloomy as a vault, and extremely dirty,' she wrote. 'Here we sat all day feeling miserable, anxious, and terrified to speak.' Alone among her companions, Mrs Harris seems to have recognized that there may well have been some justification for the uprising when she wrote: 'No doubt it is a judgment of God, and that we have greatly abused our power.'

By 4 o'clock in the afternoon it was becoming clear that the attack had failed. The firing began to slacken and groups of sepoys could be seen retiring, carrying their wounded with them. The broken ground around the Residency was littered with corpses and when, an hour later, a group advanced bearing a white flag, seeking to remove their dead, the defenders made haste to comply. That the sepoys had suffered a grievous number of casualties was evident in the great number of carts used to carry them away. At the end of the engagement, a relieved Mr Rees, powder blackened and bruised from the repeated discharges of his musket, wrote: 'A wash, a little repose, my poor dinner and a cigar after it, put me into the most enviable frame of mind.'

The garrison, although exhausted from their exertions beneath a blazing sun, were elated at the unexpected ease with which the rebel attacks had been beaten off. Casualties had not been excessive considering that the conflict had continued unabated from 9.00 am until 4.30 pm. Just seventeen Europeans killed or wounded, together with ten loyal sepoys.

The next day saw a resumption of hostilities but on a much reduced scale. The objective of the mutineers now was to secure suitable sites for mining operations. They were driven off with fierce exchanges of musketry at the Redan, but near Martin Gubbins's house they succeeded in breaking through a wall into a lane bordering the compound. Here the only obstacle between them and the house was a low barrier of earth, but the rooftop commanding the lane was occupied by the Financial Commissioner himself, armed with a pair of double-barrelled shotguns. So effective was his fire that in the short time it took to bring reinforcements, not a single sepoy succeeded in crossing the lane. Any satisfaction he might have enjoyed from that fact, however, was cut short by the sound of a heavy fall behind him – a musket ball had struck Major Banks in the head, killing him instantly. He was buried that night with the rest of the day's fatalities, much regretted by the men of the 32nd.

Hope that relief might be just a matter of days away had long been a major topic of conversation and, just before 6.00 pm on 29 July, the sound of distant gunfire and the faint echo of cheering from beyond the city suburbs gave rise to the belief that the relief column were about to break through the rebel cordon. Many in the garrison jostled their way to the roof of the Brigade Mess in order to catch a glimpse of the relief column. Mrs Case, abandoning her meal in the general confusion, thought it just as likely to be a fresh horde of rebels, but with the arrival of an angry Colonel Inglis the truth became apparent. 'It's the most absurd thing I have ever heard,' he was heard to declare. An overzealous officer keeping watch had misinterpreted the noise of musketry for the approach of the relief force – in fact, the firing had been a native salute to the newly chosen ruler of Oude. When the light faded, and with it the last glimmering hope of outside help, morale sank to a new low. Survival now seemed merely a matter of chance, and as the rain poured down and every day became ever more tedious, only a belief in their own determination to survive kept the defenders morale from crumbling entirely.

Chapter 11

THE MARCH OF
HENRY HAVELOCK

The failure of the rebel attack of 10 July had shown that, without the customary leadership of their British officers, the sepoys had been unable to co-ordinate or press home their numerical advantage. Even the artillerymen seemed to have been ill advised, for rather than concentrate on breaching the perimeter walls, the gunners chose to target the upper storeys of the building, and in this they were guilty of errors in ranging. Quite often the piece would have such a high angle of elevation set that its ball would describe a neat curve over the Residency and fall within the rebel lines on the opposite side.

Mining remained the garrison's greatest fear, with good reason, for between 10 July and 5 September, seven mines erupted with varying degrees of destruction and casualties. On the south face of the perimeter the rebel-occupied houses were so close that correct alignment of the gallery from the shaft hardly mattered. The only effective countermeasure open to the defenders was to sink shafts themselves and dig listening galleries in the area most likely to be used by the sepoys. Fortunately, the ranks of the 32nd contained a number of Cornish and Derbyshire ex-miners, and in Captain Peter Fulton the garrison possessed an experienced and resourceful engineer. It was said that he was accompanied everywhere by a devoted Sikh, carrying on his back a barrel of powder. Such was Fulton's skill that the shaft he sank would often be close enough to enable his miners to break into the enemy gallery and use it for their own purposes. It was not unusual for shafts of up to 30 feet deep to be sunk in the earth, and from them galleries would be excavated horizontally in the direction of the enemy's workings. Supports were seldom necessary since the earth was firm, and because the galleries were never of a great length, ventilation was not a problem.

143

But it was a far from comfortable task for the officer keeping a listening watch for enemy activity – for after lowering himself into the shaft on the end of a rope, he would be obliged to crawl along the gallery on his stomach to his listening post, with no way of overcoming the darkness other than by the occasional use of a candle. The heat can only be imagined, as might also be the torment from the high-pitched hum of a mosquito which was often the only sound to break the silence. Captain Fulton played a major role in these activities, often sitting for hours at a time, listening for the first faint sound of a pick which would betray the direction of the rebel workings.

On one occasion Fulton forced an entry into an enemy gallery with a crowbar. Startled by his sudden appearance the native miners fled in terror, whereupon he took away the candle they had left burning and with the assistance of his faithful Sikh, carried a barrel of powder to the point where the rebel's gallery met the shaft. Captain Fulton later recorded with justified satisfaction: 'We destroyed the whole with great éclat and enjoyment of the fun and excitement, to say nothing of the success.' Fulton was eventually to meet his end, not as a result of mining activities, but in a trench when the back of his head was smashed by a 3-pound round shot.

'He had ever been foremost in the fighting and his loss to us all was irreparable,' wrote Ensign Ruggles.

By the beginning of August the plight of the garrison was becoming desperate. 'Everyone is getting very dispirited,' commented Mrs Bartrum. 'No news of relief. They say we are forgotten and that reinforcements will never appear ... This hope deferred does indeed make the heart sick.' Such gloomy predictions and the rain which fell from a leaden sky, for the monsoon was at its height, had a depressing effect upon many in the Residency. Some, whose survival had been due as much to the exercise of caution as to good fortune, now walked casually past gaps in the defence works not caring whether they lived or died. Each death increased the workload of the survivors, weakening their resistance to such an extent that painful skin eruptions occurred with increasing frequency, as did diarrhoea.

It had been found necessary to considerably reduce the meat ration – that of the men by a quarter, and the women by a half. 'We only get 12 ounces of meat per man a day,' recorded Ludlow Smith, 'and if a man is not present at his meal at feeding time, he has to go without and as this often happens, there are a lot of half starving fellows about the Garrison ready to eat anything.' Lack of variety was another irritant to those who had exhausted their own private store, for their diet now consisted of a monotonous portion of atta – a coarse ground corn with all the husks left unsifted, and dal, an unsavoury mixture of black lentils and rice. It was particularly galling to Rees to discover that people to whom he had in the past given little luxuries, refused to return a spoonful of sugar or even a handful of flour, despite having more than enough for their own purposes. 'A siege,' thought Rees bitterly, 'was certainly the best school in which to learn character.'

With no servants to operate the punkahs, the women were tormented by swarms of flies. Especially loathsome were the bloated flies which accompanied each spoonful of food. Hunger alone made the fare palatable, for as Mrs Bartrum confessed, it was difficult to tell what it was they were supposed to be eating. 'It resembled nothing so much as a black and living mass.'

The garrison's greatest need was for fresh green vegetables as a palliative against scurvy, and many were the risks taken by individuals to gather the leaves of a lush green plant to be found growing among the ruins outside the Residency. As always, it was the very young children on a milkless diet who suffered the most. 'All the children are very bad,' confessed Mrs Harris. 'The want of fresh air and exercise, and the loss of their accustomed food, have made them all ill.' Pale faced, large eyed and weak from hunger and fear, their deaths multiplied at an alarming rate. Many of the older children were orphans who had grown indifferent to the danger which was all around them.

Doctor Gilbert Hadow was particularly touched by their plight and recorded his concern in a diary entry. 'You saw the little things drooping and dying from day to day. This was the saddest part of all.'

Katherine Bartrum went in constant fear for her little boy, but, as she freely acknowledged, there was little she could do but 'pray, cook what food there was, fan away the flies and read a psalm for comfort in tribulation'.

The one encouraging feature at this time was the steadfast attitude of the garrison's loyal sepoys who resisted every inducement to go over to the mutineers. 'Leave the infidels and come out. We'll give you good food and plenty of it,' was a typical blandishment offered to them, according to Lieutenant Anderson. 'Our sepoys would reply: "We have eaten the Company's salt. We cannot break faith with our masters like you have."'

On 10 August, the defenders of the various outposts were enjoying a morning cup of tea prepared from burnt wheat, when their attention was drawn to an unusual amount of activity within the rebel lines. It was to be the prelude to the first of three major assaults, the second coming eight days later and the final one on 5 September. The garrison was alerted at once and as the rebel artillery began its usual preliminary bombardment of the Residency, the women retired to the basement where in almost total darkness they could do little else but try to comfort the screaming children. It was to be more than an hour before a massive explosion caused Mrs Case, who had been sitting at a table writing, to rise in alarm at what at first appeared to be an earth tremor. It was immediately followed by a sound 'the like of which she never wished to hear again'.

The eruption which so terrified Colonel Case's widow and the rest of the ladies was the result of a mine sprung by the enemy close to the Brigade Mess. When the smoke and dust drifted away, the defenders manning the outposts were appalled to see that 30 feet of the wall had been totally destroyed, together with the greater part of an adjacent house. No sooner did the dust settle than sepoys were seen to be crawling through the long grass keeping up a continuous fire of musketry. Behind them came hordes of rebels screaming their hate of the infidels as they rushed towards the breach yawning invitingly before them. The defenders had not been caught unprepared, however, and the roof of the Brigade Mess, which had escaped serious damage, sparkled with flashes of rifle and musket fire. So determined was the resistance of the garrison that the rebel attack was halted in its tracks and the sepoys sent reeling back in confusion.

A second mine exploded at Sago's house, destroying several other houses and hurling two redcoats of the 32nd of Foot into the road, fortunately without serious injury, one sustaining bruises and slight burns, whilst the other, still grasping his musket, succeeded in scrambling back over the debris with bullets kicking up brick dust all around him.

In the melee which followed, Lieutenant Anderson and his men fought a savage hand-to-hand encounter knowing that defeat would mean the death of every man, woman and child in the

Residency. The sepoys were beaten off, and the men in Anderson's post were able to wipe away the perspiration and wonder whether the posts on either side of them had remained as firm in their resistance.

In fact the attack by several hundred rebels against the fortified house owned by Martin Gubbins had fared no better, despite grape from their batteries 'rattling and hammering the walls like peas in a frying pan'. A few feet from Rees a corporal of the 32nd had part of his sleeve bearing his stripes torn away by a musket ball, whilst Rees himself was showered with pieces of brick when a round shot struck the wall beside him. Partially concealed by swirling clouds of black smoke, a few determined sepoys succeeded in reaching the ditch in front of the house, but, as they quickly discovered, each defender could maintain an almost continuous fire as he had a collection of loaded muskets at his side. So the day ended as it had begun, with not a single rebel inside the Residency perimeter defences.

Although the enemy assault had been defeated, it had been at the expense of casualties the garrison could ill afford. Part of the Residency wall had collapsed burying six men beneath the rubble from which only two were taken out alive. Each day there occurred two or three deaths, due either to enemy action or to sickness, and by the beginning of September, when the siege was into its second month, more than 300 Europeans had died from various causes. So accustomed to death did the besieged become that Rees was able to comment: 'Balls fall at our feet, and we continue the conversation without a remark. Bullets graze over our very hair and we never speak of them. Narrow escapes are so very common that even women and children cease to notice them.'

Lieutenant Anderson's house was now little more than a ruin, the upper storey having been abandoned as being too dangerous even for a solitary sniper, whilst a constant artillery bombardment had reduced Colonel Inglis' house to a heap of rubble. The Residency itself had not escaped serious damage, and to many of the occupants it seemed that only a strong gust of wind was required to topple what remained of the north-east wing.

Despite the losses from enemy action and the ever-present danger from mining activities, morale in the garrison had greatly improved due in some measure to the ease with which the rebels had been defeated. The failure of Havelock's column to reach

Lucknow had understandably been a huge disappointment, but a keen watch was still kept for activity which would signal Havelock's approach, although it was becoming increasingly clear to all but the fiercest optimist that relief was a matter of weeks rather than days.

As August drew to a close the rains slackened and the stagnant pools around the entrenchments quickly dried, leaving a noxious green slime which gave rise to fears of a fever epidemic. In the event such alarms proved groundless, but deaths from cholera persisted, with the hasty business of nightly burials being conducted by the Revd. James Harris, who had succeeded the Revd. Polehampton, sometimes having to dig the grave himself. This was indeed a dangerous business for the churchyard was constantly targeted by the mutineers, and often as he read the burial service, the Minister's words would be lost in the sudden whistle of grape sweeping across the cemetery. Of necessity the service would be short and if any doubt existed over the denomination of the deceased, it was left to the senior officer present to decide between Protestantism or Catholicism.

The weight of shot directed at the Residency buildings had been immense and by September no less than 280 round shots of varying calibre were collected from the roof of the Brigade Mess alone. Mrs Maria Germon, an army officer's wife, was led to comment on the continuous artillery fire, noting in her diary that never more than a few minutes, day or night, ever elapsed without some firing taking place. Despite her bed being no more than 50 yards from the site of an 18-pounder mortar, its noise did not seem to affect her any more than if she had been accustomed to it all her life. 'Eighty days of siege life,' she explained, 'does wonders for the nervous system.'

Contact with General Neill had been made by the garrison on a number of occasions through the endeavours of a sepoy pensioner by the name of Ungud Tewari. On 16 September, having been promised a reward of 5,000 rupees should he be successful, the pensioner set off with a letter concealed in a quill in his rectum. It was written partly in Greek and partly in French, a security measure which had been used in the Afghan campaigns. Not many in the Residency expected him to return but at midnight on the 22nd, Ungud was back with encouraging news. The message he brought had been written by Sir James Outram, who disclosed that the relief force had crossed the Ganges and was even then marching on Lucknow.

Hardly daring to believe that relief could come so early, Colonel Inglis let it be known that it would be at least two weeks before Havelock could be expected. Even so, his announcement was welcomed by European and Asian alike and did much to raise the spirits of the sick and wounded. For the first time in weeks, the hospital patients were able to look forward to a measure of security and the change of air that an end of the siege would bring. Katherine Bartrum wondered whether her husband would be numbered among the relief column and, after so many months of separation, how wonderful it would be when they were at last together.

On 19 September Havelock's relief force, amounting to just over 3,000, of which 2,400 were British, crossed the Ganges by means of the reconstructed bridge of boats, and on the 21st, after another night of heavy rain, began its third encroachment into Oudh, supported by three batteries of guns and a small force of cavalry. There were, in effect, two commanders. General Henry Havelock, nominally in overall charge of the column, and Sir James Outram who, although senior to Havelock, had magnanimously agreed to waive his rank and allow his subordinate to reap the glory of relieving Lucknow. It was a gesture much appreciated by Havelock's staff. 'We all like Sir J. Outram extremely,' wrote Captain Wade after meeting him in Cawnpore. 'He is a first rate officer, very clever and amusing. His conversation you can listen to any time.'

The contents of the letter delivered to General Neill by Ungud Tewari had been disclosed to the troops, who, appreciating the need for haste, set off at an increased pace despite the treacherous going underfoot, their thoughts gripped by the plight of the women and children in the beleaguered Residency. 'Everybody is in high spirits and we hope to be back in less than a fortnight,' wrote Lieutenant Groom in what was to be the last letter to his wife. 'Then we start for Agra and Delhi ... as a second Sebastopol it will give us much trouble.'

Around 6 miles on they encountered a small force of the enemy at Mangalwar, but had no difficulty in dispersing them and capturing two cannon. The cavalry, led by Sir James Outram, immediately gave chase, killing more than 100 of the rebels although Sir James declined to use his sword, merely striking about with a Malacca cane.

General Havelock had joined Outram in the charge but had been obliged to turn back. 'The moment the charge was over,' remembered Captain Maude, 'Havelock rode straight up to my guns, his horse bleeding from four or five tulwar cuts. As the poor beast commenced to stagger, the General quickly dismounted, saying to me, with a proud but melancholy intonation, "That makes the sixth horse I have had killed under me!" and sure enough the animal died in a few minutes.'

Following this brief encounter with the rebels, Havelock led the relief force through the familiar territory of Unao and Bashiratganj, his troops splashing ankle deep in the mud of a raised road, with the crops in the fields on either side barely discernable in the flood water.

Progress was confined to a slow crawl beyond Bashiratganj, with the commissariat wagons lagging far in the rear. The breakdown in supplies led to some angry exchanges as Lieutenant Moorsom made clear in a letter to his father. 'The large commissariat wagons are the greatest imaginable nuisance – they stick and refuse to move wherever the ground affords them the slightest pretext,' he wrote. 'I would not have one of them with the force if I had anything to say to it.'

Then came a stroke of luck. When they reached the swollen River Sai the column found the bridge to be intact, the rebels having neglected to destroy it, and so Havelock's column crossed unopposed by the enemy. That night, as the troops did their best to sleep in rain-soaked clothing, they could hear the faint rumble of artillery 16 miles away in Lucknow,

In the beleaguered garrison, a further twenty-four hours would pass before a sound as of distant thunder was heard, giving rise to further speculation. In the late afternoon, kites were to be seen circling the area before flying towards the Residency from the direction of Cawnpore.

The next morning, the few observers stationed in the Residency Tower, eagerly scanning the approaches to the perimeter, reported that although there appeared to be a mass exodus of rebel cavalry, there was still no sign of the relief force; but when later that day the booming of cannon was heard, hopes were raised despite the fact that the gunfire seemed no nearer than it had been the day before.

150

No further intelligence of the column's movement was forth-coming, but early on the morning of 25 September another cannonade was heard from the south and this time the listeners were left in no doubt that relief was fast approaching. That morning, as the watchers on the Residency roof looked for signs of the column's approach, Havelock gave the order for the troops to resume their march in bright sunshine. Some 3 miles south of the Residency perimeter a cavalry patrol sent forward to recon-noitre returned with the information that large numbers of rebels were drawn up with their left flank on the Alambagh, and their centre and right wing behind a series of hillocks, their flank being protected by a marsh.

The enemy's strength was thought to be approaching 10,000, but despite the odds ranged against him, Havelock ordered a general advance on the Alambagh, his men encouraged by the news that Delhi had been recaptured. The Alambagh was soon overrun, enabling the cavalry led by Outram to drive the rebels as far as the canal south of the city. That night the relief force pitched its tents on a ridge near the Alambagh, and the troops sought shelter from yet another rainstorm which quickly turned their bivouac area into an expanse of mud.

The next day Generals Outram, Havelock and Neill debated the problem of attacking Lucknow, a city of 12 square miles. The first of the two options open to them was to advance over a canal bridge and then battle through the narrow streets, overlooked by loopholed houses, which was certainly the most direct but also the most dangerous, since it would involve lengthy street-fighting. Havelock's preference was to take a wide detour across the Gumti before coming down on the Residency from the north, which would avoid the costly casualties of the first option, but suffered the disadvantage of advancing over flooded fields, there-by seriously inhibiting the use of artillery.

The difficulties of a split command were recognized by many of the junior officers, leading Captain Maude to comment:

There was a difference of opinion between the two Generals. Outram was for taking the shortest route into the city, whilst Havelock wished to make a detour. Outram's principal, if not his only objection, having been that the surface of the ground was too soft for the heavy guns. That may have been the case, but the elephants of Eyre's battery were left behind in the Alambagh; and

151

if his guns were brought into action at all that day, which I doubt, they certainly did no good whatever.

The route eventually taken was that decided by Sir James Outram who was familiar with the area having once been the Chief Commissioner for Lucknow – a crossing of the canal before turning right through the south-eastern outskirts of the city, and then left towards the Kaiserbagh to approach the Residency by the Baillie Guard Gate. 'One is forced to the conclusion that from a military point of view, our advance was undertaken with an insouciance, of which the culpability was only redeemed by the exceeding courage of the men,' wrote Francis Maude.

At 8.00 am and in bright sunshine, General Outram, together with General Neill and his brigade, supported by Maude's battery and two companies of the 84th, advanced towards the Charbagh bridge across the canal. The plan was for Havelock to follow with Hamilton's brigade, but there was an enforced delay, Neill's men being obliged to halt for ten minutes whilst they sought to avoid casualties from the enemy's fire by lying down in the road. Since it was too narrow for Maude's guns to deploy, the brigade suffered grievously from the grape and round shot scouring the road, Outram himself being fortunate enough to escape with nothing more than a flesh wound.

Losses occasioned by this brief halt were severe, but they were to be even greater when the brigade came to take the heavily defended canal bridge and the buildings on either side. A two-pronged attack was launched, with Outram taking part of Neill's brigade to the right, whilst skirmishers from the Madras Fusiliers attacked on the left, leaving Maude's guns to silence the rebel batteries from the road. Because of the road's narrow width, it was only possible to engage the enemy with two guns, and the artillerymen came under such severe fire that Maude called out in desperation to Hamilton's brigade to 'Do something, in the name of heaven!' Upon hearing that, Neill would do nothing without the permission of General Outram, who at that moment could not be found. Major Henry Marsham Havelock rode off on the pretence of finding his father. Once out of sight, with admirably commendable initiative, he turned his horse and rode back to Neill saying, 'You are to take the bridge at once, Sir.'

Immediately the order was given, Havelock, together with Colonel Tytler and a score of men from the Fusiliers and the 84th

Regiment, dashed forward with the two senior officers at their head. They were met by a hail of bullets which killed Tytler's horse and wounded all but two of the men. Astonishingly, Havelock was left sitting in his saddle with nothing more than a hole in his cap and a graze across his forehead.

Once the rest of the brigade caught up, the bridge was overrun and the Fusiliers made good progress driving the rebels before them until the Alambagh was reached. The position there was bitterly contested by the rebels and for half an hour Maude's light field guns were engaged in a fierce duel with the enemy's batteries until a further infantry charge cleared the approach to the Baillie Guard Gate, but casualties had been heavy. Brigadier General Henry Havelock suffered a seventh horse killed under him, and Sir James Outram, looking more agitated than his adjutant had ever seen him, proposed that a halt be made whilst a less contested route to the Residency was investigated. But General Havelock could not agree. 'There is the street,' he pointed out to Outram, 'we see the worst. We shall be slated, but we can push through and get it over.'

Sir James Outram, who was suffering from his wound and not in the best of humours, grudgingly consented. 'Let us go on then, in God's name,' he replied.

Having agreed to proceed, the two generals led the way, with the Highlanders advancing along the narrow street followed by the Sikhs and Madras Fusiliers, all subjected to a continuous fire from the rebels on the flat roofs and loopholed houses.

A raking discharge of grape from three rebel batteries stripped the leaves from the trees and left the road strewn with dead and wounded. The guns were taken at a rush but there remained hundreds of mutineers to scour the streets with a punishing fire of musketry which did nothing to lessen the determination of the attacking troops, as Captain John Gordon confessed in describing his part in the action: 'I was in such a state of excitement with the cheering of the men who were running as hard as they could and yelling, that I scarcely knew what happened.'

One ball ripped through Ensign George Blake's jacket, another struck the scabbard of his sword and bent it. In a rage, the young officer set spurs to his horse and brought down the nearest sepoy with a cut which almost cleft the man's head from his shoulders.

Every house and wall overlooking the street seemed to swarm with the enemy and as Blake left a house he had been ordered to clear, General Neill passed him on his brown gelding. 'Hot work this, Blake,' the General grunted. Before the young man could reply, a sepoy fired a rifle held at arm's length and General Neill fell from his horse with a bullet in his brain. Wrote Blake in his diary later: 'Oh, I was sorry. He was the sternest and at the same time, kindest and best hearted of men and in him, we lost a good and brave General.'

Major Havelock was seriously wounded in the melee, as was Colonel Tytler, but the survivors surged forward to where the Residency building could be seen through the smoke less than 100 yards away. To the besieged, anxiously watching the progress of the fighting, it was obvious that a heavy toll was being exacted on the relief force. Undeterred by their losses, however, Havelock's troops fought their way towards the Baillie Guard Gate. There, as Scots brogue was heard above the skirl of the pipes, dozens from the garrison leapt onto the walls, heedless of the flying bullets, to cheer on the stream of Europeans and Sikhs running towards them. The shot-riddled and battered gate was thrown back for the first time in more than twelve weeks, to allow a horde of sweat-stained and powder-blackened High-landers, Madras Fusiliers and Sikhs to pour through the entrance to a tumultuous welcome from men, women and children who had all but abandoned hope. 'Oh! what welcome, what joy,' enthused Henry Metcalfe. 'Comrades shaking hands, rough soldiers embracing and kissing little ones. Women asking about friends.'

Among the new arrivals,' noted Ensign Ruggles, 'was Lieutenant Delafosse.'

Lucknow had been reached by the relief force and the pent-up feelings of anxiety, the doubts and fears of the past few weeks were released in waves of enthusiastic cheering. Even the patients in the hospital left their beds to witness an event which for many would linger long in their memory. Rees likened his feelings to the criminal condemned to death, who, just when he is about to be launched into eternity, is reprieved and pardoned. It was to be 3 o'clock in the morning before the Calcutta merchant retired to his bed.

Mrs Germon was possibly the first to recognize that the celebrations were premature, for Havelock's column, having lost 28 per cent of its strength, was in no position to conduct an evacuation of the Residency. Referring to recent events, she wrote: 'It could scarcely be called a relief seeing that we have to feed the new troops on our own scant rations and have them in consequence further reduced.'

Whilst accepting the truth of that statement, Major North was nevertheless of the opinion that 'our advance had been most timely – it saved the garrison. The Residency had been completely undermined, and the delay of even a day would have proved fatal.'

The best that can be said was that the arrival of Havelock and Outram brought a much-needed reinforcement to the beleaguered garrison. Captain Maude was scathing in his criticism of the two generals. 'It is difficult to resist the conclusion that the affair was a muddle, however gloriously conducted, from beginning to end,' he wrote. 'The officers led their men right well; but of Generalship, *proprement dit,* that day there was little if anything at all.'

Ruutz Rees, however, took a far more generous view. 'That the honour of having, under Providence, saved our lives is really due to Generals Havelock and Outram is unquestionable,' he suggested. 'But for their timely arrival, our native troops, who had up to that time behaved nobly … would certainly have abandoned us. Nor could we have reasonably found fault with them had they done so, for life is sweet, and hope had almost entirely left us.'

One cause for concern was the influx of wounded which had accompanied the relief force, for conditions in the hospital were now in an appalling state. 'The hospital is so densely crowded that many have to lie outside in the open air, without bed or shelter,' wrote Georgina Harris. 'It is far worse than after Chinhat – amputated arms and legs lying about in heaps all over the hospital.'

Katherine Bartrum's first thought, however, was for the husband she had not seen for four months. Impatient to meet him after their long separation she was overjoyed to learn from one the officers that he had shared a tent with her husband the previous night, and that he would most likely arrive with the heavy artillery in the morning. The next day Mrs Bartrum was up early and wearing the one clean dress she had kept throughout the siege. She eagerly scanned every new face for a glimpse of Robert, and in the evening took her little son to the roof of the Residency building to look for late arrivals. The rearguard was in but there was still no sign of her husband. Katherine returned to her room bitterly disappointed and sick with apprehension.

By the afternoon of 27 September it was obvious that something had happened to delay him. 'How strange it is that my husband is not come in,' she confided to the surgeon with the relief force.

'Yes', replied the doctor, 'it is strange,' before turning away to leave the room without a further word.

It was left to Mrs Polehampton to break the sad news. Surgeon Robert Bartrum had been shot dead within sight of the Baillie Guard Gate. A dazed Katherine Bartrum could not understand: 'why God had forgotten to be gracious?' She was later to suffer another blow, losing her son in February, the day before she was due to sail home to England.

The timely arrival of the relief force was crucial, for the garrison's fighting strength had been reduced from an initial total of 1,700 at the beginning of July, to 979, of which only 577 were European. Sir James Outram, who had now resumed overall command, was quick to extend the perimeter area by taking over the buildings and palaces to the east of the Residency. These not only provided accommodation for the extra personnel but also strengthened the outer defences. An added bonus for the troops was the opportunity it gave them for plunder, for as Ensign Blake confessed: 'All our baggage, our sick and wounded had fallen into enemy hands as we fought our way in and we had lost everything except what we stood up in.'

Few soldiers had any idea of the value of the property to be found in the apartments and by nightfall the ground was covered with bolts of the finest silk, divan coverings studded with pearls, cashmere shawls, dresses laced with gold thread, brass ornaments and *tulwars* decorated in gold and silver. 'Everywhere might be seen people helping themselves to whatever they pleased,' wrote L.E.R. Rees. 'Plunder was the order of the day.' Young George Blake managed to collect eleven fine pearls, but since there was precious little in the way of provisions, he was obliged to sell them to a native for 200 rupees in order to be able to satisfy his hunger.

A few days after the arrival of Havelock's column, the ration of dhal was stopped altogether, salt was reduced to 1½ ounces, beef from slaughtered bullocks to 6 ounces a day, rice to 4 ounces and ground wheat to no more than 1 pound. The wheat was often mouldy from being damp, and since there were no bakers chapattis continued to form a staple part of the diet.

After the recent excitement the monotony of siege life was becoming hard to bear and the craving of many soldiers for alcohol became almost irresistible. Their search was not without risk and inevitably the bodies of several artillerymen who had ventured outside the perimeter were recovered without their heads.

The first week of October saw a number of attacks against enemy gun emplacements which, in addition to military success, sometimes brought unexpected rewards such as chickens or other livestock, making a welcome addition to the soldiers' diet of stringy beef and dry chapattis. One soldier returning from a sortie, clutching a chicken, was stopped by Captain Anderson who asked him what success the raiding party had achieved. 'Damned the ha'porth we got, sir,' was the reply, 'but an auld cock and a hen.' Then, after a pause, he added, 'Oh yes, we did get a sepoy or two!'

The savage fighting in the streets of Lucknow, the murders of the sick and wounded who had fallen into rebel hands, and the memory of the well at Cawnpore, had blunted the feelings of many Europeans in their treatment of the sepoy. George Blake, who was by no means insensitive to the feelings of others, did his best to excuse the behaviour of some of his colleagues who showed no mercy, even to prisoners. He wrote:

> This was not a war at this stage, it was a mutiny accompanied by unexampled atrocities and was treated as such in its suppression. In the storm and stress of the Lucknow fighting however, and with the recollection of what horrors had been inflicted to their women and children, and with the day-to-day experiences of what was the fate of any soldier who fell into enemy hands, the anger of the regimental soldier can be understood.

From the beginning of October work was resumed on strengthening the defences without a break, thanks to the pool of labour provided by the camp followers who had accompanied the relief force. In examining the newly acquired rebel positions, Mr Rees was full of praise for the work the mutineers had lavished upon them. In front of the gun emplacements deep trenches had been excavated and ladders installed at intervals to enable the artillerymen to descend and keep a listening watch for

157

counter-mining. Saps reached out to the very edge of the Residency perimeter, whilst several emplacements were as close as 40 yards. All were well constructed and the Calcutta merchant could only marvel that the Residency had not been overrun. 'Truly,' he thought, 'the right hand of the Lord is manifest in all this plainly enough, for in spite of all our courage, we could never have kept them out.'

With the extension of the Residency defence works, the women and children were free to walk about in comparative safety for the first time since the beginning of the siege. To exchange a claustrophobic cellar for the pleasures of walking in the moonlight came as a welcome relief to Mrs Case as she strolled the ravaged gardens in the company of Mrs Inglis for an hour.

As October drew to a close the weather became noticeably cooler, a change which brought a degree of discomfort to the new arrivals, most of whom had nothing but their summer uniforms. Warm clothing was in scant supply and in an auction of deceased officers' effects, a mud-stained flannel shirt of Captain Fulton's fetched the equivalent of £4.50, whilst a tweed coat and trousers was sold for an equally inflated price. Captain Anderson, who viewed with distaste the sale of dead officers' clothing, expressed a somewhat pessimistic view that the purchaser had merely come into 'possession of his own winding sheet'.

For those who were by now heartily sick of the siege, there was a crumb of comfort in the news from Cawnpore. On 6 November it was reported that Sir Colin Campbell, of Crimea fame, had arrived in Cawnpore with 3,400 men and eight large-calibre naval guns under the command of Captain William Peel. Given confirmation of that report, it now seemed reasonably certain to many in the garrison that the end of a siege, which for so long had seemed nothing more than a tantalizing dream, was now close to becoming fact. On the strength of that welcome news, more than one person emptied his last bottle of wine, or smoked a long-cherished cheroot.

Chapter 12

ENTER SIR COLIN CAMPBELL

Whilst at Cawnpore, Sir Colin Campbell had learnt that the soldiers of Maharaja Scindia of Gwalior had rebelled against their ruler and the European officers, and were even now marching south towards Kalpi, with the intention of joining the Nana Sahib and placing themselves under the command of Tatya Tope, arguably the rebel army's most able general. The Gwalior Contingent as it was known, was a formidable force, reputed to have been trained to a higher standard than even John Company's sepoys. Campbell's main concern, however, was the relief of Lucknow and he rejected the advice of Sir James Outram that he should first meet and destroy the threat the Gwalior Contingent posed to Cawnpore before marching for the Residency.

Leaving just 500 European soldiers with General Windham, Campbell departed for the Alambagh on 9 November, hoping to join Sir Hope Grant who was encamped on the sandy plain with a store of provisions.

It was as well that Sir Colin refused to take Outram's advice for the latest report from the besieged garrison had told of severe hardships. Food stocks were rapidly diminishing, and only the fortunate discovery of a supply of grain stored in a plunge bath kept the garrison from near starvation.

The increase in manpower provided by Havelock's arrival had enabled the besieged garrison to extend the Residency perimeter to the north and west by occupying the palaces along the line of the river. Doing so, however, proved to be a mixed blessing, for although the extra accommodation was welcome, where previously much of the enemy artillery fire had been largely ineffective, now that the rebel guns were sited further away, a greater proportion of shot was hitting its target. Areas once thought to be relatively peaceful were becoming increasingly hazardous and casualties were mounting. An Ensign of the Bengal Artillery, making a sketch of the Residency in what he believed to be a safe spot, fell victim to a round shot which on previous occasions had sailed harmlessly overhead. 'Poor young Dashwood, while out sketching some portion of the Residency yesterday [4 November] was hit in both legs by a round shot and amputation of both followed,' reported Ludlow-Smith. 'He is now pretty well but there is very little hope for him.'

On the 6th, morale was lifted with the news that Sir Hope Grant was across the Sai on the Lucknow side of the river, less than 2 miles away, waiting the arrival of Sir Colin Campbell. A semaphore quickly set up on the Residency roof established communication with Grant's forces at the Alambagh, and the garrison's hopes of a speedy relief was renewed.

Sir James Outram was convinced that the heavy loss of life which had accompanied his and Sir Henry Havelock's storming of the Baillie Guard Gate could be avoided by using another route, and he set to work on drawing up a street map for Sir Colin Campbell which he hoped would bring about the relief with considerably fewer casualties. The route he mapped out necessitated a wide detour to the east from the Alambagh towards the Dilkusha, before turning north to cross the canal near the Martiniere, before swinging west past the Sikanderbagh towards the Brigade Mess and the Residency.

The detailed street map was obviously of great value, but there remained the problem of delivering it to Sir Colin Campbell, for unlike worded messages it could not be encoded. As it happened, one man in the Residency who had seen the map was giving serious thought to just such an undertaking.

Thomas Henry Kavanagh, a 36-year-old uncovenanted civil servant, had already gained a reputation for fearlessness having spent many hours underground with the Cornish miners of the 32nd, even on one occasion attacking the enemy miners by the light of a candle. Here lay an opportunity for further glory and he immediately volunteered his services. The fact that Kavanagh was taller than most natives, and had fair hair and blue eyes, was hardly a recommendation for success, and at first Outram refused to entertain the idea. However, in the clothes of a native irregular, and with his skin and hair stained with a mixture of lampblack and oil, Kavanagh finally obtained Outram's approval. With the General's words – 'Noble fellow! You will never be forgotten' – ringing in his ears, he left with a native guide on 9 November.

160

For a large-limbed individual with the unmistakable blue eyes of a European, it seemed a suicidal mission, but as he and his native companion crept through the darkness to the north bank of the Gumti, the Irishman had no thought of failure, despite the prospect of negotiating the streets of Lucknow. An hour later, after wading through a mangrove swamp, it did seem that fortune had deserted them when they were challenged by a group of villagers. 'They were,' explained Kavanagh 'poor travellers on their way to a village near Banni to report the death of a friend's brother.' Fortunately, their story was believed and the pair were allowed to proceed on their way. Luck remained with them, for with patches of the colouring disappearing from the Irishman's hands and arms, they were challenged again. With great relief Kavanagh recognized the shout of 'Hoo cum da?' as coming from a friendly sepoy, whose appearance heralded their arrival in the British lines, thus bringing to an end Thomas Kavanagh and Kamaujie's highly dangerous 5-mile journey.

Forbes-Mitchell was unstinting in his praise of the Irishman's feat. 'Only those who knew the state of Lucknow at that time can fully appreciate the perils he encountered, or the value of the service he rendered,' wrote the Scot in admiration.

Two days later, on the 12th, Sir Colin Campbell's column joined Sir Hope Grant's small force, having experienced little opposition other than artillery harassment which proved to be of short duration once the heavy guns of the Naval Brigade were brought into action. Before deciding to follow Outram's route, Campbell reviewed his force, now 5,000 strong, on the plain beside the Alambagh.

Apart from the 9th Lancers, the men on parade could scarcely claim to have a soldierly appearance. A lieutenant of the 84th confessed: 'I had no uniform to speak of, wearing instead a grey flannel coat and trousers and a sowar's belt and pouch I had picked up.' The men of the 75th Regiment wore khaki uniforms now 'sadly patched and worn', and although the 53rd of Foot, and the 2nd and 4th Punjab Infantry passed muster, many of the Madras Fusiliers had patched their jackets with whatever material had come to hand, some even wearing coats of green baize. As for the Naval Brigade, they boasted an assortment of sailors' attire, and were distinctive from the number of pet monkeys and parrots sitting on their shoulders. Only the 93rd, in full Highland dress complete with feather bonnet, half of whom were wearing the Crimea medal on their chests, raised a cheer as Sir Colin rode past. Delighted, the General responded with a stirring address, ending with the exhortation: 'Ninety-third, you are my own lads. I rely on you to do the works.'

In the early hours of the 14th, Sir Colin Campbell set off at the head of his force for the Dilkusha, leaving Sir Hope Grant with a small garrison of 300 at the Alambagh. Warned of Campbell's approach, the rebels fell back to the Martiniere College, whose pupils had long since made themselves useful in the Residency. Before the Mutiny the Dilkusha had been a park filled with spotted deer and other fauna. There was still game to be had and the officers made sure of roast venison for dinner, both for themselves and the men they commanded. After a good breakfast, the troops left the park on 16 November having spent the night patrolling in a different direction in a bid to deceive the rebels as to their approach to Lucknow.

Nearing the Martiniere the 93rd came under fire from a concealed battery of six cannon. A Highlander was eviscerated by a ricocheting 9-pound shot near to Forbes-Mitchell, whilst another ball cut down several of the Light Company. As the 93rd began to shuffle uncomfortably, the Colonel sought to calm them. 'Keep steady, men,' he called. 'Close up the ranks and don't waver in the face of a battery manned by cowardly Asiatics!' In the opinion of the Adjutant, Lieutenant William MacBean, this was altogether the wrong advice and he called out sharply, 'Damn the Colonel, open out and let them [the cannon balls] through. Keep plenty of room, and watch the shot.' The exasperation in his voice broke the tension and as the round shot continued to bound across the turf, the men joked among themselves that there seemed to be 'a guid wheen footba's kicking aboot Lucknow'. The 93rd's ordeal was short lived, however, for the heavy guns of the Naval Brigade quickly dispersed the enemy and Leith Hay's men advanced across the plateau to reach the wall of the Martiniere without further casualties.

Two guns which had been brought to bear upon the British cavalry screen were driven off in a similar fashion, and when a battalion of mixed infantry companies advanced on the College the rebels hastily abandoned the building and retreated across the canal bridge hotly pursued by the cavalry. With the Dilkusha and the Martiniere abandoned by the rebels after little more than two hours, and the ground up to and including the canal bridge in British hands, Campbell's troops bivouacked for the night fully accoutred and ready for whatever the next day might bring.

The night air was chill and damp as the surgeon of the 93rd stood close to the fire with two companions speculating on what action could be expected on the morrow. As they whiled away the hours, the tropical sun rose abruptly above the horizon and Surgeon Munro turned to admire the dawn display of colour. He felt a touch on his arm and Captain John Lumsden, an officer on temporary assignment, remarked in a quiet voice, 'That is the last sunrise that many will see, and God knows to which of us three standing by this fire, it may be the last.' Shortly afterwards the Regiment was called to assembly and the three shook hands before going their separate ways. They never met again, for in the space of two hours Munro's two companions were dead, killed in the very forefront of the battle for the Sikanderbagh, having displayed a degree of gallantry 'which excited the admiration of all who followed them'.

The mutineers presented a solid front at the Sikanderbagh, where a concentrated fire of musketry raked the exposed flanks of the advancing troops, and for a while the situation verged upon the critical. Impatient at being kept waiting for an hour whilst the artillery endeavoured to widen a breach in the palace wall, a sergeant known to Forbes-Mitchell as 'Dobbin' called out to Sir Colin Campbell, 'Sir Colin, your Excellency, let the infantry storm; let the two 'Thirds' at them and we'll soon make short work of the murderous villains!'

Campbell, who had a good memory for names and places, addressed the Sergeant. 'Do you think the breach is wide enough, Dobbin?'

Back came the reply without a moment's hesitation. 'Part of us can get through and hold it until the pioneers widen it with their crowbars to allow the rest to get in, sir.'

The Sergeant's enthusiasm moved Sir Colin and he turned to Colonel Ewart commanding the 93rd. 'Bring on the tartan,' he urged in his strong brogue. 'Let my own lads at them.'

From the shelter of a mud wall, Lieutenant Gordon Alexander looked at the spurts of dust being kicked up in the road from a shower of musket balls, and wondered for a moment whether even a rabbit could escape unscathed. It was no time for hesitation, however, and the young subaltern joined the men of the other six companies in leaving his shelter to face a storm of musketry the like of which he had not seen since the crossing of the Alma. Led by the pipes, the Highlanders dashed towards the breach accompanied by the men of the 53rd and the Sikhs.

Forbes-Mitchell thrust himself through the narrow opening close upon the heels of a taciturn Scot known as 'Quaker' Wallace, renowned for quoting verses from the Psalm 116 whenever he bayoneted a mutineer. Barely had Forbes-Mitchell gained the other side of the wall before a ball struck the thick brass clasp of his waist belt with a force sufficient to cause him to stagger back amongst the rubble. Lying winded on the ground, he distinctly heard Colonel Ewart's voice as he passed, 'Poor fellow, he's done for!'

No quarter was given, or asked for, by the 2,000 rebels in the Sikanderbagh, for the atrocity of the well at Cawnpore was fresh in the memory of the Highlanders, and shouting 'Cawnpore! You bloody murderers, Cawnpore!' the Scots surged forward in a sea of waving plumes and tartans, closely followed by the 53rd Foot.

In a savage encounter during which the mutineers fought with a fury born of desperation, some even hurled their muskets, bayonet first, like javelins, whilst others drew *tulwars* and threw themselves beneath outstretched bayonets to slash at the Highlanders' legs. The sepoys were gradually driven from court to court and from room to room. In more than two hours of continuous fighting, described by Forbes-Mitchell as 'a horrible and brutalising war of downright butchery', every corner of the palace's four towers was contested until the last defender had been killed, and his body thrown out of the window to fall on the stone paving below. 'Dreadful sight,' noted Major Bingham, 'the dead were lying in some places twenty deep.' The fact that sixty-four mutineers threw down their weapons and surrendered to the Sikhs did not save them – they were slaughtered to a man.

The ghastly mounds of bodies, in which the dying were entangled with the dead, horrified young Fred Roberts. 'There they lay in a heap as high as my head,' he wrote. 'One of those sights which even in the excitement of battle and the flush of victory make one feel strongly what a horrible side there is to war.'

In this atmosphere of death, thick with smoke and the pungent smell of burning flesh, Surgeon Munro went in search of the wounded. In one corner of the court, more than 100 bodies lay

164

smouldering, a sight which nauseated the surgeon of the 93rd, and yet he could not rid himself of a feeling of satisfaction that the massacre at Cawnpore had been well and truly avenged. Later that evening, having attended to the wounded, Munro went to look for the bodies of the two officers he had shaken hands with in the company of Captain Lumsden. He discovered that they were to be buried close to the breach, and as he raised the covering, Munro looked down 'on such calm and peaceful expressions that but for the peculiar pallid hue which marked the rigid features, I might have been gazing upon the faces of men hushed in the sound sleep of weariness and not of death'.

Now that the Sikanderbagh was in British hands, there remained one more obstacle to be overcome before the Residency buildings could be reached – the Shah Najif, enclosed in a garden surrounded by a high stone wall. Seizing this tomb of the first king of Oudh looked to be a difficult and dangerous operation, but whatever the cost it was a necessity since it barred the way to the Residency, and Campbell was determined that its fall should be accomplished before nightfall.

A hail of musketry poured down on the assembled Highlanders from the castellated top of the building, stopping them from making any appreciable headway. The defenders included a body of archers whose arrows flew 'with great force and precision'. One soldier of the 93rd who raised his head incautiously above the shelter of a wall paid for the rash act with a shaft through his brain which projected more than a foot from the back of his skull. 'Boys,' Forbes-Mitchell heard a senior NCO say, 'this is no joke. We must pay them off.' After very nearly three hours, as bullets rained about them with a noise like 'stones being thrown at a saucepan', and in which the heavy artillery and rocket batteries of Peel's Naval Brigade had made little impression against the massive stone walls, there occurred a noticeable slackening in the enemy's fire. It was then, when the infantry were about to retire, that Sergeant Paton of the 93rd stumbled upon a narrow gap in the wall, half concealed in the undergrowth. Followed by his comrades he reached the tomb, only to find it deserted. The mutineers, after witnessing the Naval Brigade's rockets dipping and twisting in a trail of fire which had come roaring above the wall, had abandoned their post and fled.

165

Whilst Campbell's men had been engaged in the bloody business of storming the palaces, Outram had been doing his best to create a diversion. It had never been his intention to merely watch Campbell's progress from the roof of the Residency, and on his orders a battery was set up in a garden no more than 100 yards from the Shah Najif. Possessing a good field of fire, his guns began to pound the two buildings in which the rebels had sought shelter. Each was strongly held, but a bugle call sounding the advance was greeted with a storm of cheers by Outram's men, seething for action after the frustration of the past two weeks, and the rebels quickly discovered that with no artillery to support them their places of refuge were indefensible.

Only a short distance now separated the Residency from the relief force, and Outram and Havelock's men spent the hours of darkness in a fever of excitement, watching shells from Campbell's mortars describe a fiery arc against the eastern sky.

To Forbes-Mitchell, the Residency buildings seemed invitingly close as he endeavoured to seek some warmth from a bivouac fire, but the glow which threw the trees and bushes into sharp relief brought little warmth to the Scot, for without his greatcoat he soon discovered that the kilt afforded scant protection against the chill night air. Unable to sleep, he spent the night listening to the men reliving their terrible experiences of the day in their fitful dreams.

The next morning, the 17th, having secured his left flank by occupying the suburbs adjacent to the canal, Campbell ordered the guns of the Naval Brigade to open fire against the old Mess House of the 32nd, whilst he sent in a mixed battalion against another palace, the Mothi Mahal. By mid-afternoon the Mess House had fallen to the 53rd led by Captain Hoskins, but the Mothi Mahal proved a harder nut to crack. At length, the rebels were driven from its orange and lemon groves and the last obstacle to reaching the besieged garrison was overcome.

At the Engine House, Generals Outram and Havelock were conferring with their staffs. The question of how best to render assistance to the relieving force was a vexing one and they broke off in irritation at the sudden appearance of a tall, bearded, jack-booted figure in the quilted jacket of a staff officer, and wearing a pith helmet.

Suddenly, one of the officers raised a delighted shout. 'It's Kavanagh! He's the first to relieve us.'

166

In the congratulations which followed, Kavanagh almost forgot the point of his visit. Turning to Outram he asked, 'Are you willing, Sir James, to join the Commander-in-Chief at once?'

An open space of almost half a mile, occasionally the subject of musketry, separated the generals but, giving way to the excitement of the occasion, Outram, Havelock and Kavanagh, accompanied by six other officers, hurried towards Sir Colin Campbell waiting at the Mothi Mahal. It was a journey not without risk and inevitably four of the officers were wounded. Havelock narrowly escaped with his life when a shell, rebounding from a wall, burst at his feet. The General was knocked on his back, but to the astonishment of his aides he regained his feet and continued slowly on his way showing not the slightest concern.

With this meeting on 17 November, the relief of Lucknow had become an established fact. 'Oh! How thankfully we welcomed them,' confessed Mrs Huxham, and then, conscious of the part played by the garrison, she added: 'Over 400 of the brave defenders of our garrison lay buried in the graveyard and the remainder who have been fortunate enough to survive were now to bid adieu to the trials and harrowing scenes that had been their lot for six months.'

To the gaunt, ragged and louse-infested garrison troops, the relatively smart appearance of their rescuers was something to marvel at. The Naval Brigade excited particular attention and the children gazed wide eyed at the sailors led in by Captain William Peel. The unfamiliar uniform, particularly the straw hats, so impressed the Asians in the Residency that they spoke of the sailors in awestruck tones, of being a strange race of men 4 feet high and 4 feet wide, of enormous strength, who carried 24-pounder cannon on their shoulders with ease.

As they stared at the shot-encrusted walls, the tumbled ruins and the foul trenches, the soldiers of Campbell's relief force could only admire the fortitude of those who had defended the Residency for 140 days against the many thousands of rebels who still swarmed the streets of Lucknow. That night Brigadier Inglis warned the women that they should make preparations to withdraw from the Residency the following evening, and that luggage was to be limited to that which could be easily carried in a small bundle. Mrs Inglis and Mrs Adelaide Case exchanged concerned glances. 'How are all the wounded and sick people, and women and children to be got off in such a hurried manner,' asked Mrs Case, 'at only a few hours notice?'

It did not seem to have been a concern for Mrs Katherine Bartrum. 'Well!' she exclaimed upon hearing the news, 'I can only carry my baby, and my worldly effects can be put into a very small compass, since they consist merely of a few old clothes.'

Only Mrs Germon seems to have been fully prepared. She noted in her diary that as soon as she heard that the Alambagh had been captured, she began to pack, 'for if the troops come in, we may be sent off at a moment's notice'.

In fact, the women were given an extra day in which to prepare for the evacuation, but it was still received with mixed feelings, not only by them but by a few civilians who bitterly resented abandoning positions to the enemy that they had held at such cost. Mrs Case nevertheless celebrated the announcement with a fruit pie for dinner, something which she and the others in her room had not tasted for weeks. The restriction on the number of possessions they would be allowed to take with them caused a great deal of consternation among the ladies, many of whom spent the day feverishly packing away as many valuables as they possibly could. Capacious pockets were sewn into dresses to accommodate jewelry, linen was folded into pillow cases or packed into boxes. Mrs Germon wrote that she donned

> four flannel waistcoats, three pairs of stockings, three chemises, three drawers, one flannel and four white petticoats, my pink flannel dressing gown, skirt, plaid jacket, and overall my cloth dress and jacket that I had made out of my old habit, then tied my cashmere shawl sash-fashion round my waist and put on a worsted cap and hat and had my drab cloak put on the saddle ... I also had two under-pockets, one filled with jewelry ... the other with my journal and valuable papers.

'Much comment was made on some of the ladies turning out so well dressed,' remarked a sympathetic Ensign Ruggles, 'but this arose from their very natural wish to save the best of their wardrobe.' Only Katherine Bartrum remained relatively unencumbered, for all she possessed in the world were a few clothes and her little son Bobby.

The rigours of the siege had not improved the disposition of several of the soldiers' wives who passed the picket at the shattered gateway with surly expressions and scarcely a word of thanks to the men who had rescued them. Some even complained of the inadequacies of the transport provided, a criticism which reached the ears of Sir Colin Campbell, who rebuked them with the words 'Ladies – women, I mean – you ought to be thankful that you have got out with your lives, for I do not know how it might have been in two hours more with you.'

At 10.00 am on 19 November, the first stage of the refugees' long journey to Allahabad, by way of Cawnpore, began with a stream of carts, palanquins and carriages drawn by coolies, some ladies riding ponies, and the sick and wounded being carried on doolies over the 4 miles to the Sikanderbagh, a large house in its own grounds within the confines of the city. To guard the refugees from unwelcome attention, British marksmen in the Shah Najif, and artillery at the Moti Mahal, were put on alert and the slow-moving column eventually arrived unmolested, to be greeted with every sympathy by the men and officers who provided them with much-needed refreshment and rest before the time came for their departure to the Dilkusha, a journey not without its difficulties and alarms.

'We were obliged to halt frequently, because of the water-logged ground,' wrote Major North, 'and each time we stopped, those in the rear, unconscious of what was passing in front, suf-fered all the terrors of uncertainty.' Eventually the long column of refugees arrived with a new escort just before midnight.

There, in sharp contrast to their reception at the Sikanderbagh, they met with total confusion. 'No one could tell us where to go,' complained Mrs Brydon, 'and it was in vain to look for a servant in such a crowd and in the dark.'

Having been refused entry to a building which, she was told, already housed 1,100 sick and wounded, at 2.00 am Mrs Adelaide Case was too tired to do anything but lie down fully dressed where she was, under a *rezais*, and try to sleep.

Mrs Germon fared a little better. After confronting a stranger with a lantern and asking him where she might go, she was directed to some tents a long way off:

After tumbling over a lot of tent pegs and ropes we reached them and lay down on the ground for the night. It was impossible to find my pony with my bedding, but we got a *duree* [rug] to lie upon and I put my head on my basket – the tents were so open that I of course got a cold – however daylight soon appeared.

In the morning order was restored and the breakfast served by the 9th Lancers beneath the trees was such as to banish entirely the discomforts of the previous night.

Among the delicacies not seen for many months by the refugees were cold beef and mutton, tea with milk and sugar, and biscuits and jam. 'I don't think that we ever enjoyed any meal in our lives so much,' admitted Mrs Huxham.

Most welcomed by the children was the sight of fresh white bread with butter. 'Oh Mamma!' shrieked a little girl. 'There is a loaf of bread on the table. I am certain of it. I saw it with my own eyes.'

'We had none of us tasted bread and butter since the 30th of June till today,' wrote Mrs Harris, 'so it was indeed a treat.' The one occurence to mar their enjoyment, of the meal was the death of the popular Ensign Charlie Dashwood.

There was to be one further incident which led to a deep feeling of dismay affecting the whole community. General Sir Henry Havelock had contracted dysentery in Lucknow and now lay dying in a soldier's tent at the Dilkusha. He would permit of no assistance save that proffered by his son Harry, who read him passages from the Bible. He died peacefully in his son's arms soon after dawn on 24 November and was buried at the Alambagh. Curiously, only the letter 'H', carved on the trunk of a mango tree, marked the position of his grave.

The withdrawal of the Europeans and loyal sepoys of John Company's army did not begin until three days after the evacuation of the non-combatants. 'We left Lucknow on the night of the 23rd November at mid-night in silence,' recorded Captain Anderson, 'and as we left our outposts, the rascals were firing on our outer walls. We got safe out without the loss of a single man.'

By 4.30 am on the 23rd, most were encamped in the Dilkusha park to join the others for the next stage of the journey to the Alambagh.

'Left the Dilkoosha Palace in carts which had been provided for us,' entered Mrs Katherine Bartrum in her diary dated 24 November. 'We arrived at the Alam Bagh late at night, tired to death by our weary march.'

'Never shall I forget the scene – as far as the eye could search on all sides were strings of vehicles, elephants, camels, etc.,' recalled Maria Germon. 'The dust was overpowering. We went across country to avoid the enemy – our road lay over cultivated fields and such ups and downs it was a wonder how the vehicle got over them.'

That day had been intensely hot and the dust stirred up by the slow-moving column was at times so dense that as Mrs Brydon noted, 'even to see the children in your arms' was scarcely possible. It was difficult to obtain even the bare modicum of food, for every village on their route had been deserted by the inhabitants who feared the ill humour of the redcoats, and it was not long before Mrs Brydon's small store of edibles was reduced to 'some carrots and a little sugar candy'.

Adelaide Case wrote:

> We left the Alumbagh at half past ten o'clock and had a most tedious day's march. I think we were one hour and a half sitting in the carriages without moving. To imagine the sight of so many hackeries, camels, carriages of all kinds, riders, camp followers, is quite impossible. The whole column was nine miles in length. The name of the place where we are encamped tonight I do not know, but it is about nine miles from Allumbagh. Even getting over that short distance took us more than seven hours.

Each halt had been plagued with a swarm of flies and such was the disorganization that although there was no shortage of tents, many of the evacuees were obliged to sleep in the open, with no protection from the elements.

Meanwhile, at the Residency, having heard nothing from General Windham by 27 November, Sir Colin Campbell became increasingly concerned about the bridge of boats across the Ganges. The 93rd were drawn up on parade and Campbell explained to the men that in the event of the bridge falling into the hands of the rebels, they would be cut off in Oudh, with the responsibility of protecting the women and children against an army of mutineers in their rear and to their front. 'So, Ninety Third,' he concluded, 'I don't ask you to undertake this forced march in your present tired condition, without good reason. We must reach Cawnpore tonight at all costs.'

Leaving the task of maintaining a watch on the Lucknow mutineers to Sir James Ourtram at the Sikanderbagh, Sir Colin Campbell had been among the last to leave the Residency, and in negotiating a particularly rough piece of ground on the arm of Lieutenant Gordon Alexander, he suddenly asked him, 'Well, young man, what's your opinion of the move?'

171

Taken by surprise, the subaltern answered, 'I don't understand it, sir, but it looks as if we are running away.'

'Of course we are,' replied the General, adding, 'but il faut reculer pour mieux sauter!' and roared with laughter at his own joke.

About 40 miles to the south-west, preparations were being made to lodge the Lucknow refugees in the compound of the old Cawnpore Hotel. Furniture, crockery and other domestic items thought necessary to their well-being were being collected from the bazaars, and a score of tents were pitched for the accommodation of the women and children. The Assembly Rooms were made ready, servants were taken on and consideration was being given to hiring a number of vehicles to meet the column as it neared Cawnpore. In the midst of all this activity, the forced march which had begun early on the morning of the 27th was having a deleterious effect upon Corporal William Forbes-Mitchell's physical well-being. After eighteen days of continuous duty without the opportunity of a bath or a change of clothing – even a change of socks – had exhausted the young Highlander as he freely admitted: 'I shall never forget the misery of that march. However, we reached the sands on the banks of the Ganges, on the Oude side of the river opposite Cawnpore, just as the sun was setting, having covered the forty-seven miles under thirty hours.'

As the weary troops covered mile after mile in dogged determination, the faint noise of artillery had grown from 'a sound of distant thunder' to an intensity which caused an anxious General Campbell to urge the men to make even greater exertions. With typical Gaelic phlegm, Forbes-Mitchell sought to make light of it. 'There is nothing to rouse tired soldiers like a good cannonade in front,' he confessed. 'It is the best tonic out.'

The fact that Windham had been hard pressed at Mangalwar was readily apparent from the spiralling columns of smoke rising from the battered township, but to Campbell, who had earlier received a note from Windham urging his assistance, the sight of an undamaged bridge of boats across the Ganges was one of unsurpassed relief. After a forced march of 28 miles, Campbell's 'exhausted men and officers, having had nothing to eat except those who were lucky enough to bring something with them' – wrote Major Bingham – finally reached Cawnpore on 18 November. News which undoubtedly lifted his spirits was shortly to greet him, for Major Bingham was promoted to Lieutenant Colonel on 20 December.

Chapter 13

THE FALL OF LUCKNOW

The long winding procession of refugees, carriages, hackeries, doolies and bullock-drawn carts had been left far behind by General Campbell, but now, as the column continued its slow progress towards Cawnpore, Mrs Brydon's sense of anticipation was heightened by the sound of firing and the sight of 'smoke rising in many places'. She was further encouraged from being told that the bridge of boats would soon be reached.

At length, ten days after vacating the Residency, the weary women and children, and the sick, crossed the bridge of boats from the Oudh side of the Ganges, to be confronted by the grim sight of Wheeler's old entrenchment with its background of smoke-blackened walls, charred timbers and the stumps of once leafy trees. 'Those few houses in cantonments that had escaped hitherto,' wrote William Shepherd, 'were on this occasion reduced to ashes.'

'Nothing,' in the opinion of Mrs Adelaide Case, 'could look more wretched and miserable than this dreadful place as we came in by the light of the moon. The station of Cawnpore, once so familiar, was a desolation.'

Mrs Georgina Harris evidently shared this view when she entered in her diary the observation:

> I never saw such a sad scene of desolation as this station. There is not a house left standing; it is enough to make one cry to look at the blackened ruins of what once were beautiful bungalows, and then to think of the awful fate of all those who so lately inhabited them – a fate too which we so narrowly escaped.

Despite the general air of gloom, for one member of Windham's garrison there was cause for celebration. Among the last of the refugees to cross 'was my friend Lieutenant Delafosse,' exclaimed Mowbray Thomson, 'reduced to a most emaciated condition from the continued effects of fever and dysentery.'

173

Over the next few days the Lucknow survivors were given time to recover from their experiences whilst arrangements were made for the final stage of the journey to Allahabad. On 3 December they left with a small escort, much to the relief of Sir Colin Campbell who was now able to devote the whole of his attention to the overthrow of Tatya Tope and Bala Rao. Three days later, he struck.

Earlier in his attempt to relieve the Lucknow garrison, a Calcutta newspaper had referred to the General as 'Sir Crawling Camel', alluding to his slow progress through Oudh, but now that he was relieved of responsibility for the refugees, the alacrity with which plans were drawn up to free Cawnpore from the grip of the Gwalior Contingent amazed even officers on his own staff. Campbell's tactics laid emphasis on exploiting the vulnerability of Tatya Tope's right flank. In a subsequent despatch to the Governor General, Sir Colin wrote:

> It appeared to me if his right were vigorously attacked that it would be driven from his position without assistance coming from other parts of his line, the wall of the town which gave cover to our attacking columns on our right being an effective obstacle to the movement of any portion of his troops from his left to right.

The rebel army facing Campbell amounted to just over 13,000 infantry and was split into two bodies: the Gwalior Contingent on the right across the road to Kalpi; and on the left, holding the city and the ground beyond it to the Ganges, were stationed the regular and irregular troops loyal to the Nana Sahib and led by Bala Rao.

To face these forces, all that Campbell could muster were 5,000 infantry, including some new arrivals from Britain, 600 cavalry and 35 guns.

At precisely 9.00 am on the 6th, General Windham began a heavy bombardment of the rebel-held ground between the city and the river, concentrating on Tatya Tope's position along the Ganges Canal, which lasted for two hours before lifting to allow the infantry to advance. The Rifle Brigade were sent to occupy the two villages near the canal, from where their fire effectively prevented the enemy gunners from harassing two other brigades which had left the fort to proceed across the open plain towards the brick kilns. Lieutenant Frederick Sleigh Roberts, who had been born in Cawnpore, wrote:

It was a sight to be remembered, that advance, as we watched it from our position on horse back, grouped around the Commander-in-Chief. Before us stretched a fine open plain, to the right the dark green of the Rifle Brigade battalions. Nearest to us, the 53rd Foot and the 42nd and 93rd Highlanders in their bonnets and kilts, marched as on parade although the enemy's guns played upon them.

To Surgeon Munro advancing with the 93rd, it seemed that he was 'moving within a circle of fire'. Behind him, Windham's batteries belched forth their noisy discharges, whilst to his right there could be heard the continual rattle of musketry, described by Munro as 'at one moment sounding near in crashing volleys, at another, rippling away slowly in the distance'. William Munro was no stranger to the passage of round shot – 'a rushing sound like the concentrated essence of an express train' – and the whistling of musket balls, but he had never before heard the deadly sound of grapeshot. As his regiment advanced, it appeared to him that 'the sound of birds in rapid flight' was above and all around him. At this strange and terrifying noise Munro instinctively lowered his head and turned to present his side to it in an effort to make as small a target as possible. No sooner had he done so than his orderly tugged at his sleeve, saying reproachfully, 'A'm ashamed for ye, doctor, Laud yer front tae't mon, 'tis only grape ye're hearin'.'

As the surgeon watched the men of his regiment go into battle with 'waving plumes and flowing tartans', even as a non-combatant he was conscious of a mounting sensation which, he wrote, 'enthralled the soul and made that day one worthy to be remembered with a feeling of pride and satisfaction'.

It was whilst he too was engaged in observing the movement of the enemy, that Colonel John Ewart fell victim to enemy action just as he was in the act of dismounting from his horse, as he recorded in his memoirs:

> I was aware that I had been struck violently on the left side, but did not know what had actually taken place, until I looked down and saw the bleeding stump. The blow did not knock me down, nor did I feel any inclination to fall, but a soldier of the 93rd ran up at once and tied his handkerchief tightly around the stump.

Ewart was later carried off to the field hospital where what remained of his left arm was amputated. 'This caused universal regret in the regiment,' commented Corporal Forbes-Mitchell, 'he being the most popular officer in it'.

John Ewart confessed:

> What took place I do not know, but when I came to myself again, another piece of my arm was gone and the wound had been nicely bandaged up. I was then replaced in the doolie, and had the leisure to think over what had occurred ... not that I could do so in perfect peace, as the shells continued to fall around the bungalow.

For a short time the rebels fought with tenacious fury until a spreading cloud of white smoke interspersed with streaks of orange flame signalled the commencement of a fierce bombardment from the large-calibre naval guns and Windham's field artillery, which poured round after round into the enemy's position with telling effect.

Under this punishing fire the Gwalior Contingent was driven back beyond the Kalpi road with Campbell's infantry in hot pursuit. 'Our time had come at last,' enthused Hugh Gough, 'we were in amongst them, driving them before us, a disorganised, flying rabble.'

A young officer in Peel's naval brigade also found it difficult to contain his excitement. In a letter to his parents, Edmund Verney wrote:

> I can't tell you how jolly it was seeing the brutes run. I could hardly believe my eyes. I felt perfectly mad, and our men got on top of the guns, waving their hats and yelling ... we pursued them to their camp, found it all deserted, tents, horses, ponies, baggage, bedding, swords, muskets, everything lying about, hackeries loaded with all manner of treasure.

By 1.00 pm the 7,000-strong Gwalior Contingent, which had considered itself to be invincible, had become a flying rabble with the sepoys seeking whatever cover they could find, either in the jungle or the fields of tall sugar cane. Meanwhile the cavalry, which had been drawn up along the Grand Trunk Road, received orders to cross the canal and join the pursuit. Standing close by Sir Hope Grant, Forbes-Mitchell heard the Colonel give the word of command 'Squadrons, Outwards', and watched them wheel in response as if 'at a review on the Calcutta parade ground'. The bridge was crossed and the infantry spread out leaving the cavalry to sweep round each flank.

Despite having taken the wrong road, Hope Grant's cavalry caught the remnants of Bala Rao's command crossing the Ganges and captured what was left of their artillery without suffering a single casualty. 'On we went still, right through the camp and after them across the fields and roads at a tremendous pace,' Lieutenant Verney continued to write. 'We chased them for about 10 miles ... We took seventeen guns, loads upon loads of ammunition, all their luggage, treasure and everything – there's for you!'

At one stage of the chase, Hugh Gough found himself keeping pace in a fast gallop with Sir Colin Campbell, who, carried away by the excitement of it all, remarked, 'By Jove! You fellows can go.'

'His whole face was beaming with delight,' remembered the young subaltern. 'I felt I would have gone anywhere for the plucky old man.'

'What a chase we had,' confirmed Lieutenant Frederick Roberts. 'We went at a gallop, only pulling up occasionally for the battery to come into action, to clear our front and flanks.'

Harried upon every side, the sepoys scattered, many throwing away their weapons and discarding their distinctive red jacket in the hope of being mistaken for a harmless village peasant.

For many of the captured sepoys the method of punishment was swift and merciless. Those suspected of committing atrocities against Europeans faced a method of execution which had been practised by the Moghul Emperors as recently as 1825. An officer who was a witness to one such multiple execution described it thus:

> Their eyes were bandaged and they were bound to the guns with their backs against the muzzles, and their arms fastened backward to the wheels. The port fires were lighted, and at a signal from the artillery major, the guns were fired. It was a horrid sight that then met the eye; a regular shower of human fragments – of heads, arms, and legs – whistling through the smoke; and when that cleared away, these fragments lying on the ground – fragments of Hindoos and Musselmans mixed together – were all that remained.

This grisly death was perhaps one of the few which held any real terror for either a Hindu or a Muslim. The same anonymous officer explained with some candour:

177

If he is hanged or shot he knows that his friends or relatives will be allowed to claim his body, and will give him the funeral rites required by his religion. But if sentenced to death in this form, he knows that his body will be blown into a thousand pieces, and the thought that perhaps a limb of someone of a different religion to himself might possibly be burned or buried with the remainder of his own body, is agony to him. So great is the disgust we all feel for the atrocities committed by the rebels, that we had no room in our hearts for any feeling of pity.

It was an attitude of mind which Corporal Forbes-Mitchell seems to have shared:

The inhuman murders and foul treachery of the Nana Saheb and others put all feeling of humanity or mercy for the enemy out of the question, and our men thus early spoke of putting a wounded Jack Pandy *out of pain*, just as calmly as if he had been a wild beast; it was even considered an act of mercy.

It was impossible, however, despite the degree of indifference prevalent among most Europeans for them not to feel admiration for the way in which those mutineers faced their end. 'Of the whole forty only two showed signs of fear, and they were bitterly reproached by the others for so disgracing their race,' admitted a witness. 'They certainly died like men.'

The Nana Sahib had not stayed to see the outcome of the battle for Cawnpore but had retired to his palace in Bithur where he made an effort to recover as much of his treasure as possible before crossing into Oudh with his followers.

Lieutenant Frederick Roberts, who was one of those who had pursued the Nana's forces to Bithur, was told by a native on 12 December that the Nana had slept at the palace the night before, Roberts observed, 'but hearing of our approach, he decamped with all his guns, and was now at a ferry some miles up stream trying to get across the river and make his way to Oudh'.

Since there was little to be gained by a forced march which would result in the troops arriving at nightfall, a halt was made in Bithur for 'rest and refreshment'. The palace was found to be in a good state of order and in one of the many rooms Roberts discovered a great many letters addressed to Azimullah Khan. Of those written in English, the majority appeared to be from female admirers. 'Not a few from ladies of rank and fashion,' he noted, 'some opened and some extremely interesting.'

There was treasure in abundance. After being drained, a nearby well was found to contain valuable artefacts, among which was a massive golden bowl weighing 40lb. A rumour that the soldiers in Hope-Grant's detachment were to share in the distribution of prize money prompted many to labour through Christmas, but their expectations were in vain for it was eventually decided that most of the treasure, to the value of two million rupees, had been looted from the Cawnpore garrison and therefore was the property of the State. 'We never got a pice,' complained Forbes-Mitchell bitterly. 'All we did get was hard work. We even had to pay from our own pockets for the replacement of our kits which were taken by the Gwalior Contingent when they captured Windham's camp.'

When the sun rose, the pursuit of the mutineers was resumed but to little avail, as Lieutenant Roberts had predicted, and he and the rest returned to Cawnpore. The Nana and his force had boarded the boats waiting at the Serai Ghat to ferry them across the river into Oudh, having abandoned all but two of their seventeen cannon and a train of carts, leaving them to sink in the mud.

The defeat of the Gwalior Contingent and the capture of their camp with all its stores had ensured that Campbell's line of communication along the river was safe, and with reinforcements pouring into Bengal from Burma, Ceylon, Persia, Mauritius, and from England via the Cape, his army was rapidly gaining strength for a punitive thrust into Oudh and the expulsion of the vast numbers of rebels threatening Outram at the Alambagh. Transport was still a problem, some of it having been taken for the conveyance of the Lucknow refugees to Allahabad, but Campbell did not let the shortage deter him and he left Cawnpore on Christmas Eve, knowing that the hot weather season was almost upon him. His first objective was to occupy Fatehgarh, the last rebel-held city in the Doab, midway between Allahabad and Delhi, and orders were issued that several converging columns were to advance on the city, which he hoped to reach by the beginning of January. Of greater interest to Corporal William Forbes-Mitchell and his fellow Scots, however, was the opportunity it gave them for a bathe in the Ganges. 'The condition of our flannel shirts is best left undescribed,' confessed Forbes-Mitchell. 'We sent our shirts afloat in the sacred waters of mother Ganges, glad to be rid of them, and that night we slept in comfort.'

179

Meanwhile the first Christmas of the Mutiny was celebrated in Cawnpore by the sailors of Peel's Naval Brigade in time-honoured fashion with a double allowance of rum. A young naval cadet with fond memories of his mother's plum puddings wrote: 'We had a very good cosy little Christmas dinner, some of these natives are excellent cooks and it is quite wonderful how they do it considering the material they have.'

Campbell's force, having recently replaced the carriages taken by the Lucknow refugees thanks to a column from Delhi, was averaging 25 miles a day in a long winding column of wagons and naval guns drawn by elephants, leaving a vast horde of camp followers in their wake. By 2 January Fatehgarh had been taken with a minimum of casualties and now that he had secured the city, Campbell turned his attention to the reduction of the neighbouring district of Rohilkhand. However, he was dissuaded from this by the Governor General, for Lord Canning held the view that Oudh should not be afforded any respite from military action, and by 15 February Sir Colin had returned to Cawnpore.

By the end of the month British military strength had grown to 17 battalions of infantry, 28 squadrons of cavalry and more than 100 cannon of varying calibre, including mortars, all of which had turned the sandy plain around Cawnpore into one vast encampment. While he waited to join those shortly to cross the bridge of boats into Oudh, Lieutenant Vivian Majendie of the Royal Artillery had time to inspect Wheeler's old cantonments, and as he traced the paths and flower beds of what had once been well-kept gardens, but were now covered inches deep in pulverized brick dust, he was conscious of a feeling of acute depression, writing: 'There is something indescribably sad about Cawnpore. You may yet through the ruins of razed houses, trace the walks and beds of what once were gardens ... wondering where the hand is that used to tend them so carefully.'

Where previously had stood the much-admired Assembly Rooms, shops, houses, large shady trees and a flourishing bazaar, there was now an empty space. The shattered barrack blocks stood as a reminder of past events, but the Bibighar had been demolished and the trees around the courtyard uprooted. The only memorial to the victims was a wooden cross near the well, put up by the soldiers of the 32nd Regiment as a mark of respect to the memory of their wives and children.

'It was a horrid spot,' William Russell informed his readers. 'Rows of gorged vultures sit with outspread wings on the mouldering parapets, or perch in clusters on the two or three leafless trees. Again I am struck by the scowling, hostile look of the people,' he added. 'The banniahs bow with their necks, and salaam with their heads, but not with their eyes.'

In his preparation for a renewed assault on Lucknow, Sir Colin Campbell held the view that it would be to his advantage to advance upon the town from the north, an approach never previously attempted and which could reasonably be expected to possess fewer defence works. Campbell was correct in this for the mutineers had neglected to construct any appreciable defence on the city's northern side, believing that the British would never consider a crossing of the River Gumti, with all the difficulties that would entail.

As previously mentioned, there were three lines of defence around Lucknow. The outer was in the form of a deep canal which enclosed the city on its eastern and southern sides until it bore away to the north-east where it joined the Gumti. The second subtended an angle formed by the river and the suburb of Hazratganj, and included the Mess House which had proved so troublesome in the November assault. The third was formed by a rampart around the Kaiserbagh, a palace whose 400-yard square and enclosure formed the rebel citadel. To man these natural and artificial defences and resist an assault on the town, the Maulvi of Faizabad, who repeatedly led attacks on Outram at the Alambagh, had upwards of 100,000 trained sepoys and armed civilians. No less impressive were the 127 pieces of artillery at his disposal, among which were several 18-pounders and large-calibre mortars.

At his meeting with Sir Colin Campbell, when referring to Jung Bahadur's generous offer of 8,000 troops and 120 guns, the Governor General emphasized the importance of including the Gurkhas in his operations in Oudh, since recruiting additional troops from England was far from certain. When in Cawnpore, Campbell had lost no time in appointing senior commanders to lead the various divisions to be employed against Lucknow. Brigadier General James Hope Grant was given command of the cavalry division, Major General Sir James Outram, Major General Sir Edward Lugard and Brigadier General Robert Walpole, the three infantry divisions, whilst command of the

181

artillery was to go to Brigadier General Archdale Wilson and of the engineers to Colonel Robert Napier.

The appointments were not without controversy and were resented by some senior staff recently arrived from England, but as Campbell explained to the Duke of Cambridge, for an officer unfamiliar with Indian affairs it would be difficult for him 'to weigh the value of intelligence ... he is totally unable to make an estimate for himself of the resistance the enemy opposed to him is likely to offer'.

Having crossed the Ganges the force was halted at Banthira, a few miles into Oudh, for two days while Campbell awaited the arrival of the Gurkhas promised by Jung Bahadur. For a while all was peaceful until a sudden shout of 'Get up! Get up! The sepoys is a-coming!' galvanized the camp into action. Lieutenant Vivian Majendie, hearing the shouts and the general pandemonium, scrambled out of his tent in pyjamas to join officers in shirtsleeves feverishly buckling on their swords, others swearing and trying to mount their horses in what Majendie termed 'the very hottest of hot haste', going on to suggest:

> A dead silence pervades the camp now, and one could not help thinking that 'Jack Sepoy' would be a sad fool if he chose this moment for making his attack, and I suppose 'Jack Sepoy' thought much the same, for he did not put in an appearance that day, and indeed, I believe he had never had the slightest intention of doing so, the whole being a false alarm.

One officer, added Majendie, 'wondered what on earth this inexperienced army would do when the enemy really did appear'.

Order having been restored, the march was resumed on 2 March, through cultivated fields and beneath the welcome shade of mango trees, to approach the Dilkusha the next day, where many of the newcomers saw for the first time the remains of mutineers killed by Outram's soldiers from the Alambagh. 'Lying,' wrote Majendie, 'in all sorts of unnatural and distorted positions, with their fleshless limbs contorted, and the white teeth imparting a horrid grin to the ghastly skulls. Some of their old rags yet clung to them, the mouldy remains of their red coats and uniforms as decayed as themselves.'

Now that the Dilkusha was occupied, Campbell split his force into two. One part under Outram was given the task of crossing the Gumti and advancing along the Faizabad road to within a mile of Chinhat where he was to set up his heavy guns on the rising ground. The other half, led by Sir Colin himself, would cross the canal north of the Martiniere before mounting an attack against the city's main citadel, the Kaiserbagh.

On the morning of 9 March, Outram began his advance towards the Chakar Kothi with the Bengal Fusiliers and a regiment of Sikhs. For many of them it was to be their first experience of battle and the building was taken at the expense of one officer and twenty men. Most of the casualties had been inflicted by a small group of rebels desperately defending a room on the ground floor. Rather than risk further casualties, Outram ordered up two of his artillery pieces to shell the building, and when the smoke of the last round had drifted away, the Sikhs charged forward to storm the shattered entrance. Lieutenant Majendie wrote that:

> It was most exciting to see them racing up to the place, where, when they reached it, there was for a moment a confused scrambling at the doorways, then a sharp report or two, then a sort of shout and scuffling, then bang! bang! bang! Sharp and distinct, and finally there burst from the building, with loud yells, a crowd of Sikhs bearing among them the sole survivor of the garrison.

Enraged at the loss of a popular officer, the Sikhs attempted to tear him in two by seizing his legs. 'Failing in this,' continued Majendie, 'they dragged him along stabbing him with their bayonets as they went. I could see the poor wretch writhing as the blows fell.' Worse was to follow. 'Whilst still alive, though faint and feeble from his many wounds, he was deliberately placed on a small fire of dry sticks, which had been improvised for the purpose, and there held down in spite of his dying struggles.'

Commenting later upon this incident, Lieutenant Majendie expressed his horror that:

> in this nineteenth century, with its boasted civilisation and humanity, a human being should lie roasting and consuming to death, while Englishmen and Sikhs, gathered in little knots around and looked on without attempting to interfere. The whole business was done so quickly and with such noise and confusion, that to me who beheld it from a short distance, it seemed almost like a dream, till I rode up afterwards and saw the black trunk burned down to a stumpy, almost unrecognisable cinder.

After waiting in vain for the Gurkha detachment, Sir Colin Campbell had begun an operation against the Martiniere on the other side of the river. The attack was pressed home to such good effect by the Highland Brigade that the defenders were forced into a precipitous retreat, during which their musketry became so wildly inaccurate that only the tall, feathered bonnets of the 93rd suffered damage from the high-flying musket balls. 'Nae doot the niggers think our brains are higher up than ither men's,' remarked one amused Scot to Surgeon Munro. The doctor of the 93rd smiled, but as he later commented: 'An inch or two lower would have found the brains of several officers and a number of the men and increased the list of our casualties considerably.' The Martiniere was captured with remarkably few casualties, the most notable perhaps being Captain William Peel who had sustained a severe thigh wound from a musket ball.

Now that particular building was in his possession Campbell ordered his force to cross the canal, and on the morning of 11 March he launched an attack on the Begum Kothi with troops commanded by Major General Sir Edward Lugard. Two large-calibre guns manned by sailors of the Naval Brigade were ranged upon the high wall surrounding the palace, and after a four-hour bombardment from no more than 50 yards, a practicable breach was made. Surgeon Munro, who was close to the storming party, wrote:

> Each man stood leaning on his rifle, wrapt in his own thoughts ... Thus they remained for a second or two, when the tall form of their favourite leader, Adrian Hope, appeared and his right hand waved the signal for the assault. Then a cry burst from their ranks. It was not a cheer, which has a pleasant ring in it, but a short, sharp, piercing cry which had an angry sound which almost made one tremble.

The Highlanders and the 4th Punjab Rifles rushed towards the breach with howls of rage, and such was their fearsome appearance that many of the defenders immediately turned and fled.

There remained a fanatical body of some 700 men who were determined to fight to the death, however, and a confused melee spilt from court to court and from room to room. Forbes-Mitchell came upon a group of mutineers when leading a section of the 93rd and, rather than risk casualties by following the rebels into a room, he sent for a few bags of gunpowder. As he waited, Major William Raikes Hodson approached, sword in hand, demanding to know the whereabouts of the group of sepoys. Forbes-Mitchell pointed to the closed doors. 'It's certain death, sir,' he told the Major. 'Wait for the powder, I've sent men for powder bags.' Hodson, who really had no valid reason to be involved in the battle, brushed aside the warning and, bursting through the doors, paid with his life for his rash action. Afterwards, bags of powder with slow matches attached, were brought as requested and, wrote Forbes-Mitchell: 'Two or three bags very soon brought the enemy out, and they were bayoneted down without mercy.'

'A running fight was going on in the street all this time,' wrote Lieutenant Majendie. 'Little knots of desperate rebels, here and there, shut themselves up in houses where they fought fiercely, necessitating an infinity of small sieges on our part to drive them out.'

After two hours of brutal hand-to-hand combat in which more than 800 rebels were killed, Sir Colin Campbell could not find praise enough for his favourite regiment. Clapping his hands together, he cried, 'I knew it! I knew it! I knew my Highlanders would take it!'

On 14 March, the Imambara, a large mosque between the Begum Kothi and the Kaiserbagh, was taken without loss. It had not been Campbell's intention to advance as far, but so relentless had been the pursuit of the rebels that by early evening even the Kaiserbagh and the Mess House had fallen to his troops.

Nightfall did nothing to lessen an orgy of looting. William Russell, *The Times* correspondent, was the first civilian upon the scene and he was appalled by the behaviour of the British soldiers:

> At every door there is an eager crowd smashing the panels with the stocks of their firelocks or breaking the fastenings by discharges of their weapons. Here and there officers are running to and fro after their men, persuading or threatening in vain ... The men are wild with fury and lust for gold – literally drunk with plunder. Some come out with china vases or mirrors, dash them to pieces on the ground, and return to seek more valuable property.

Few had any notion of the value of their loot and Russell saw them breaking up sporting guns and pistols to get at the gold filigree mountings and the jewels set in the stocks.

185

Campbell's troops were not alone in the search for valuables. William Russell, stumbling over ground littered with corpses bloated by the fierce heat, had been almost suffocated by the stench of death, but nothing had revolted him so much as the hundreds of camp followers crowded together in the Hazratganj – so named after the Begum of Oudh. 'They were,' he informed his readers, 'as ravenous as vultures, packed in a dense mass in the street afraid or unable to go into the palaces, and, like the birds they resembled, waiting until the fight was done to prey on their plunder.'

An unofficial estimate of the day's plunder put the figure at £1¼ million sterling, but given the British soldier's suspicion of the bounty system, probably less than a quarter found its way into the Treasury. It was Forbes-Mitchell's belief that a good number of diamonds, pearls and emeralds were concealed in the uniform cases of even the prize agents. Whatever the truth of the matter, the prize money awarded to each private soldier amounted to less than 18 rupees, a miserable reward by any standard.

'I could myself name over a dozen men who served throughout every engagement, two of whom gained the Victoria Cross,' stated Forbes-Mitchell, 'who have died in the almshouses of their native parishes, and several in the almshouses of the Calcutta District Society.'

The next day, 15 March, was spent in consolidating the various gains and in mopping up small pockets of resistance. The capture of the Residency took less than half an hour before the artillery turned its attention to the crumbling walls of the Machi Bhawan, the old fort half a mile away. The final confrontation with the rebels in Lucknow occurred on the 21st when a strong body led by the Maulvi of Faizabad was defeated at the Shadatganj in the centre of the city by men of the 93rd and the Punjab Rifles. In the pursuit which followed, a great many were killed by Hope Grant's cavalry, but the Maulvi was among those who escaped to cause further trouble in Rohilkhand and north-western Oudh.

As the last of the rebels in Lucknow were killed and the more fortunate escaped across the river, Campbell's officers strolled about the devastated city, now but a travesty of the once most magnificent in all of India. Lieutenant Vivian Majendie was fortunate enough to accompany a brother officer who had experienced the siege and he found the personally conducted tour to be most informative. 'That long windowless, shot riddled ruin was a hospital,' he was told. 'This old, haggard skeleton of a gateway, pitted with bullet marks and with the ragged plaster dropping from its sides, is the Baillie Guard Gate. That shell pocked building the Racquet Court, the house which the ladies occupied, and that, the Gubbins House.' As he gazed at the ruins and listened to his friend expound upon a particular thrilling incident, Majendie felt that he was standing among the remains of buildings 'replete with associations half mournful, half joyous, but always glorious'.

As the days passed, the once deserted streets slowly came back to life, and when Vivian Majendie passed the bazaar for the last time, he found it thronged with merchants, beggars, chattering children, and the usual sights and sounds that were typical of an Indian bazaar, so far removed from the scenes that had been common-place not so many days before.

Although the Mutiny was approaching its final stages, the prospect of spending further time in India had become less than attractive, even to seasoned campaigners, and many officers sought their release on medical grounds. Mr A.N. Bradshaw, an assistant surgeon, was quite indignant. He wrote:

> It is remarkable how greatly love of England became developed in officers during the Campaign. I have learnt that as many as 300 have tried either to resign or get leave to go home on urgent private affairs. But old Colin is inexorable: 'No private affairs here, if you please gentlemen, rumour says was his dry answer to applications. Were it not for the pay which is a good bait for the higher ranks but a mere pittance for us subalterns, it would be absolutely impossible to keep gentlemen in India; the climate and the natives are barely supportable even in the comfort of cantonments, but on service they are intolerable.

The fall of Delhi had been instrumental to a successful prosecution of the campaign in Oudh and now with the occupation of Lucknow, the cause of the mutineers had been lost, although the rebellion was far from being suppressed. Much of Oudh, Rohilkhand and a vast track of central India had still to be pacified, and it was not to be until 8 July 1859 that Earl Canning would announce that a 'State of Peace' now reigned throughout India.

Chapter 14

THE DEMISE OF THE NANA

The rebel leader most wanted by the British, next to the Nana Sahib, was Tatya Tope. In company with Rao Sahib he had fled across the Chambal river into Rajputana with an army of 5,000 and ten guns, using guerrilla tactics to harass the British troops sent in pursuit, for the next seven months.

He was overtaken at Rajgarth by Major General Sir Hugh Rose in September 1858 and forced to give battle, where he was defeated, losing all of his artillery. But he escaped capture and with a number of supporters, joined forces with Rao Sahib again in the following October. At the end of the month, having lost half their men from sickness and desertion, the two rebel leaders decided to march south to Nagpur territory hoping to raise support for their cause. The peasantry there were unsympathetic and, harried by Rose's column, they recrossed the Nerbudda river before meeting up in January with Firuz Shah, a Moghul prince, at Indragarh, a town in Rajputana.

Hotly pursued by the British, their forces suffered another defeat at Sikar on 21 January and the three rebel leaders decided to part company. Tatya Tope took to the jungle around Paron, whilst Rao Sahib and Firuz Shah successfully evaded the patrols sent to apprehend him, and sought refuge in the jungles of Sironj.

Chasing the remnants of the Gwalior Contingent 'from the Jumna to the Dekkan and back again, had given the grey beards of our service a lesson in marching which had never entered their philosophy,' wrote John Henry Silvester, a 27-year-old cavalry surgeon. 'The energy thrown into the pursuit was immense ... Force after force and column after column pulled up dead beaten.'

In April 1859 Tatya Tope was betrayed by Maun Singh, the Rajah of Narwar, acting on the promise that the British would help him regain territory confiscated by the Maharajah Sindhia, a supporter of the Raj. On the pretext of seeking his advice on the

188

possibility of throwing in his lot with Firuz Shah, he requested a meeting, to which Tatya Tope agreed. They did in fact have a long discussion, after which the rebel leader rested. At a signal, sepoys who had lain in ambush closed in and arrested him, Maun Singh himself securing his arms. On the 15th, a court martial convened at Sipree charged Tatya Tope 'with having been in rebellion and having waged war against the British Government between June 1857 and December 1858 in certain specified instances'.

The rebel leader's defence rested upon the fact that he was merely obeying his master's orders, and in referring to the massacre at the Satichaura Ghat, he was careful to absolve both himself and the Nana of any responsibility. 'I went out and got ready forty boats, and having caused all the gentlemen, ladies and children to get into the boats, I started them off to Allahabad,' he explained to the Court. He went on to say, 'I only obeyed, in all things that I did, my master's orders up to the capture of Kalpi and afterwards, those of Rao Sahib. I have nothing to state except that I have had nothing to do with the murder of any European men, women or children.'

The Court refused to accept his statement and sentenced him to be hung at 4.00 pm on 18 April. His execution at Sipi was witnessed by many hundreds of natives and troops of General Rose's command. After the execution it was said that 'a great scramble was made by officers and others to get a lock of his hair'.

Rao Sahib evaded capture until 1862 when he too was betrayed. Rao Sahib was tried before an Indian jury who were unconvinced by the evidence put before them, and only returned a guilty verdict of 'modified rebellion'. The judge, however, overruled them and sentenced Rao Sahib to death. He was hanged at the Satichaura Ghat on 20 August. As for Firuz Shah, he survived the Mutiny, escaping to Mecca where he died in poverty in 1877.

There remains something of a mystery concerning the fate of the Nana Sahib.

Earlier intelligence of the Nana's movements was often contradictory and when on 10 February 1858 a rumour had it that he had crossed the river with the intention of entering Bundelkhand, it was greeted with scepticism. Lieutenant Roberts, who at that time was encamped at Unao, certainly gave little credence to the report. 'Wolf had been cried so often with regard to him,' he wrote, 'that but little notice was taken until my faithful spy, Ungud Tewari, brought me intelligence that the miscreant really was hiding in a small fort about 25 miles from our camp.'

This was at Fatehpur Chaurasi, a village on the banks of the Ganges, and Hope Grant was sent to investigate. The General set off with a detachment of cavalry and reached the fort early on the 17th only to discover that the Nana had made a hasty departure only hours before. Subsequent reports proved to be just as frustrating. One sighting had it that he was near the River Dogra with his entourage, and this was followed a few days later by news that he was at Shajahanpur on his way to Bareilly.

Other sightings quickly followed but early in April, confirmation that the Nana Sahib had crossed the Ganges near Bithur with an escort of 500 horsemen in a bid to reach the Jumna was received by General Sir James Hope Grant, who was soon on his track and the Nana was obliged to retire on Rohilkhand. Towards the end of the month he was back in Shajahanpur where he again avoided a party of cavalry which had crossed the Ranganga in pursuit of him.

Capturing the fleeing Nana was now one of the principal British war aims – not only was there a price upon his head of Rs.100,000, but an unconditional pardon was to be the reward of any mutineer whose information led to the apprehension of 'the beast of Bithur'. The offer, although leading to nothing of value, did have the effect of producing a letter addressed to Queen Victoria, supposedly from the Nana since it had his seal. Dated 29 April 1859, it read:

> I have committed no murders. All I could save by any means I did save, and when they left the entrenchments I provided the boats in which to send them down to Allahabad. Your sepoys attacked them. By means of entreaties I saved the lives of 200 English women and children. I have heard they were killed by your sepoys and budmashes at the time my soldiers fled Cawnpore and my brother was wounded.

John Lang, a barrister who had once acted for the Rani of Jhansi before the uprising, was doubtful whether the Nana could in all fairness be blamed for the massacre at the Ghat. In his book, *Wanderings in India*, he submits that:

> Nana Sahib had seen so much of English gentlemen and ladies, was personally (if not intimately) acquainted with so many of the

sufferers, that it is only fair to suppose, when he ordered the boats to be got ready, he was sincere in his desire that the Christians should find their way to Calcutta, and what ensued was in violation of his orders and the act of those who wished to place for ever between Nana Sahib and the British Govern-ment an impassable barrier, so far as peace and reconciliation were concerned.

With regard to John Lang's submission, it is not unreasonable to suppose that the massacre resulted from a mass hysteria quite beyond the Nana Sahib's ability to control, and that the order for the killings at the Bibigarh could in all fairness be attributed to Hussaini Khanum, the Nana's mistress and Begum of the Bibigarh.

For six months following the suppression of the Mutiny, the pursuit of the Nana and his followers was relentless, with the Nana always one step ahead of his pursuers.

In December 1859, both he and the Begum of Oudh were reported to be in the town of Bahraich. Sir Colin Campbell, or Lord Clyde as he then was, acted promptly by crossing the River Gogra from Faisabad, to reach the town on the 17th. Again the Nana evaded capture and nine days later Lord Clyde's troopers entered Buridiah, a fortified village 17 miles from Bahraich where the Nana was said 'to have stayed for a few days'. Early the next morning the punitive column closed on the fort of Majidiah – 'a dun coloured parapet of mud with three embrassured bastions' was how an observer described the fort before artillery reduced it to so much rubble.

'I do not think we have the slightest chance of catching him,' observed an officer engaged in the hunt, 'as the country is so covered with clumps of trees and high crops that a mounted man can disappear in a few minutes.'

The terrain bordering Nepal as it then was, abounding in rivers and forests, dotted with swamps and completely bereft of roads, was largely unfamiliar to the British military, nevertheless, despite the hard going and the uncertainty of whether Lord Canning would sanction a pursuit across the Nepalese border, Lord Clyde's column pressed steadily onwards. As William Howard Russell reminded the readers of *The Times*: 'The mere chance of capturing the Nana Sahib, killing and dispersing some of the desperadoes around him before the old year closed, seemed to justify an undertaking which was esteemed hopeless by those most conversant with Indian warfare.'

Christmas Day 1859 was spent by Lord Clyde's forces close to the Terrai and celebrated by the officers and men as if they had been in England. The tables, set up in the brightly lit tents, groaned beneath barons of beef, turkeys, mutton, game, fish, and other 'other delights not often found even in the best of camps', explained one delighted officer. Even *The Times* correspondent, as he looked with satisfaction on 'beakers of pale ale from distant Trent or Glasgow, Champagne, Moselle, Sherry, curious old Port – rather bothered by travelling 20 miles a day on the back of camels – plum puddings and mince pies', could not help thinking how different campaigning was in India compared with his experiences in the Crimea.

Later, on New Year's Day, word reached Lord Clyde that rebel troops were concentrating in the town of Bankee, close to the Nepalese border. The chance of taking them by surprise was slight, and a night march across unfamiliar country was hardly to be desired, nevertheless, despite the difficulties, the troops detailed for the operation set off at 8.30 pm, with just a glimmer of light from a lantern tied to the tail of an elephant to guide their path. Contrary to expectations, the vanguard made such good progress that a halt was made near a tope of trees and, wrapped in their greatcoats against a bitterly cold wind sweeping down from the Himalayas, the Rifle Brigade and a battalion of the 20th of Foot enjoyed the unexpected treat of a few hours of refreshing sleep.

Early the next morning, as the column neared Bankee, 93 miles NE of Lucknow, a strong picket of rebel cavalry were sighted by a patrol of Hussars, who spurred forward to take them completely by surprise. A captured *sowar* told Russell later that the first indication they had of the proximity of the British 'was the sound of their carbines opening fire on the rebels' rearguard'. In spite of the enemy taking up a position between 'a long deep swamp' to their front and 'a dense high wall of jungle' behind, the outcome was never in doubt. The one disappointment lay in the fact that the Nana Sahib, warned of the approach of the British, had loaded an elephant with treasure and made haste to cross the Raptee.

'The Nana was in the wood a couple of miles in the rear,' *The Times* correspondent reported. 'He at once gave orders for flight, had his eight elephants loaded, and made straight off to the Raptee, which he crossed, no doubt long before our cavalry reached its banks.' From his observation post on the high ground overlooking a spreading plain, William Howard Russell saw that the retreating rebel force had split into two groups, one heading towards the river pursued by the Hussars, whilst the other dashed for a belt of jungle growing as a dense wall of foliage as far as the eye could see.

A rebel battery of six cannon had been ranged across the river against the British cavalry, but in an action which Russell described as being 'one of those wonderful spectacles only to be seen in actual war, and of which peace has no counterpart', the Hussars stretched their horses into a mad gallop as they ran the gauntlet of shell bursts along the river's bank, in an attempt to close on the ford. As Russell watched, the mutineers urged their mounts into the water and within minutes the river was awash with struggling men and horses. The fast-moving current was equally treacherous to both sides and several Hussars and *sowars* were swept away and drowned. Among those unfortunates was the Colonel of the 7th Hussars. When his body was recovered later from a deep recess in the bank, it was seen that he had a firm grip on two of his assailants.

The next day a number of rebel leaders rode into the British camp at Bankee to surrender their arms, but neither the Nana nor any of his relatives were among those seeking an amnesty. His brother, Bala Rao, had escaped to seek refuge in a partially ruined fort 12 miles from Bankee, to be joined soon after by a local rebel leader by the name of Muhammad Hussain. Their combined strength, however, failed to check an attack mounted by General Hope Grant and the rebel band was forced to flee eastward towards Kandakot, a half-ruined fort on the edge of the jungle close to where two streams converged to form the Rapti.

On 4 January 1860, following up their recent engagement, Hope Grant's cavalry had no trouble in driving out those who remained, for, as reported by the General: 'All the courage had been driven out of the faint hearted wretches, they would not stand for a moment, running away like wild fire and leaving their 15 guns in our possession.'

With the defeat of the Nana and his brother Rao, the sepoy uprising was virtually at an end. Lord Clyde returned to Lucknow leaving his army to keep a careful watch on the passes, and with the exception of one incident in April when a group of mutineers crossed into Oudh and caused a disturbance near the town of Sikrova, the province was left in peace.

Shortly after Sir James Hope Grant's confrontation with the rebels at Kandakot, a native brought him a message allegedly from the Nana. In it he bitterly condemned British rule, ending his protest with the words: 'What right have you to occupy India and declare me an outlaw? Who gave you the right to rule over India? What! You, Firangis, are kings and we thieves in this our country?'

If the message was indeed genuine, then it was probably one of the last the Nana wrote, for on 13 May, the Commissioner for the North-West Provinces was notified that as 'the Nana had failed to avail himself of the terms of the Royal Proclamation, those terms would no longer be extended to him. If he did approach the authorities with an offer to surrender, he must be told that he would be granted "a fair trial and nothing more".' Faced with this uncompromising situation, the Nana had little choice but to take flight for the foothills of the Himalayas.

In his escape from Bithur the Nana had carried away much of his jewellery and family treasure, a provision no doubt appreciated by Jung Bahadur, the less than sympathetic Prime Minister of Nepal, who, whilst not actually offering the Nana sanctuary, nevertheless agreed to aid his progress towards Tibet. The most valuable piece in the Nana's collection was a long necklace of high-quality pearls, diamonds and emeralds. As a condition of his agreement of support, Jung Bahadur offered to purchase the necklace at a fraction of its true worth. Nana Sahib was hardly in a position to bargain, and given an assurance that he could rely upon the protection of the Prime Minister, he accepted the offer before resuming his flight westward towards the district of Butwal. Five months later, in October 1860, the British Resident at Katmundu was informed by Jung Bahadur that the Nana had died on 24 September from fever contracted in the Dang district of the Nepal Terrai. Major Ramsay, who telegraphed the news to the Governor General, was inclined to believe it, reckoning that the rainy season, together with the unhealthy reputation of the Terrai, had also taken its toll of the Nana's supporters. However, he added a note of caution: 'It is not unlikely that the Nepalese Government may have connived at his escape into the mountains, but I have no grounds for asserting that they have done so.'

Further reports seemed to confirm the truth of Jung Bahadur's message and by the end of the year it was widely assumed that the Nana had indeed died in the jungles of Nepal. One person who did have doubts was the Secretary of State, Charles Wood, who wrote to Lord Canning early in 1861 that Ramsay's report on the death of the Nana was 'not decisive', and that he believed it was 'very desirable that further efforts should be made to place the matter beyond reasonable doubt'. Colonel Ramsay, as he now was, was unable to provide firm evidence that the Nana still lived, and on 22 July 1861 wrote:

> I have exhausted all the means of enquiry that I possessed but without being able to obtain any intelligence calculated to throw additional light upon the matter ... if the Nana be still alive the secret is buried in the breast of the Maharajah Jung Bahadur, known only to himself and to the very few confidential agents here and in the district to whom he may have chosen to entrust it.

Later, in the autumn of that year, Colonel Ramsay began to have serious doubts himself as to the reliability of Jung Bahadur's report, and notified the Indian Government that he now had what he termed 'fair presumptive evidence of the Nana's existence'. He was reasonably certain that the story of his death had been circulated 'to favour his escape and to aid his concealment in the Nepalese territories'.

His assumption relied upon one eyewitness. A fakir had told Ramsay's orderly havildar that he had been in the Nana Sahib's camp for some weeks after the death of Bala Rao, 'until after Jung Bahadur went down in the terrain with his army in the cold weather. On reaching Butwal,' the fakir continued, 'Jung Bahadur sent for all the Pugree wallahs but Nana Sahib feared treachery and would not see him. He was resentful of the fact that Jung Bahadur had taken his money and now refused to give him any assistance.' The fakir added that the Nana subsequently journeyed into the hills, 'but he did not know whether he was alive'.

The mendicant's tale had the ring of truth, but much to Colonel Ramsay's disappointment he could not be traced to provide a sworn statement. His account did much to confirm Ramsay's belief that there had been collusion between the Nana and Jung Bahadur over the account of the Nana's death, and he was reasonably sure that the Nana was 'still alive in the hills between the shrine of Muktineth and the Omaon frontier'.

No further action was taken, for it was now the official view that rumours of the Nana's continued existence might well lead to a hard core around which disaffection would grow. The reward for the Nana's capture was not withdrawn, but the report of his death was generally accepted despite the possibility that it had been his brother Bala Rao, and not the Nana, who had died in the jungle. John Sherer had little doubt that the Nana had indeed died in the jungles of Nepal. Prior to being hanged at Cawnpore, Jwala Prasad, the Nana's brigadier, confessed to Sherer that 'he was not present when the Nana died, but that he attended when the body was burned. He spoke,' wrote Sherer, 'apparently without attention to deceive, and I fully believed him.'

Stories concerning men resembling the Nana surfaced from time to time, and in October 1874 Mowbray Thomson was sent to interview a prisoner taken by the Maharajah of Gwalior. He did not at first think that he was the Nana, but when changes were made to the man's dress and hair, Thomson thought he bore a close resemblance to the Nana Sahib. 'The likeness was remarkable,' wrote Mowbray Thomson. 'Though I am unable to positively swear to him, so many years having elapsed since we met, I strongly believe him to be the rebel Nana Sahib.'

But the authorities could not agree. 'I saw Colonel Mowbray Thomson yesterday,' reported Lord Northbrook, 'who inclines to think that the prisoner is the Nana, but his evidence is worth very little, for he had only the kind of acquaintance with the Nana that a subaltern has with a Rajah near cantonments.'

For many years rumours concerning the Nana persisted, but with the passage of time interest in his demise waned until a curious incident in a small town in Gujerat created a stir among the authorities in 1895. An old man who had been causing a disturbance near the police post was arrested. The following morning, a young police officer was told that an old man dressed as a mendicant had spoken in his sleep of Nepal, and had appealed for the protection of Jung Bahadur. When questioned, the would-be mendicant claimed to be the Nana Sahib and 'that if he had his rights he would be the Peshwa'. A physical examination disclosed marks on his body closely resembling those the Nana was said to possess, and an urgent telegraph was sent to Calcutta.

'Have arrested the Nana Sahib. Wire instructions.' Back came the reply which no doubt astonished the young police officer.

It was brief and incisive: 'Release at once.' The Government, conscious of the likelihood of the Nana becoming a martyr, was determined to put an end to all further speculation. Whether the old man's claim was genuine or not is impossible to say, but there is some irony in the Nana being deliberately ignored by his enemies and left to wander the countryside, claiming to be the infamous Nana Sahib, only to be ignored and scorned by his own people for a homeless old man 'whose brains God had filled with illusion'.

Nana Sahib left no heir, and in celebrating the centenary of the outbreak of the Mutiny, the Government of Uttar Pradesh erected a memorial to the Nana at Bithur. It stands as a bronze statue on what had once been part of the palace grounds, and the inscription on the pedestal, loosely translated, reads: 'India will always remember Nana Sahib Dondu Pant's self sacrifice and that will glorify India for ever.'

Another to escape justice was Hussaini Khassum, the infamous Begum of the Bibigarh, who fled to the hills with the Nana's entourage. Not so fortunate was Sarvur Khan, the bodyguard she had employed to slaughter the women and children. In February 1858, Sergeant William Forbes-Mitchell encountered a native hawker whilst encamped at Cawnpore, describing him as 'a very good looking, light coloured native in the prime of life. Speaking good English, the native told the sergeant that his name was Jamie Green and that he had General Hope Grant's authorization to sell his wares in the camp. Although amused by 'Jamie Green's' attempts to persuade the Highlanders to part with their money, Forbes-Mitchell took an exceptional dislike to his companion, a 'villainous looking Eurasian named Mickey'. The next day he discovered that both had been arrested and condemned to death, the one for spying for the Lucknow rebels, and the Eurasian for having been identified as Sarvur Khan. 'Jamie Green' later confessed to Forbes-Mitchell that he was no native Christian but Mohammad Ali Khan, who had travelled to London with Azimullah. Questioned by Forbes-Mitchell on the reason for the massacre of the women and children, Mohammad Ali Khan replied, 'The murder of the European women and children at Cawnpore was a woman's crime for there is no fiend equal to a female fiend; but what cause she had for enmity against the unfortunate ladies I don't know. I never enquired.' He and Sarvur Khan were hanged shortly afterwards.

The fate of other prominent mutineers is less clear, apart from Firuz Shah who died in poverty at Mecca in 1877. Baba Bhutt, the Nana's adoptive brother, together with an ailing Azimullah Khan, were observed travelling towards Calcutta. Azimullah, so it was rumoured, died of smallpox before reaching their destination. Another version of his fate has it that he fled from India in the company of a Miss Clayton, only to be murdered in Istanbul following the death of Miss Clayton in old age.

The generals responsible for the successful outcome of the operations to re-occupy Cawnpore and Lucknow, fared considerably better, as one might expect, although upon being elevated to the peerage as Lord Clyde, Sir Colin Campbell was heard to remark, 'It's too late. There is nobody alive to whom I care to tell the news'.

Sir James Outram left Calcutta in April 1858 to take up an appointment as the Military Member of the Governor General's Council, until reasons of health caused him to resign the office two years later. He sailed for England in July to be welcomed as a hero and fêted at a banquet given in honour of himself and Lord Clyde. He died peacefully in his armchair in 1863 at Pau in the South of France, and is buried in Westminster Abbey, to be joined there a few months later by his old comrade, Lord Clyde.

Concerning the fate of the junior officers and officials closely connected with the events in Cawnpore and Lucknow, none achieved a greater claim to fame than Frederick Sleigh Roberts VC, who became the most distinguished soldier of the Victorian Age. As Field Marshal Earl Roberts of Kandahar he was to play a notable role in defeating the Boers in 1902. Lieutenants Mowbray Thomson and Henry Delafosse both survived a shipwreck on their journey home to England before pursuing their military careers with distinction. Both served on the North-West Frontier and retired as generals, Mowbray Thomson eventually receiving a knighthood. He died in his bed at Reading sixty years after the event which had made him a popular Victorian hero. His old friend Henry Delafosse preceded him by twelve years, dying in 1905.

William 'Jonah' Shepherd, greatly disturbed by his experiences during the siege, resigned his position as Head Clerk in the Commissariat division and left Cawnpore for Agra. He was given a grant of land and Rs.1,000 as a reward for 'services rendered during the siege of Cawnpore', but finding it barely adequate to both support himself and the villagers he was responsible for, having bought the village, he rejoined the service, dying in 1891 at the age of sixty-six.

Amelia Horne, after witnessing the brutal murders of her family at the Satichaura Ghat, was rescued by a *sowar* who in the general confusion succeeded in concealing her from the other mutineers. Later, dressed as a Mohammedan female, she was forcibly converted to Islam and spent ten months as the mistress of her captor, Ismael Khan. Eventually, acting on the promise of a free pardon to rebels who delivered up their prisoners, he released her in Allahabad. In 1858 she settled in Calcutta where she met and married a William Bennett. Recovering slowly from her horrific experiences, she spent the rest of her days in relative poverty, giving piano lessons and writing her memoirs.

Of the two soldiers who escaped the massacre with Mowbray Thomson and Delafosse, Private Murphy of the 86th of Foot found employment as the first custodian of the Memorial Garden in Cawnpore, but fate dealt a tragic blow to Gunner Sullivan, who enjoyed just two weeks of freedom before being struck down by cholera, dying shortly after the four survivors reached the safety of Havelock's camp.

Even as late as November 1859 the area which had been the site of the cantonments in Cawnpore remained as a desolate sandy waste. After paying a visit on her return from Lucknow, Lady Charlotte Canning recorded her impressions in a letter to Queen Victoria:

> I am tomorrow to go over the sad scene with Captain Mowbray Thomson, one of the survivors of the massacre ... I suppose it is one's impression of the horrors which have happened here which throw such a gloom over the place, but I think I never saw anything so hopelessly arid and gloomy. Ruined houses everywhere and every spot with a story of horror. We are to choose the site of the memorial church tomorrow & lay out the ground round the well. The design of the memorial monument will be chosen from some expected from England.

She ended her letter by stating: 'I never knew what heat was till I came here & the damp moist air of Calcutta is to me far less trying than this parched climate.'

It was a design of Lady Canning's which was eventually adopted as the basis for a marble statue, *Angel of the Resurrection*, sculptured by Baron Marechetti, which became the central feature of a memorial garden established shortly after law and order had been restored to the province. The sculpture never received the universal acclaim expected of it. In a handbook for visitors to Cawnpore, H.G. Keane described it thus: 'The result is not wholly satisfactory. The statue is monotonous and unmeaning in design, rough and inartistic in execution. The ogee doorway and cast iron doors are the only decent feature.'

Percival Landon was even more forthright in his condemnation. Writing in 1906, he told potential visitors: 'the cheap German Gothic screen and clap trap angel who stands with crossed palm branches over the well head might surely have been spared to those who hold the ground sacred ... the well head itself is in the same deplorable state as the angel and the screen.'

The garden remained under the control of the military authorities until 1863, during which time anyone of Indian birth was refused entry. This ban remained in force right up to the day of independence when all restrictions on entry were removed by the State Government of Uttar Pradash in 1947. Two years later, the Angel and its screen were moved to the compound of All Souls Memorial Church near the site of Wheeler's entrenchment.

Because of its Mutiny fame, Lucknow enjoyed a special status with the British during the time they governed India, and indeed the Union flag which had been raised above the ruins of the Residency in 1858, remained there in spite of its tattered condition for almost ninety years until August 1947, when independence was declared.

Commenting on his experiences during the Mutiny, William Forbes-Mitchell remarked:

> It was a war of downright butchery. Whenever the rebels met a Christian or a white man he was killed without pity or remorse, and every native who had assisted any such to escape, or was known to have concealed them, was as remorselessly put to death whenever the rebels had the ascendant. Conversely, whenever a rebel in arms was met upon whom suspicion rested, his shrift was as short and his fate as sure.

William Swanston, the civilian volunteer from Allahabad, was in no doubt as to why the sepoys had mutinied:

> It was entirely a matter of caste. I have little doubt that the principal instigators will be found to be the Mohammedans ... The annexation of Oudh, though I believe a wise and necessary

200

measure, has been no doubt the straw that has broken the camel's back, though in a way we never expected. That the villainous and barbarous deeds committed have, with few exceptions, been perpetrated by the Mohammedans there is little doubt; and however guilty the Hindoo soldiery may be, the Hindoos as a race have generally been the people to save and protect the Christians.

In his summing up of the causes, John Sherer raises some interesting and relevant points which are worth quoting:

It must not be overlooked that there were large parts of India which experienced no mutiny, and other parts where what mutiny occurred did not excite the people. On the whole the native princes behaved very well; the large states did us little harm, and some of the small ones who took part against us would sooner have remained neutral if the rebels would have allowed them to do so. That the Moslem section of the army should have gathered at Delhi, and made the Emperor's name a rallying cry, is not to be wondered at.

He goes on to pose a question:

But what made the Hindoos take the same course, and cluster around the long disused throne of the Great Mogul? It cannot be supposed that the Hindoo soldiers could really wish for a Mohammedan government; they must have merely thought that Moslem enthusiasm would serve well as an influence against the British rule. There can be no doubt that the power of the Brahmins amongst the soldiers was very great. And the Brahmins have been always the inimical force which is discontented with British supremacy. Not because it is British, but because it is Western ... because the political principles of the West are all opposed to any belief in caste – that is, caste as understood in India.

Despite the reforms which followed the Mutiny, chief among them being a Bill which transferred the functions of the East India Company to the Crown, the Government still relied to a large extent upon the support of Indian soldiers to maintain its authority. It will always remain open to doubt as to whether the uprising could have been suppressed without the support of those sepoys who remained loyal to the Raj. History has recorded little of their fate and it is appropriate that a remark made by a veteran present at the unveiling of a memorial at Lucknow in 1876, to those sepoys who had fallen in the service of the East India Company, should be recorded for posterity. The surviving loyal sepoys of the Lucknow garrison, dressed in their old uniforms and wearing their medals, were presented to the Prince of Wales.

It was an occasion to be remembered by all who were there, and one old Lucknow veteran, perhaps thinking of the rewards his years of service should had brought him, could not resist putting in a word about his pension – '14 rupees a month, Sharzadah! It's not much, is it?'

SELECT BIBLIOGRAPHY

Allen, Charles, *A Glimpse of the Burning Plain*, London, 1986.

Anderson, R.F., *A Personal Journey*, London 1858.

Bartrum, Katherine Mary, *A Widow's Reminiscences of Lucknow*, London, 1858.

Bingham, G.W.F., Diary (typed copy), National Army Museum, ref. 5903-105.

Case, Adelaide, *Day by Day to Lucknow*, London, 1858.

Chand, Nanak, Diary Cawnpore, National Army Museum, ref. 1857 (54).

Dawson, Lionel, *Squires and Sepoys*, London, 1964.

Germon, Maria Vincent, *A Journal of the Siege of Lucknow*, London, 1858.

Harris, Georgina Maria, *A Lady's Diary of the Siege of Lucknow*, London, 1858.

Harris, John, *The Indian Mutiny*, London, 1973.

Hibbert, Christopher, *The Great Mutiny*, New York, 1978.

Huxham, Mrs G., A Personal Narrative of the Siege of Lucknow, National Army Museum, ref. 7303-24.

Majendie, Vivian Dering, *Up Among the Pandies*, London, 1859.

Maude, J.F., VC, *Memoirs of the Mutiny*, London, 1908.

Metcalfe, H., *Reminiscences of the Great Mutiny*, London, 1953.

Moorsum, H.M., Letters, India Office Library, ref. mss Eur. E299.

Munro, W., *Reminiscences of Military Service*, London, 1883.

North, C., *Journal of an English Officer*, London, 1858.

Rees, L.E.R., *Personal Narrative of the Siege of Lucknow*, London, 1858.

Ruggles, J., *Recollection of a Lucknow Veteran*, London, 1906.

Russell, W.H., *My Diary in India*, London, 1859.

Shepherd, W., *A Personal Narrative of the Outbreak and Massacre at Cawnpore*, Lucknow, 1886.

Sherer, J.W., *Daily Life During the Indian Mutiny*, London, 1898.

Smith, Ludlow, Journal (typescript), National Army Museum, ref. 1857 (54).

Swanston, W.O., *My Journal by a Volunteer*, Calcutta, 1858.

Ward, Andrew, *Our Bones are Scattered*, New York, 1996.

Watson, F.S., Journal (typescript), National Army Museum, ref. 92 WAT.

INDEX